The Health Care
of the Arabs in Israel

Published in cooperation with the
International Center for Peace in the Middle East,
Tel Aviv

The International Center for Peace in the Middle East (ICPME)
gratefully acknowledges the Ford Foundation for making this project
possible. The views expressed in the publications of the ICPME are
those of the authors and do not necessarily reflect the views of the
trustees, officers, or staff of the ICPME.

The Status and Condition of the Arabs in Israel
A project under the direction of Professor Henry Rosenfeld

The 750,000 Israeli Arabs are a national minority making up 17 percent of the population of Israel. In 1987 the International Center for Peace in the Middle East, together with Professor Henry Rosenfeld, director of the project, initiated a comprehensive research project on the status and condition of the Arabs in Israel. The focus of the research is on the Arabs' legal status, health and social services, and local government in Arab communities. The books prepared by the project members report the empirical findings of the project and offer a penetrating analysis of the degree of social, economic, and political integration between Arabs and Jews, the extent of discrimination, and the degree to which rights and opportunities are shared by all.

The Health Care of the Arabs in Israel
Nira Reiss

A study of the development of modern medical health services in Palestine until 1948 and in Israel, this book focuses on the interaction of state policy, class relations, voluntary organizations, and professional practice as they affect the level of participation of Arabs in the emergent health system.

Nira Reiss is a lecturer in anthropology at the University of Haifa, Israel.

The Health Care
of the Arabs in Israel

Nira Reiss

Westview Press
BOULDER • SAN FRANCISCO • OXFORD

Westview Special Studies on the Middle East

This Westview softcover edition is printed on acid-free paper and bound in library-quality, coated covers that carry the highest rating of the National Association of State Textbook Administrators, in consultation with the Association of American Publishers and the Book Manufacturers' Institute.

Published in 1991 in the United States of America by Westview Press, Inc., 5500 Central Avenue, Boulder, Colorado 80301, and in the United Kingdom by Westview Press, 36 Lonsdale Road, Summertown, Oxford OX2 7EW

Library of Congress Cataloging-in-Publication Data
Reiss, Nira.
  The health care of the Arabs in Israel / by Nira Reiss.
    p. cm.—(Westview special studies on the Middle East)
  ISBN 0-8133-7763-3
  1. Palestinian Arabs—Medical care—Israel. 2. Palestinian Arabs—
Israel—Social conditions. 3. Palestinian Arabs—Legal status,
laws, etc.—Israel. I. Title. II. Series.
  [DNLM: 1. Delivery of Health Care—Israel. 2. Ethnic Groups—
Israel. 3. Health Services—Israel. 4. Social Welfare—Israel.
W 84 J19 R3h]
RA396.I75R45 1991
362.1′0899274—dc20
DNLM/DLC
for Library of Congress   89-70441
                                                                      CIP

Printed and bound in the United States of America

The paper used in this publication meets the requirements of the American National Standard for Permanence of Paper for Printed Library Materials Z39.48-1984.

10   9   8   7   6   5   4   3   2   1

CONTENTS

TABLES

PREFACE

This study examines the origins, development and distribution of Western health care in Palestine as of the mid-19th century and in Israel (within its 1967 borders) and describes the implications of successive political regimes—Ottoman rule, British Mandatory administration, and the State of Israel—for the Arab population living in these configurations. While the interaction between Islamic and European medical cultures has had a long history, the expansion of the western powers into the area in the 19th century brought with it new medical practices and European modes of institutional organization for health (cf. Ullman 1978, Worsley 1982, Gran 1979).

The changing political and social situations of the Arabs in Palestine and in Israel have affected their fundamental conditions of health, including their participation in the emergent system of medical services. There has been no previous comprehensive study delineating the development of modern health care and the changing health needs of this population.

Beyond this descriptive goal, the aim of the analysis of conditions within the Israeli context is corrective. Indeed, the research was motivated by the assumption that inequalities in the provision of public services in Israel should be remedied. The primary goal of the research was then to provide an assessment of the health services available to the Arabs in Israel.

For a number of years after the establishment of the state an account which began and ended with the favorable comparison of health conditions of the Arabs in Israel with pre-state conditions had some force of truth. There has indeed been an improvement over the situation which existed before 1948; lags in the services were attributed to pre-state neglect of the Arab population and to a lack of a pre-existing basis. These constructions have worn off by now, since enough time has passed within a declaredly universalistic framework to make equal distribution of health resources the only valid criterion for public action.

Initially in this study the relative access of the Arab population of Israel to the public health system was therefore analyzed with regard to the infrastructure of water supply and sanitation, quality and quantity of public preventive and curative services, coverage by medical insurance, and local participation in health services.   An attempt was made to assess the health status of this population with regard to life expectancies, infant mortality rates, and rates of adult illness and mortality.   In extending the research toward an understanding of processes which have affected this population, my approach has been historical, with a Marxist emphasis on the relation between political power, social class, health services and health (Rosenfeld and Carmi 1976; Navarro 1976, 1978; Waitzkin 1983).

The research on which the study is based was conducted primarily from 1985 to 1987 and included interviews with persons active in the provision of health care and of related services in the present and past, observation of health facilities in various Arab and Jewish communities, and a review of published and unpublished materials.   The sources reviewed included publications and unpublished surveys by the Israeli government and the public sick funds, as well as other health-related institutions; archival material in the State Archive and at the Israeli Ministry of Health; books and articles in academic journals; and M.D.   theses in Israeli medical schools.

The spelling of place names in this book is consistent with that of official Israeli government publications, such as Central Bureau of Statistics 1985a. The map on page xv was made by the University of Haifa Computer Cartography Laboratory.

In Chapter One I present the origins of modern health services in Palestine in the latter half of the 19th century, when the prevailing positivist European medical culture was brought into the area. I point out the differential distribution of this sectorially organized system of medical care—introduced primarily by Christian missions and Jewish voluntary organizations—to the various populations of Palestine: Arabs and Jews, Muslim and Christian Arabs, rural and urban residents.

Chapter Two focuses on the implications of colonial rule during the period of the British Mandate (from 1917 to 1947) to the development and distribution of health services to Arabs and Jews. The role of the government with regard to the two national communities and the differences between the two groups in training, resources, class formations, labor organization and national priorities are related to the expansion of medical institutions for Jews and to their late development among Arabs. Some of the medical problems which differentially affected the various subgroups in the population are also discussed.

In Chapter Three I consider the consequences of the establishment of the State of Israel in 1948 for the system of public health services which had emerged during the Mandatory period. Topics of particular interest are the state's interaction with the health care institutions which were developed by the labor movement, and the struggle for control between the Israeli Ministry of Health and the Histadrut's Sick Fund. Following discussion of the range and the limitations of the state's responsibility for health care and insurance, and of the political contexts of decisions affecting the distribution of health services, the consequences for the Arab population are delineated.

The subject of Chapter Four is the role of the voluntary sick funds in providing medical services and insuring the majority of the Jewish and Arab populations in Israel. I analyze the predominance of the Histadrut's Sick Fund—which has dominated medical care and health insurance in Israel—and its current relative decline, and describe the competition between sick funds (and the organizations they represent) for various class-based and political constituencies. The process of expansion of the sick funds along lines of social and political affiliations into Arab communities in Israel is also described, along with its implications for the rates and the scope of medical insurance.

Chapter Five deals with conditions and developments in the Arab population which have bearing upon the relative availability to Arab communities of local public and private health care. These conditions include, on the one hand, the inferior status of Arab communities vis-à-vis the state and the quasi-state agencies and, on the other, an increasing availability of Arab professional medical manpower and a rising demand in the Arab population for an equitable share in the public health system. Changes in the class situation of the Arabs in Israel are presented as background for these processes and because of their relevance to the health of this population.

In Chapter Six, statistical information on life expectancy, infant mortality, and causes of death and hospitalization is supplemented by a review of case studies and analyzed for an indication of the relative health status of the Arab population. This discussion is important in giving an overall impression of trends characterizing the Arab population in Israel and of the medical problems which affect it.

The research on which this book is based was funded by the Ford Foundation, through the International Center for Peace in the Middle East, as part of a research project on 'The Condition and the Status of the Arabs in Israel' (Project Director: Professor Henry Rosenfeld). The Research Authority and the Faculty of Social Science at the University of Haifa provided financial support and services which made the completion of this book possible. An earlier version of some parts of this study was published in *Asian and African Studies* 1989, 23/1-2:245-269.

I would like to especially thank Professor Henry Rosenfeld, who proposed the research, encouraged my work on it, and made many helpful comments throughout its successive phases. Ms. Judy Blanc participated in and contributed to the early stages of the research. The following people have generously made available their expertise in various topics, and some of them read earlier versions of some of the chapters: Mr. Sa'id Rabi, Dr. Hatem Kana'aneh, Professor Judah Matras, Dr. Deborah Bernstein, Professor Gabriel Warburg, Dr. Hedy Frank-Blum, M.K. Victor Shemtov, Ms. Pnina Tzadka, Mr. Gerald Sack, Engineer Fuad Farah, Dr. Adiya Barka'i, and Ms. Anat Shemesh. Ms. Sarah Rumney helped in compiling the bibliography and, along with Ms. Rajda Zo'abi, participated in processing data on the distribution of health services.

Finally I wish to thank, for their indispensable help in bringing the book to its final form, Mr. Dick Bruggeman for his meticulous editorial improvements and for proofreading the work, and Ms. Heather Kernoff for assiduously word-processing it. Thanks are also due to Mr. Amos Zubrow, Ms. Christine Carson and Ms. Martha Leggett of Westview Press for their help, patience and efficiency in producing the volume.

Nira Reiss

MAP OF (MAIN) PLACES MENTIONED

1. Akko
2. Baqa al-Gharbiyye
3. Beer Sheva
4. Gaza
5. Hadera
6. Haifa
7. Hebron
8. Jenin
9. Jerusalem
10. Kafr Yasif
11. Karmiel
12. Ma´alot-Tarshiha
13. Metula
14. Nablus
15. Nahariyya
16. Nazareth
17. Upper Nazareth
18. Netanya
19. Rahat
20. Ramallah
21. Shefar´am
22. Taiybe
23. Tel Aviv-Yafo
24. Tiberias
25. Umm al-Fahm
26. Zefat
27. Zikhron Ya´akov

Chapter 1

THE COMMUNAL BASIS OF WESTERN MEDICAL
INSTITUTIONS IN PALESTINE
TOWARD THE END OF THE OTTOMAN PERIOD

In the 19th and early 20th centuries the population of Palestine, affected by widespread poverty, was subject to malaria, smallpox and cholera epidemics, and to typhoid, dysentery and other enteric diseases. Measles and other childhood diseases, as well as influenza and pneumonia, were highly mortal diseases. In addition, disabling ophthalmic infections (trachoma and others) affected a majority of the population, and contagious skin and scalp diseases were common (Avitzur 1972, Eliav 1978, Yofe 1971, Livingstone 1925, Rosenau and Wilinski 1928, Grant 1921). The conjunction of poverty and disease patterns produced a high rate of infant mortality, poor health in survivors, and a low life expectancy estimated at 35 years at the end of this period (Eisenbach 1978:67).

Water was scarce and often of poor quality. The supply of drinking water was undependable, and obtaining it was a major household expense especially in the towns. In some towns the situation affected everyone equally. Thus in Akko, where aqueducts built by the Romans were maintained, water was good, while Tiberias, where sewage flowed into the lake, was known as a hotbed of cholera. In other towns, the distribution of drinking water varied according to means, and thus reflected class differences. In Jerusalem and Hebron the rich paid for spring water brought to them, while others drank rainwater in all seasons. Poor urban residents suffered most from water scarcity in the summer months. Arab villages in the proximity of springs had a good supply, but on the coast villagers had to purchase well-water from contractors in summer. In the new Jewish rural settlements then first being established by Zionist immigrants, digging wells was an essential activity (Avitzur 1972:42-45).

The integration of the Middle East as periphery in the capitalist world system brought about a shift in the class-tied medical pluralism which had characterized Muslim society throughout its history, so that medicine among Muslims as of the mid-19th century consisted of three different cultures (Gran 1979):

1. A 'folk' (homeopathic) tradition among peasants and nomads, practiced by female midwives and male curers and evolving in the direction of increased reliance on saints and shrines.

2. A 'spiritual' (holistic) medical culture, radically Islamic, rooted in psychosomatic Avicennian medicine, and practiced among the Muslim urban middle class.

3. The emergent 'positivist' (western allopathic) medicine, favored by the ruling classes. Positivist medicine had an empiricist attitude in common with the 'rationalist' (physical) medicine which evolved in interaction with Greek medical thought in Islamic states before 1550, where it was frequently practiced by physicians belonging to minorities (Christians and Jews) who served the ruling class.

For most of the Ottoman period, the peasants and nomads (and probably the urbanized Muslim poor) in Palestine relied principally on traditional medicine (Canaan 1914). Characteristic of these classes, however, was an eclectic attitude toward medical practitioners which enabled them to comfortably make use of any element of the other medical cultures which was made available (Gran 1979).

In the towns there were 'physicalist' specialists in pharmacy, bloodletting and leeching, cauterization, wound-piercing, and bone-setting (Avitzur 1972). As of the 19th century there were also some professional practitioners who had assisted army physicians as medical orderlies in the Turkish army. Primarily Jews and Armenians, they practiced mainly in towns but made rounds in some villages. During the second half of the century, a number of immigrant Jews who had acquired experience as medics in European armies or as assistants to European physicians also began to dispense medications and to treat patients (Avitzur 1972). In addition, some licensed physicians—most of them Turkish but toward the end of the period including some Jews and Arabs— operated as part of the military in army hospitals, and as part of the Ottoman health service. Some of them also saw patients privately.

Hospitals for the poor, based on *waqf* property (property dedicated by its owners to religious charity either for the benefit of the community or for safeguarding the family's inheritance), had been set up by the Caliphs in many of the towns of the Domain of Islam as of the end of the seventh century (Rosen 1974). With Ottoman rule beginning in the 16th century, this system deteriorated. Voluntary Arab health organizations were late in developing in the Middle East primarily because in the Islamic state central government was held responsible for local administration and for the provision of local services. This view, which accounted for the fact that active municipal organization was developed in the Arab world only toward the end of the Ottoman period, accounted for the lag in developing the infrastructure for health as well as for the historical absence of voluntary health institutions (Baer 1963, 1969).

Ottoman westernizing reforms included attempts to incorporate western science and medicine, but in the peripheral region of Palestine in the 19th century state involvement in problems of medical care was minimal. The Ottoman public health service in Palestine consisted mostly of the on-the-whole ineffective quarantine at port of cholera and other cases of potential epidemics, and of the appointment of municipal medical officers in some of the towns who were responsible for isolation and disinfection procedures during epidemics and for the bureaucracy of permits and licences (Livingstone 1925, *Survey* 1946, Yofe 1971, Bar-El 1985). Licensing regulations issued in Constantinople for the practice of physicians and pharmacists appear to have been enforced, but local sanitary control through municipal licensing of foodshops was ineffective. Toward the end of the period, two houses donated as *waqf* property were opened as government hospitals in Jerusalem and Nablus (*Survey* 1946:609, Cagan n.d.).

The increasing penetration of western powers into Palestine in the second half of the 19th century brought with it the expansion of western medical culture in the area (Eliav 1978). In Europe, hospitals were established by voluntary, charitable organizations, often religious ones (Rosen 1974). The budding western personal health services in Palestine were funded by several church-based groups and by Jewish external philanthropists and voluntary organizations in cooperation with the communal institutions of local Jewish urban communities. They were provided mainly by European physicians, Jews and Christians, who introduced recent European medical science. The first European clinic was opened in Palestine in 1842 by the Anglican mission in Jerusalem together with a physician (Dr. MacGowan) sent as medical missionary by the London Society for Promoting Christianity Among the Jews (Kass 1989). The Jewish religious leadership reacted by imposing a ban on the clinic, and in 1843 the Jewish English philanthropist M. Montefiore sent the first Jewish physician and pharmacy to Jerusalem. As Christian mission activities increased, and not least in order to protect Jews from their influence, more physicians and medications were sent by Jewish philanthropists and various European Jewish communities (Eliav 1978). Christian and

Jewish providers engaged in ongoing competition, often matching one facility against a rival in the same urban locale.

British, German, French and Italian missions established hospitals or clinics in the towns. Jerusalem, Tiberias, Zefat, Yafo, Hebron, and Haifa, where both Arabs and Jews lived, as well as Nazareth, Ramallah, Nablus, and Gaza, whose residents were overwhelmingly Arabs, all had mission medical facilities by the beginning of the 20th century (Grant 1921). In the traditional communities—Jerusalem, Tiberias, Zefat and Hebron—where Jews were concentrated, subsisting on funds transferred from Jewish communities overseas, clinics and hospitals were established for them with moneys collected abroad. In the developing Jewish urban communities in Yafo and Haifa, residents also contributed toward this goal. The staff of Jewish facilities was, whenever possible, formed by the trickle of arriving Zionist physicians, appointed as salaried community physicians to treat members of each Jewish community in the clinics for little or no individual charge (Bar-El 1985). In one of the first Jewish public clinics in Jerusalem the procedural custom was as follows: An assistant to the physician would sit in the pharmacy in the morning and write down the names of the people the physician would then visit for free at their homes at noon. He would also distribute numbers for patients who wished to be seen at the clinic in the afternoon and evening. During the morning and evening hours the physician would make home visits for a small fee (Margalith 1970:274). What appears from this description, beyond the physician's long hours, is that even the most indigent Jews were provided with medical care, including home visits, at least at times of urgent need.

Jewish physicians in the towns most often combined a salaried position for the benefit of members of Jewish communities with a private practice for all patients who were able and willing to pay—generally little, given the poverty and hardship of the time (Yofe 1971, Avitzur 1972). Contracts with these physicians differed in their terms, but in general the poor and the indigent of the community received free or nearly free care in the clinics and subsidized or free care at home, according to a specified schedule. Some contracts permitted significant charge of the rich Jewish patients of the community and others did not (Eliav 1978, Margalith 1970, Bar-El 1985). In the course of their careers, a number of Jewish physicians took on different positions in communities of both the traditional and the new Zionist settlement, in both public and private practice. A few were appointed by the Ottoman governor as municipal physicians. On the whole Arabs were charged for care, and physicians hoped especially for rich patients who could help guarantee their livelihoods (Yofe 1971).

Some Jewish physicians practiced in predominantly Arab areas; in 1885 there was a Jewish physician in Nablus and one in Bethlehem (Assaf 1970:35). The fact that physicians who were members of minorities were a familiar feature of Muslim society may have facilitated their practice. Others included a large number of Arab patients in their practice (especially in Jerusalem, Haifa, and Tiberias). Outpatients, including Arabs, were treated for free in the clinics of the two largest Jewish hospitals in Jerusalem (Eliav 1978:233, 423). But hospitalization without charge in all Jewish hospitals was limited to members of the community. Others could be hospitalized, but the requirement that they pay, or at least guarantee payment before being admitted made hospitalization relatively inaccessible for those without financial means, such as the poorer Arabs, or Jewish socialist immigrants who were not members of the existing Jewish communities (Shapira 1961).

In the Christian mission facilities inpatients and outpatients were treated without pay. Medications were generally free, except in the English facilities, which collected a nominal fee since they were philanthropically funded whereas other missions were supported by their respective governments. Mission physicians also made home visits, and some if not all charged urban patients for private care (Eliav 1978, Livingstone 1925).

Of the towns in which medical services were concentrated, Jerusalem served as the major medical center not only for its own urban residents and rural periphery but for much of the region. Jewish hospitals were opened there by the Rothschild family, by the two main Jewish ethnic groups—the Sephardim, initially for their own community but later for all Jews, and the local German-Ashkenazim with the support of the Jewish community in Germany—and by a voluntary fundraising society of local women. Most of these hospitals were rebuilt and expanded by the end of the century. Because of the variety of medical institutions in Jerusalem (including a major central English mission hospital, an English hospital for eye diseases, and several German institutions), its relative number of physicians (18, eight of them Jews, for a population of 30,000) was higher than that of European towns (Avitzur 1972).

The urban rich and small middle class, Arabs (most Christian) and Jews, benefited most from having access to services provided by Jewish and Christian agencies and individuals, because they could best afford home visits and medications at need and thus buy accessibility, frequency, and continuity of attention. Poor Jews received care sponsored by their community. Of the Arabs, the Christian minority—mostly urban, more affluent, and at ease with the missions— benefited most. Poor urban Arabs received free care in the mission clinics and hospitals and in some of the Jewish hospitals, and could see Jewish and mission physicians privately, to the extent that they took the initiative of seeking such care. The majority Muslim rural population of peasants were furthest removed from the penetration and benefit of western medical care.

Social and religious traditions in the Jewish community of volunteering to visit the ill, institutionalized in the form of visiting societies, were meaningful in organizing charity and mobilizing mutual aid at times of personal and communal crisis, including on matters of health. There were old-age homes and hospices for the chronically ill and for the old of the various ethnic groups in Jerusalem, Tiberias and Zefat. Development and support of communal institutions was more advanced among Ashkenazi communities than among the Sephardim, who tended rather to distribute funds to individuals. In spite of such differences and divisions, Jewish communities were united especially at times of crisis. At times of epidemics, the councils which led the Ashkenazim and Sephardim cooperated in coordinating isolation and treatment. During a cholera epidemic in Yafo in 1902 the better care received by urban Jews resulted in the fact that only 20 Jews died while there were hundreds of Muslim casualties (Eliav 1978:423).

Soup kitchens for poor Jews were also common in Jerusalem, and their increase in the early 20th century indicated an increase in the number of poor as well as in the attempts to aid them (Eliav 1978:424). In 1913, the first public health nursing service in Jerusalem, initiated by the American Jewish women's group later known as 'Hadassah,' was staffed by two American nurses and supported by American Zionist and philanthropical aid (Adams 1987). Its models were the urban neighborhood health centers then current for immigrants in the USA (Rosen 1974).

Mutuality was no less a feature of Arab Muslim society. Income from *waqf* property was used to support institutions for distributing food to the needy and to some extent as direct allocations for food subsistence (Assaf 1970:312-314). In addition, aid for the ill or disabled was given by members of the patrilineal kin group. However, while on this familial basis support was aimed to assure the basic subsistence needs of the ill and disabled, no attempts were made to develop services or to achieve improvements beyond the maintenance of existing conditions. Communal mutual aid was undertaken as religious collection and allocation of charity to individuals and families, but not in the form of communal development of voluntary facilities and services. During Friday sermons imams would collect moneys (*zaccah*) to be distributed to the needy by religious councils. Each year during Ramadan, there was a major charity undertaking in which each of the religious submitted 2% of his property for the poor, and these funds were used to support the needy, especially the disabled.

Where alternatives were absent or inadequate, religious opposition by Muslim and Jewish authorities could not counteract the need for treatment met by the Christian missions (Eliav 1978:422). This was true of the Jews, and no less true of the Muslims who had still fewer alternatives. Dr. Torrance, who established a medical practice and set up a hospital in the Galilee in the 1880s sponsored by the London Society for Promoting Christianity Among the Jews, reports seeing dozens of patients per day in Tiberias and in Zefat. A majority of them were Jews who continued to arrive in spite of religious bans, and despite the fact that a salaried, albeit unpopular, community physician had been appointed for them by the Jewish community to provide treatment for which patients did not have to pay (Livingstone 1925:139). Jewish agricultural colonists in the Galilee who required hospitalization were also hospitalized in this mission hospital in the years during which the Jewish hospital in Zefat was inoperative.

In the new rural communities being set up by immigrant Jews, the creation of medical institutions served as an integral part of the settlement effort. Services for medical care were initiated, as in the towns, along a principle of a community responsibility toward the health of its members. Several physicians appointed by Baron Edmond de Rothschild in the agricultural colonies (*moshavot*) which he sponsored (twinning economic motives for patronage with national identification and the impetus of nation-building) opened medical clinics along with pharmacies and nurses to provide communal care for the farmers (Yofe 1971, Bar-El 1985). Such care included not only treatment but also attention to sanitary conditions and some preventive measures against malaria—most significantly, leadership in attempts to reduce the marshes and other measures of environmental sanitation. (Later on, the Palestine Jewish Colonization Agency [PJCA] which took over administration of the moshavot toward the end of the century took on responsibility for the appointment of physicians, but Rothschild continued to support the facilities).

Jewish socialist Zionist immigrants who were employed as agricultural laborers in the moshavot were treated by physicians in these facilities according to the determinations of the Baron's representatives and the farmers. Except in those few settlements in which Rothschild remained most directly involved (and in the period of his maximal involvement), where he instructed physicians to treat all workers—including Arabs—who came for help, treatment was considered a favor rather than a duty, since colony rules stipulated free care only to farmer-members (Bar-El 1985:74, Shapira 1961). Refusal of medical care was used by farmers in an attempt to defeat their Jewish employees' union-organizing activities (Eliav 1978:343). These laborers were also dependent on the goodwill and identification of individual physicians: While some physicians invested their best efforts for free in order to improve the health of laborers both at work and in their living quarters, others could refuse to treat them even when payment was possible (Yofe 1971, Shapira 1961:241). Being neither members of the old communities nor members of the moshavot, and having no affinity with the Christian missions, Jewish immigrant laborers, mostly young men and without familial support, found themselves without dependable and independent access to whatever services were available. Laborers in Judea and in the Galilee started mutual aid by instituting sick-watch for the ill by their companions. In 1911 the nascent union of laborers of Judea, which consisted of workers employed in the colonies as well as in the town of Yafo and its surroundings, negotiated with the Jewish hospital in Yafo to admit workers in emergencies on the basis of promised payment. In 1912 they founded a sick fund designated as insurance for treatment by physicians and for medication, for transportation to hospital and for hospitalization and convalescence, as well as for aid to dependents of the ill and disabled. A similar fund was then founded by the union of laborers of the Galilee.

Voluntary medical insurance in Palestine, along with communal workers' kitchens which attempted to provide better nutrition for Jewish workers and along with communal laundries, began therefore as mutual aid for these groups of laborers committed to creating services for themselves but also for the nascent Zionist labor movement as a whole in the context of its national aims (Tzahor 1981). Their goals and commitments were from the first moment expansive within a Zionist scope and went beyond their own immediate needs, their first effort being a temporary clinic set up to treat the (uninsured) sick Yemenite laborers in Petah Tiqwa (Shapira 1961). Only a socialist minority of Jews arriving in Palestine from Russia organized themselves in this way, and groups of unorganized laborers such as Yemenite laborers remained unprotected despite the token gesture of solidarity. As the first institution common to urban and agricultural laborers which went beyond local communities on the basis of movement identification and encompassed in its aims more than its own members, the sick fund expressed social ambitions which were for the time being also beyond the movement's abilities; there were serious difficulties in collecting membership fees (Tzahor 1981).

Organizing for mutual aid was made possible by the small number of Jewish agricultural laborers: In 1912 there were only 750 of them in the moshavot of Judea and the Galilee (Eliav 1978:346). Moreover, medical service and facilities were already in existence or being established by and for other Jewish groups in towns and in the moshavot, so that a measure of independence could be achieved merely through insurance. The socialist ideology and consciousness of these laborers was an important stimulus, but crucial, along with their own efforts, in making medical care available to these Jewish laborers was the sympathetic attitude of a number of activist Zionist physicians who not only provided care but acted in their behalf to elicit funds from philanthropists and from the World Zionist Organization (WZO) and thus established their right to receive medical services (Yofe 1971, Margalith 1970). In this way a hospital in the moshava Zikhron Yaakov, funded mostly by Rothschild, was designated not only for farmers but for laborers as well, and attracted patients from far beyond the local area.

While farmers on the moshavot did not willingly assume responsibility for the health of any of their employees, some Jewish laborers were thus able to partially escape dependence with regard to medical needs. Arab agricultural laborers, who outnumbered them by far, were unable to do the same. The ongoing struggle for paid agricultural work between the relatively expensive immigrant Jews and the more poorly paid local Arab laborers, which the Jews at this stage lost, made joint organization in this matter out of the question (Shafir 1989). For Arab migrant laborers, among them former tenants expelled from lands sold by landowners, whose living conditions were even worse than those of their Jewish competitors, the sponsorship of the missions was most distant. Some received treatment from Jewish physicians of the moshavot, in the clinics and where they lived (Yofe 1971, Bar-El 1985:42).

For the rural Arab majority, consisting of peasant-tenants and Bedouin pastoral nomads, as well as for the agricultural laborers around the moshavot, western medical services were scarce. The peasants, subject to landowners' usurpation and state overtaxation, had no patronage or benefactors with regard to health except the Christian missions, which were concentrated in the towns and reached out only partially to rural areas. Most acutely deprived were peasants and Bedouins in the periphery farthest from the center and from towns. Peasants came to the towns to be treated by foreign physicians as much as the distance from the towns and the difficulty of transportation allowed. In the winter in the Galilee they were isolated (Livingstone 1925).

Visits to peasant villages and Bedouin camps by town physicians were irregular and rare, although some mission doctors reached out through mobile clinics. Dr. Vartan, an Armenian English-trained MD who opened the first hospital in Nazareth in 1861 and continued to head it under the auspices of the missionary Edinburgh Medical Society, rode out to villages within a 30 kilometer radius of Nazareth to provide treatment (Bar-El 1985). Dr. Torrance reports a visit to the villages and Bedouin camps of Transjordan as a summer campaign, in which he found patients eager for medical care, and in addition to treatment (some of it explained simultaneously to groups of patients who shared the same medical problem) administered smallpox inoculations (Livingstone 1925). Village Arabs and Bedouin were charged only for medications on visits, but these were few and sporadic, and appear to have slackened off considerably if not stopped altogether in winter. Some of the Jewish physicians on the moshavot also made visits to villages (Yofe 1971).

The efforts by the Jews as of the latter part of the century to develop their own health institutions primarily for the benefit of their own community—rather than to rely on the Christian missions—were successful as professional practice was imported with the Zionist immigration of physicians to Palestine. Among the Arab population a comparable institutional development was unlikely at the time, if only because of the lack of European-trained Arab physicians in Palestine until toward the end of this period. By the turn of the century the first Arab graduates of the recently established American Medical College in Beirut did began to practice, independently or as assistants to mission physicians (Livingstone 1925, Grant 1921:193). Grant (1921) refers in this context to Dr. Ma'alul of Ramallah. Other Arab physicians (not necessarily from Palestine) who had studied in Beirut and practiced in the Galilee in the 1890s include Dr. Daud of Damascus and Dr. Sa'adi, who substituted for Dr. Torrance in Tiberias, Dr. Faris of Beirut, who practiced in the mission in Zefat, and the Lebanese Christian Dr. Imeglala of Jedida and Dr. Amin of Deir Mimas, who served for a while as visiting doctors of the moshava Metula. Three Arab physicians in Haifa served as municipal, port and railroad public health doctors in 1912; Dr. Ibrahim Effendi is mentioned both in a municipal role and as a private practitioner (Bar-El 1985:27, 37, 69). Eventually during this period Jews and Arabs born in Palestine began to study in Europe and in Beirut. Dr. T. Canaan of Jerusalem appears to have been the first of the Arab Palestinian MDs to have graduated in Europe (Canaan 1914). The Mandatory government's *Survey* (1946:703) reports that there were 68 Palestinian physicians in 1921, the majority of them Arabs. Deducting from these 68 the number of Jewish Palestinian natives, further deducting the number of physicians licensed since 1914, and assuming the rate of increase in the number of physicians to be greater in the years following the First World War, the calculation shows a number of Arab Palestinian western-trained physicians in the country during the Ottoman period which was indeed small. Whatever their absolute number, and given the likelihood that most were sons of the urban landowning elite, the number of those who came from and practiced in villages could only have been infinitesimal in proportion to the large rural population.

Arab laborers on the moshavot had the benefit of access to physicians there, but their often abominable living conditions offset much of that advantage (Yofe 1971). There is no reason to doubt that Arab patients received dedicated care, when they received it. Still, Jews were the main focus of attention of Jewish physicians and, even with the best intentions, when it came to the need for investing resources beyond their own labor, individual physicians were unable to obtain for Arabs what could be obtained for Jews. For example, since free medication such as quinine was made available by the PJCA for Jews only, a situation could arise where even when the physician was eager to treat Arab patients, the cost of medication prevented this. In 1913 the moshava Yisud Hama'ale in the Upper Galilee, a place of exacerbated conflict between Jews and Arabs, was only beginning to receive regular medical care through the PJCA. The physician distributing quinine to farmers and to Jewish laborers wanted to distribute it to Arab laborers as well. The latter were willing to pay, evidently on the basis of future wages, but the farmers refused to put up an advance payment as guarantee (Yofe 1971:303). On the other hand in Zikhron Yaakov, Rothschild had specified that Arab laborers should receive free care and medications at any time, and quinine there was distributed to them (Yofe 1971:286).

A number of Jewish physicians in the towns and in the moshavot had leadership positions in the Jewish community. Their scope of commitment varied, but some if not all saw their main constituency as the community as a whole, and the new Zionist settlement especially (Margalith 1970:266-375). Twelve of these activist physicians from the new Jewish town Tel Aviv and from the moshavot in 1912 formed the Hebrew Medical Association, which was expanded in 1913 to include physicians in the rest of the country. Their primary commitment can be seen in the Association's agenda: The organization was perceived by its members as being primarily for Jews (Christian physicians were invited to attend conferences as free listeners), serving mainly Jews (Yofe 1971:282). Their stated goal was to improve health conditions in Palestine and especially the health of Jewish agricultural workers, and they engaged in public scientific and educational activities, such as the improvement of medical records, conferences and publications (Assaf 1970, Margalith 1970). In Jerusalem (where in 1890 there existed a professional physicians' association of Jerusalem consisting of both Jews and Christians) a separate association of Hebrew-speaking physicians was formed, evidently concerned much more with differentiation from and professional competition with Christian mission physicians (Margalith 1970).

The issue of paying for medical services, and of fees relative to economic situation, was a significant one at this time. For all physicians, collecting payment from those who could afford to pay was a question of livelihood and of professional practice. But for the physicians of the Zionist settlement, demanding such payment was an ideological and social issue as well as a practical one. The conception of medicine as work to be paid for rather than offered as charity was part of a desire to base livelihoods, not least their own, on productivity. The demand for such payment was an expression of the struggle between the values of the traditional and the new Jewish communities (Eliav 1978). Dr. Yofe instituted payment by patients who were able to pay for hospitalization in the hospitals he directed in Zikhron Yaakov and in Yafo even if they were members of that community (Yofe 1971). Dr. Auerbach of Haifa as of 1909 successfully competed with Christian mission hospitals while charging patients of all religions in his hospital clinic (Bar-El 1985). Ideological and professional stances joined, generated by an emphasis on self-reliance rather than dependence on charity and consequently the belief that those who can should help themselves, and the complementary belief in the right of physicians to make a living by practicing medicine. And, in some cases the sponsors' (Rothschild and the PJCA) insistence on self participation was a powerful motive in trying to provide services with limited means.

Similarly, although the missions for the most part operated as charitable institutions, some missionaries did take payment. Dr. Vartan in Nazareth and Dr. Torrance in Tiberias agreed on the professional importance of charging fees for home visits to urban Arabs, while on visits to villages they did not expect pay (Livingstone 1925).

By the end of the Ottoman period there were 15 hospitals and clinics operated by European missions and charities in Palestine (*Survey* 1946:613). Six were British, four French, three German and two Italian. There were two government hospitals for Muslims, in Jerusalem and in Nablus, which served also as prison hospitals and which employed, in 1914, at least one western-trained physician (Cagan n.d.). There were nine Jewish hospitals: Four in Jerusalem, one in Yafo, established for all Jewish groups by the Jewish community there with the aid of German Jews, a small hospital in the moshava Rishon Letzion and a more substantial one in Zikhron Yaakov financed by Baron Rothschild for the benefit of the new Zionist settlement as a whole, a hospital in Haifa whose expansion was assumed and a brand new Jewish hospital in Zefat (1912) supported by Rothschild, which was not opened until after the War. A Jewish hospital in Hebron was under construction. Two malaria research centers were also established. Competition between the two centers, the Malaria Research Center in Jerusalem sponsored by the Jewish American philanthropist N. Strauss (1912) and the Anti-Malaria Service centered in the Galilee and funded by Rothschild (1913), had a personal basis in competition between the local physicians who were their directors, but represents also the first of the series of duplications of services and conflicts on both professional and ideological grounds between local Zionist physicians and institutions and those directed from the USA (Yofe 1971).

From the moment modern medicine was introduced into Palestine a mixture of public voluntary and private practice thus emerged which, even when actual practitioners and manner of treatment were the same, articulated distinctions between Jews and Arabs, between rich and poor, and between sectors of the Jewish public, through differences in communal responsibility for provision of services, and through differences in patients' responsibility for payment. These factors affected the immediacy, frequency and continuity of care, and therefore both the availability and effectiveness of treatment.

The small size of the Jewish community made it possible to organize from within and to support from outside. In the early 1880s the Arab population of Ottoman Palestine numbered approximately 350,000, and the Jewish population about 24,000. By 1914 there were about 600,000 Arabs and 85,000 Jews (Gilbar 1989, Gertz 1947). Jews received medical care as members of communities and under the principle of a community's responsibility for its own members. Moreover, despite some exceptions, the boundaries of communal identifications extended in general beyond the local and even beyond the political to an allegiance to the total Jewish community in Palestine. Within that national allegiance, different levels of commitment by both physicians and their sponsors to patients outside of each Jewish group were expressed to a lesser or greater degree in the manner of payment demanded and in the degree of initiative taken in providing care.

Except in the two government hospitals, Arabs received care in mission hospitals and clinics, the Christian Arabs as members of religious groups, the Muslims as objects of possible religious conversion along with assistance. This patronage was communal to the extent that the missions began treating Arabs as a favored community, at first perhaps to a degree by default, increasingly by design. Mission physicians sometimes took it upon themselves to visit villages, but in practice rural regions were most deprived.

From the services established and given by Jews, Arabs received care for the most part on an individual basis and through their individual initiative in seeking it—free of charge in at least some of the outpatient clinics of Jewish hospitals and moshavot clinics, and privately from individual physicians and as patients in Jewish hospitals, according to their ability to pay and to the dispositions of particular physicians and institutions. Some Jewish physicians treated Arabs on occasion in Arab villages. Arabs could also see Christian physicians privately. Since most of the Arab poor were rural rather than urban and had no local services designated for them, poverty must have inhibited seeking care which had to be paid for. On such a dependent and to a great extent individual basis, Arab patients were more than the Jews subject to the differential determinations of class and place.

Although not all sectors of the Jewish community had equal access to services, by the end of the Ottoman period a serious start had been made toward providing health services to all of them. Rural communities of the Galilee lagged behind, but were nevertheless reached. In the north of Palestine the penetration of western medicine had begun (in Zefat and Tiberias) two decades later than in Jerusalem and medical manpower was more scarce. Arab residents of the north sometimes traveled for treatment to Beirut, the closest major medical center, whereas for Jews as of the 1890s the medical center was the hospital in Zikhron Yaakov. Bar-El (1985:76) counts in the 1890s in the north from Hadera to Metula (where the population was about 70,000) a total of 14 licensed physicians and in addition medics, pharmacists and nurses. By 1914 there were 26 physicians, and the population numbered 137,000. In Haifa in 1914 there were seven physicians for a population of 20,000 (three of these physicians were the Ottoman municipal, railroad, and port physicians, one was a Jew, and three were European Christians); in Zefat there were five physicians for a population of 13,000; and in Tiberias three per 8,000. The availability of physicians in the villages themselves was of course on a minor scale.

Moshavot of the lower Galilee were at first served by town facilities and by visiting doctors from Tiberias. As the number of Jewish settlements and people in the rural sector doubled from 1900-1914 (while Jews remained mostly urban), the PJCA appointed physicians in the moshavot and the WZO paid the salary of physicians in other new settlements. A contract by the moshavot of the lower Galilee for the joint employment of one physician stipulates a salary paid by the councils of the moshavot, and spells out duties, rights to private practice, and housing in residence. The physician born in the moshava Rosh Pina, who had returned to practice in the Galilee, was allowed to receive other patients in addition to making rounds in the moshavot (Bar-El 1985:65). The practice of Arab village MDs (to the small extent they existed in Palestine) in the villages was also not limited within one community, but they must be assumed to have operated on a private basis through personal and familial ties in line with the kinship basis of village organization, without an institutionalized formal arrangement.

Given the structure of voluntary and for the most part sectarian sponsorship that established modern medical care in Palestine, the determinants of differences in access to services were physical proximity to facilities and personnel in the towns or the moshavot; social, cultural and political proximity to the providers and sponsors of care; and the requirement and ability to pay. Most of the Jewish physicians were on public salary which paid for at least a part of their livelihood, and on that basis were employed primarily for the benefit of Jews, whether with philanthropical, religious, or Zionist funding. These positions were designed to provide access to and affordability of care to the Jewish public. Arab physicians were extremely few, and in any case medicine without an institutional base could not compare with that backed by communal investment. Arab patients were more than the Jews at the mercy of individual physicians' goodwill, and most importantly, at the mercy of the communal sponsorships which differentiated between members of the two groups on the levels of both investment and expectations. The professional matter of treatment was tied, sometimes more loosely than others, to the dynamics of nationbuilding by the Jews, and, for the Muslim majority, to the dynamics of foreign religious activity by the missions. With regard to the availability of western health care (including the visibility of physicians' commitments), in a context which was sectarian to begin with and becoming more so, the majority of Arabs at this stage were outside its realm.

The years of the First World War exacerbated health conditions in Palestine. Lack of money and budgetary collapses in health institutions caused many of them to cease or drastically limit their operation, in particular the extent of free treatment. Assistance for the Jewish sector included increased activity by American Zionists, and local Jews organized for mutual communal aid, whereas Arabs relied primarily on their family networks and on indigenous medical care. By the end of the War the population of Palestine was diminished and exhausted by famine, diseases and displacement.

Chapter 2

THE DEVELOPMENT AND DISTRIBUTION OF MEDICAL SERVICES DURING THE PRE-STATE PERIOD

2.A. The Mandatory Government's Public Health Service

The British began to institute a public health service in 1918, with several epidemic stations, hospitals, and traveling hospitals on camels (Assaf 1970:290). The British civil administration, which governed Palestine as of 1920, established a Government Department of Health (GDH) through which measures against sanitary neglect, and the continuing advances in bacteriology, immunization and curative treatment of infection began to be applied.

The public health service was initially designed first and foremost to protect British personnel, secondly to protect and further the political interests of administration, and thirdly, and only reluctantly, to improve in restricted ways the conditions of the local population outside of such direct interests, in response to demands from both communities. Beyond operating government hospitals and attempting control of infectious diseases through basic preventive and curative measures, the administration preferred to take on an uncostly advisory and coordinating role. A mixture of self-interest and a restricted humanitarianism, motivated by the professionalism of some of the GDH civil servants, guided the level and priorities of government effort. Its reluctance to seriously invest in prevention as in curative services was commensurate with its general lack of interest in developing the social services in the country (Wellesley 1937).

Initially GDH policy was to deliver elementary preventive services but to leave medical treatment of all but dangerous infectious diseases to the voluntary agencies (Samuel 1925). In the face of Jewish public health initiatives, of some responsive Arab activities, and of demands by both Jews and Arabs for increased government involvement and investment, government efforts were somewhat extended, but on the whole remained partial and limited. Since the administration left much of the responsibility for environmental and personal preventive services and for most curative care to the voluntary agencies and municipalities, these active forces in the Jewish community continued to expand services, while medical institutions in the Arab community were not developed. Under these circumstances, the low level of government spending maintained the gap between Arabs and Jews.

A Sanitation Department in the GDH was responsible for the quality of drinking water, including chlorination. Plans were made for improving water supply and for building pumping stations in every community. Actual development of water supply was undertaken mainly in urban municipalities, but some rural well pumping stations were also built. Programs were established for the prevention of typhoid as well as malaria through pest control, and for the prevention, through food hygiene and the sanitation of milk, of typhus and the dysenteries. Public health licensing ordinances were made renewable, and thus in principle more enforceable than they had been during Ottoman rule, but there was no strict enforcement in fact of such regulations as the required pasteurization of milk. Government health supervisors reportedly did not necessarily reach villages regularly or do much there (Washitz 1947:200).

The British introduced modern house sanitation, plumbing and drainage in the cities and in some rural localities. But garbage and rubbish collection, sewage and other environmental sanitation measures were defined as municipal responsibilities, and little progress was made in these areas (Rosenau and Wilinski 1928, ESCO 1947). An exception was an anti-hookworm campaign in which the GDH installed 25,000 latrines and fined offenders (GDH 1938:11, GDH 1940:4). Otherwise, even when local town planning committees adopted sanitary regulations, there were no plumbers to carry them out. By 1948, only the three largest cities had central sewage.

In addition to quarantine and isolation of communicable diseases, the GDH played a supervisory role in the anti-malaria campaign of draining swamps, canalizing marshy streams, and covering wells and cisterns. The campaign was re-initiated after the War by the Malaria Unit sent to Palestine from the US by the American Joint Distribution Committee (a voluntary Jewish-American philanthropic organization [AJDC]) for the benefit of Jewish settlers, and carried out by these settlers (Samuel 1925, Rosenau and Wilinski 1928). The GDH introduced a malaria survey section and water laboratories and a government Malaria Center and dispensaries which coordinated activities with the Jewish agencies active in this area, the AJDC, the Hadassah Medical Organization and the Malaria Research Center (founded in 1913) which became affiliated with the Hebrew

University, the PJCA, active in malaria prevention since the Ottoman period, and the Jewish National Fund.

The Supreme Muslim Council (SMC), in charge of *waqf* funds, also supported anti-malaria activities. Arab municipalities and some villages carried out campaigns in their own localities, under the supervision of government medical officers and engineers (Samuel 1925:11, Wellesley 1937). Such local responses were hampered by the fact that 50% of the population lived in villages and tribal areas without recognized local authority, and were thus unable to elicit government participation (Committee on Village Administration And Responsibilities 1941:8). By the end of the Mandate malaria had virtually disappeared among Jews, but in spite of improvements in environmental conditions and of some actions motivated by activist attitudes, there were still thousands of cases among Arabs (Assaf 1970:296).

The GDH declared and attempted a policy of involving local communities in health care and ultimately devolving it upon them. On these terms, the government took responsibility for serving the Arab population by providing for them services like those introduced in the Jewish sector, particularly and increasingly assuming patronage of the Muslims in line with attempts to counteract the effects of the Balfour declaration of a National Home for the Jews. Such a policy, a priori with respect to the Jews, who were already engaged in providing communal health services, meant that Jewish institutions received some allocations and subsidies, but were mainly left to develop under their own devices. The government concentrated on activities in Arab towns and some villages (*Survey* 1946:632).

In the areas of personal preventive and clinical care other than for malaria, the GDH began in the 1920s to prepare and administer immunizations against typhoid and cholera, introduced compulsory immunizations for smallpox and voluntary immunizations for tetanus and whooping cough, and opened eye clinics in the towns, and later in some villages, for the treatment of trachoma (estimated to have affected in 1922 75% of Arab children and 50% of Jewish children) as well as a center for treatment of ringworm of the scalp. In the treatment of eye diseases, it combined forces with the Christian Order of St. John (GDH 1924:3, GDH 1933:11). The government also initiated a school medical service and established infant welfare centers in some of the small towns, where vaccinations and inoculations were administered within three months of birth (Assaf 1970:289, Rosenau and Wilinski 1928:630). All of these projects were preceded by programs run by Jewish voluntary organizations, particularly the Hadassah Medical Organization, and some had been projects of mission and other Christian philanthropic organizations. Later the GDH also opened outpatient curative clinics in Arab towns and weekly clinics in villages.

There was limited government involvement in hospital care, as some government hospitals were built (or taken over from Ottoman military and civil facilities) primarily in order to serve British nationals, and secondarily for the isolation of dangerous communicable diseases and for some care of the indigent (Wellesley 1937). In the course of time these hospitals came to serve also as general hospitals. Toward the end of the period, most government hospital beds were still used either for government personnel, for isolation, or for mental inpatients, but in addition more than 10% of all general and maternity beds were in government hospitals (GDH 1942:10-12). Government hospitals added to the services available in Jewish, mission and other Christian voluntary facilities, and along with the missions provided mainly for the Arab, especially Muslim, population. There were complaints, however, that admission to government hospitals was limited to the well-connected (Washitz 1947:199).

During the Second World War the government increased spending on hospital facilities (but not the overall percentage of the budget spent on health), and in the 1940s its hospitals surpassed mission facilities and continued to expand, providing a third of hospital beds by 1944. By 1945 there were ten government hospitals: general and infectious diseases hospitals in Jerusalem, Nablus, Yafo, Tel Aviv, Beer Sheva, Gaza, and Haifa, and hospitals for infectious diseases only in Jerusalem, Zefat, and Bene Beraq). There were also three GDH mental hospitals and a maternity hospital (*Survey* 1946:611-618). A lack of needed facilities was noted in the Arab towns of Ramle, Jenin and Akko, and in areas of Jewish settlement.

Although hospital services were in principle available for use by both Jews and Arabs, in practice most patients in government hospitals (except in the new Jewish towns of Tel Aviv and Bene Beraq, and in the mental hospitals) were Muslim Arabs and most patients in Jewish hospitals were Jews (ESCO 1947:325). Rosenau and Wilinski (1928:637) noted in 1927 that the non-British staff of government hospitals were usually Arab and not Jewish. Jews were reluctant to go to hospitals where Arabs were treated and vice versa (Wellesley 1937:230ff). In 1944, 85% of the patients in government hospitals were Arabs (*Survey* 1946:611). By then some of the staff—immigrant doctors from Germany and in a lesser number nurses—was also Jewish, and Jewish patients were being admitted to GDH hospitals somewhat more than before.

The GDH operated 21 urban outpatient clinics. All but the one in Tel Aviv were in Arab or mixed cities: Ramallah, Hebron, Jerusalem, Beer Sheva, Yafo, Ramle, Gaza, Majdal, Haifa (2), Akko, Nablus, Tulkarem, Jenin, Beishan, Zefat, Nazareth, Bethlehem, Tiberias and Qantara). It conducted weekly village clinics in 19 (out of about 1,000) Arab villages, urban ophthalmic centers, 41 village ophthalmic clinics and a traveling clinic, a school medical service for Arab children, 20 urban and 18 village infant welfare and maternity centers, four prenatal and gynecology centers staffed by two woman physicians in Haifa, Akko, Jerusalem, and Nablus; and anti-rabies centers. There were also five hospital training centers for nurses and a school for midwives (*Survey* 1946:616-634; but a former nurse trained at a hospital center in 1940 has described to us much exploitation of young Arab nursing students' labor, and callousness with regard to the safety of students, Arabs and Jews).

The number of weekly clinics reported as held in Arab villages toward the end of the Mandate ranges from 19 (above) to 54, in either case indicating quite limited involvement (GDH 1923:33, GDH 1946:22). In the Nablus region, two government physicians were responsible for a population of 94,000, and reached some villages once a month. In the south, deprivation of services was even more acute: In the Beer Sheva region one GDH physician was responsible for a population of 100,000 (Washitz 1947:200). As to the infant welfare centers (46 in 1946), they also did not become sufficiently widespread, although wherever they existed they were popular (GDH 1929:7, 1946:26, Economic Advisory Council 1939:8). It is clear from reports of various evaluating committees that the Mandatory government recognized the value of extending preventive and curative services, but did not do much in this matter (Committee on Development and Welfare Services, 1940:34).

The government school service provided vaccinations on entry to schools, medical examinations on admission and twice more, treatment for communicable eye and skin diseases, and training in hygiene. But the reach of these programs to the villages was partial at best, since rural schools were limited in number and even in villages which did have schools not all children were included. A joint building effort by the government and village local authorities (which constructed and maintained school buildings and paid the salary of supplementary teachers) succeeded in developing the extent of public primary education so that by 1945 there were 426 village schools with 49,000 students (*Survey* 1946:646-50). Overall in 1944, out of 300,000 rural and urban Arab children aged 5—14, less than one-third were enrolled in schools. Nearly all Christian children were in school, but schooling for girls in the villages was barely existent (*Survey* 1946:638-9). As partial as was the medical screening received by schoolchildren, those who did not attend—girls especially—had no re-inoculations even in those cases where inoculations had been administered in infancy, and no further necessary medical attention at all. In the majority of smaller village schools, especially those more remote from the Jewish sphere of influence, where access to Jewish private or public physicians was rare, and where the Christian missions did not reach, children were medically isolated.

The Jews had entered this period with a higher level of expectations of medical care and of demand from their own community for its provision, and with a leadership capable of and interested in demanding it of the government. The levels of expectation and of demand for health services among the Arab population were initially low. The Arab poor and especially the peasants did not expect much of government health services, having previously experienced neither the goodwill of rulers nor the effectiveness of their own leadership in this regard. Under Ottoman rule, they had demanded little except perhaps relief from mounting exploitation. Passivity in this regard changed as the level of expectations increased, stimulated by the increasing availability of medical care and by the example of the Jews in this matter.

Confronting the basic colonial policy that colonies be self-sustaining in terms of expenses (e.g. Fieldhouse 1981), there were conflicting national claims for a piece of the budgetary and employment pie. The Arabs complained that the government provided services to Arabs much below the bare minimum of needs. The Jews complained that government participation in the health services was inadequate and the share of Jews in it was too low, considering the contributions of Jews to government income; that work on village water supply and sanitation did not benefit Jews sufficiently; that government hospitals did not provide for adequate care of Jewish patients while Jewish facilities served Arab patients; and that the government discriminated against Jewish physicians. They complained that in 1930 the GDH employed only six Jewish physicians (ESCO 1947:413, 1138, Wellesley 1937). On the other hand, the Muslims, as tension between them and Christians increased as a result of government policy, charged that the government discriminated in favor of Christians in that out of 53 Arab physicians employed by the government in 1930 only six were Muslim, one of them about to be fired (Arnon-Ohana 1978:186).

The administration's answer to budgetary demands, self-serving with regard to the Jews and condescending with regard to Arabs, was that Jews did not pay taxes at the rate paid by citizens in England, so that Palestine was too poor to afford, and that its Jewish inhabitants could not expect, as high a level of services as they were demanding. Furthermore, the administration claimed that since 'the Jewish requirements are so much higher than those of the Arabs in general at their present stage of development' equity in medical care and equipment was in any case impossible and a per capita calculation irrelevant (Wellesley 1937:317). In fact, during the 1930s the Jewish population received a greater share of government services than warranted by its share in the labor force, but less than its tax payments to the government were worth (Ofer 1967). The government did not find the budget to finance even services under its expressed jurisdiction, such as tuberculosis hospitals, and explicitly eschewed responsibility for planning and providing curative services despite the fact that it did establish clinics (Committee on Development and Welfare Services 1940:63).

Undoubtedly a public health service functioning on a regular even if restricted basis was a prerequisite for introducing the advances in public health which were being made during the period, particularly with regard to subtropical diseases. The limitations of government policy and practice became more apparent as control of that class of diseases became more effective and diseases whose prevalence and incidence depended even more on socioeconomic factors began to become dominant. The translation of government policy, minimal to begin with, into structures and activities was further constricted by a reduced health budget (in 1928-1936 4.4% of the total budget and from then 3.5% of the total (Survey 1946:630, Gov't of Pal. 1936-37:137). The government's differential dispensing of health care on ethnic- religious criteria promoted ethnic divisiveness, but finally its colonial policy of spending as little as possible left more substantive developments for the benefit of the Arab sector to the responsibility of Arab civic and voluntary organizations, as it had to the Jews. Given the much greater ability of the Jews to fend for themselves the disparities grew, and Jews in both the rural and urban sectors by the end of the Mandatory period were enjoying the benefits of development more than before, while the Arab rural majority remained behind. Only during the years of prosperity of the Second World War did forces in the Arab community capable of communal enterprise toward creating medical facilities and institutions begin to gather.

2.B. Christian and Jewish Voluntary Agencies

The Christian Missions

Following a philanthropic view which emphasized curative services, the Christian missions continued to expand their facilities in the towns and to provide treatment to patients in hospitals and clinics for small fees. Other Christian charitable agencies such as the Order of St. John and the American Colony Aid Society (both in Jerusalem) were also active.

By the end of the Mandate there were 22 mission hospitals, including outpatient clinics (11 British, four French, four German, and three Italian); five of the seven added since the First World War were British. All of them were in towns, and they provided 29% of all inpatient beds compared with the GDH's 33%. No longer the major benefactor of Arabs in the matter of health as the government increased its activities, the missions offered medical care particularly to Christian Arabs, although their facilities remained available to and used by Muslims (see also 2.D, below). Only two missionary societies attempted village outpatient clinics: in 1938 they reported treating a total of 6,400 Muslim patients (GDH 1938:78, Washitz 1947:199).

The Histadrut Sick Fund

In the Jewish sector, while the voluntary activities of religious communal aid and of some philanthropic groups continued, the major health-care development was the expansion of the labor movement's voluntary medical insurance sick fund. Until 1918 there were four separate regional mutual aid sick funds: for the workers of Judea, the Galilee, and the Shomron, and for the Guardian defense militia (Berriman 1962:42). In 1919 the two competing Jewish workers' political parties (Ahdut Ha'avoda and Hapo'el Hatza'ir) established instead two separate funds. When workers' union organizations united in 1920 to form the General Federation of Hebrew Workers (the Histadrut), the cooperative institutions they began to develop included a common Histadrut Sick Fund (HSF). In the context of political divisions between Jewish socialists, the fact that the Histadrut was formed as a supra-political organization in order to unite workers' organizations was crucial to its ability to foster comprehensive ambitions and to create social and political institutions. While workers did not always have an unambiguous definition of the function of the Histadrut, certainly the medical services offered to members were not the least of its attractions; as the only health security for workers, medical insurance and the subsequent availability of clinics were primary motivations for joining the union (Tzahor 1981:146,165, Horowitz and Lissak 1977).

The first union clinics had already been opened before 1920—a central clinic staffed by a physician and a nurse in Yafo, and smaller ones, with a nurse only, in the moshavot Petah Tiqwa and Rehovot. But most medical aid was given by private physicians associated with the four existent sick funds (Berriman 1962:42). After the formation of the Histadrut, local urban and rural branches opened clinics according to their own initiative: National connections were few, as throughout the 1920s HSF facilities developed as a little-coordinated network according to specific union participation and possibilities in each place (Tzahor 1981:156). In 1927 the HSF Central Office was established within the union charter, and budgetary planning became national (Berriman 1962:28).

Expanding to serve the increasing population, the HSF emerged not only to insure but also to provide preventive, curative, and rehabilitative care to hired urban and rural workers in the Histadrut and in affiliated religious workers' organizations, as well as to members of cooperative agricultural settlements, kibbutzim and moshavim. (The moshavot, consisting of private farmers in class opposition to their employees—the agricultural laborers who were the union founders—were outside the realm of the HSF). The Histadrut's commitment to socialist agricultural settlers is indicated in the placement of its first hospitals in the centers of such settlement—the first in kibbutz Ein Harod in the Yizrae'l Valley in 1923 (transferred to the neighboring Jewish town of Afula in 1930), and the second near Petah Tiqwa in the mid-1930s—and in the initiation of rural clinics.

The first union sick fund had been formed in 1911 by 150 members. The HSF had 2,000 members in 1920; 15,000 in 1930; and by 1945 it insured and served 140,000 members of the Histadrut who, including their families, were 270,000 persons, nearly half of the Jewish population at that time (Wellesley 1937, Tzahor 1981:363). The importance of the HSF to this population was even greater considering that as the sick fund became more and more successful the Jewish community's dependence on it became more widespread. With WZO's support, it took responsibility for medical care to immigrants, and subsidized health care for thousands of family members of Jewish soldiers in the British army (Berriman 1962).

By 1946 the HSF was operating two hospitals, 274 clinics and additional stations in cities, towns, and rural settlements including five major outpatient clinics in the cities, and physicians and nurses provided in 50 agricultural settlements.   Only five agricultural settlements founded since 1920 were not served by the HSF.   In addition it had convalescence and rest homes, institutions for chronic patients, a laboratory section,   X-ray institutes, electrotherapy institutes, dental clinics, and pharmacies and a central pharmacy depot. It also operated stations for infant welfare and prenatal care, a school health program and a program for public education, nurses' training centers, training for school teachers in hygiene, and anti-rabies measures (Kurland 1947:110, *Survey* 1946:759, ESCO 1947: 388-393).   HSF expenditures in 1944 were more than twice the government's expenditures on health, and its budget for 1946 was two-thirds of the budgets of all the Jewish medical services in Palestine (*Survey* 1946:728, Kurland 1947:108-9).

The Histadrut owed its success among Jewish workers not only to its collective ability to improve working and living conditions (including medical care), but also to its ability to influence employers to hire Jewish labor in the first place in a situation where Arabs, prepared to work for lower wages, had an advantage in competition for unskilled jobs created by the importation of Jewish capital.   From 1919-1931 115,000 Jews entered Palestine, most of whom went to work as urban laborers, menial and skilled. In the following years, when the Jewish population increased at an even more rapid pace through the immigration first of Jews from Nazi Germany in the 1930s and later of refugees from the War in the 1940s, labor immigration was still substantial enough to account for half of the Jewish entries to Palestine from 1919-1947. The majority of these workers joined the Histadrut and were insured in the HSF: By 1927 70% of wage earners were in the Histadrut and by 1930 75% were members, constituting a distinct large subgroup in the Jewish community (ESCO 1947:388-393, Tzahor 1981:299).

The emergence of the Histadrut as a general federation of Jewish labor, recruiting as of its first years the majority of wage earners and engaging in substantial cooperative economic enterprises, made it possible to create substantive medical institutions and facilities. Its initial successes put it in position to also request, channel and absorb funds from the WZO. In spite of some contempt expressed in the labor movement for the WZO (considered bourgeois), there was a mutual dependence: The WZO in the 1920s did not set up its own institutions, but rather allocated funds collected abroad through its financial arm, the Palestine Foundation Fund. The Histadrut and the HSF, as the institutions of the Jewish labor movement at the forefront of settlement in Palestine, represented (along with the rural cooperatives) to Jews overseas the legitimacy of the Zionist enterprise, and were accordingly favored in support. The Palestine Foundation Fund supported the HSF through its first years (Tzahor 1981:177, Kurland 1947:114).

A permanent tax according to income was adopted in 1920, but in the early years, when underemployment and low wages were the norm collecting membership fees was a constant problem. The special hardship of Jewish women workers who were unable to pay fees and had no protection at times of illness is noted in 1926 (Bernstein 1987). In some places the HSF had to collect its own fees, members did not always pay and used the services without registration when they could (Tzahor 1981:140-141, 299).

Increasingly, however, services were financed by the union dues paid by organized workers and by the dues they succeeded, through collective bargaining, in getting their employers to pay. As of 1937 the Histadrut collected from its members a uniform fee for all the social services including workers' sick fund, disability fund, unemployment fund, widows and orphans fund, old age fund, and social assistance (Kurland 1947:106). Thereafter it came close to balancing its budgets as the workers' share increased rapidly, while employers' contributions rose slowly. In 1946 72% of the budget came from workers' contributions, another 10% from workers' collectives and institutions, 15.7% from employers through collective agreements, and only 1.1% from the government. Since 20% of this budget was made up of extra payments for some services, it appears either that the fee did not insure full coverage, or that use of the services by non-members for pay was common, or that both of these were the case (Kurland 1947:108-9, 114).

The HSF's hospital facilities were limited, and its main service was provided in the clinics (through which home visits on emergency were also arranged). The pattern of public queuing, established in the previous century in the communal clinics for the poor of Jerusalem, was adopted with a connotation of working-class egalitarianism —ideological pride and practical inconvenience complementing rather than contradicting each other in this matter. Those members of the Histadrut who were identified less with class solidarity and more with the benefits of medical insurance, and could besides afford to pay physicians privately at need, continued to do so. On the other hand, members close to the HSF bureaucratic or professional staffs were able to expedite clinical treatment.

In relation to Arab workers, the Histadrut had before it primarily the interests of the Jewish workers. Where there was competition with Arabs for work in the Jewish sector, the Histadrut's policy was one of a 'closed shop' (Mansur 1937, Shafir 1989). In the government's employ, where Arabs and Jews sometimes worked together, it

attempted to encompass the Arab workers as well. For this purpose
it set up in 1927 a 'Palestine Labor League' (PLL). Its charter called
for the Histadrut to be the Jewish unit of the League, while other
national groups—i.e. Arabs—were to eventually organize as
autonomous national units within the League. In fact the League
arrangement was an uneasy compromise fraught with contradictions,
since it was as much a way of isolating Arab members from Histadrut
membership as it was an effort at organizing them.

Notwithstanding a marginal faction within it which called for
binational cooperation, the Histadrut did not cease to be a declaredly
Jewish institution which originated in competition with Arab labor and
thrived on it. Within these tensions, the HSF was prepared to insure
Arab workers on the occasions that they organized in specific
configurations (usually as government employees) under the
patronage of the Histadrut, as part of the PLL (Tadmor 1981). There
were not, however, many such occasions, since such client Arab
organizations were opposed as cooptative by Arab national and labor
leaders and were unsuccessful. While the PLL increased its activities
with the formation of an Arab department in the Histadrut in 1943, in
1946 it had a total of 5,000 nominal Arab members, only a minority of
them with fees-paying status, entitling them, for example, to sick fund
treatment (Kurland 1947:113, 162-163, Washitz 1947:173).   With
pressures from both Jews and Arabs toward separatism increasing
segregation in most work-place, the Histadrut's attempts to recruit
members to its 'separate but equal' activities in the Arab sector
remained marginal.

The Hadassah Medical Organization and Other Agencies

Simultaneously with the rise of the HSF in the Jewish sector, the
Hadassah voluntary organization (the Women's Zionist Organization
of America), representing the increasing involvement of American
Zionists in Jewish affairs in Palestine after the First World War,
assumed the role of major external benefactor among the
philanthropic agencies providing health services. In 1918 the
American Zionists' Medical Unit (Hadassah medical mission, recruited
by H. Szold) arrived on a visit to Palestine, and in 1921 took on
permanent status as the Hadassah Medical Organization (HMO), and
established a hospital in Jerusalem in 1922. Administered from
abroad, the HMO engaged in sanitary and anti-malaria work, programs
against tuberculosis and trachoma, six hospitals in Tel Aviv, Haifa,
Jerusalem, Zefat, and Tiberias, as well as urban outpatient clinics,

laboratories and pharmacies, and sponsorship of dental clinics operated by local dental societies (ESCO 1947:388-393). The HMO focussed especially on children from birth through adolescence, and in addition to a school health program and luncheons its preventive health services were family oriented, ranging from district hygiene nursing to infant and mother centers providing pregnancy, obstetric and postnatal care, including a milk kitchen dispensing 'a drop of milk' formulas. In 1927 the HMO had 17 mother and child welfare centers in Palestine; by 1946 it had built a network of 90 such centers.

The HMO also, in cooperation with the Farmers' Association of the moshavot, founded a rural People's Sick Fund in 1931 and set up rural curative clinics (Grushka 1959:2, Halevi 1961:615). The farmers of the moshavot were ineligible for the workers' sick fund founded by their employees, and were not served by the HSF's expanding number of clinics. The new sick fund continued for them the communal health care established in Baron de Rothschild's day. The HMO's alliance with this group reflected an alignment in which HMO facilities, while available to all, served especially the middle class, while the HSF served especially the labor movement of which it was an integral part. In the situation of division in the Jewish community between the socially activist labor left and the majority constituted by the middle class, petite-bourgeoisie, and independent agriculturalists, the relation between the two major voluntary agencies providing health care to the Jewish public emerged as an aspect of the competition for primacy and for clientage—especially that of the ideologically uncommitted employed constituency in the increasing Jewish middle class which was eligible for Histadrut membership.

The conflict between a philanthropic agency funded from the USA, which required no self-participation of its clients and inevitably projected some dependency upon them, and a locally rooted socialist cooperative institution based on mutual aid and stressing self-reliance, continued the argument begun during the previous period about paying for medical services and about fees relative to economic situation. The issue was still that of the importance of productive independence, but now the terms of the argument were no longer the confrontation between the values of the traditional and the new Jewish settlement in Palestine, but rather the increasing tension between the rising labor movement's class-conscious socialism and the growing middle class's decided lack of political organization for class confrontation.

Here as in the previous period considerations of ideology and professional livelihood conjoined, producing conflict from the beginning between veterans of the developing local institutions and the arriving American doctors of Hadassah (not withstanding the HSF's dependence on HMO hospitals, and the HMO's support of the construction of the first HSF hospital in Afula; Halevi 1980). The competition between Jews for employment was furious. Thus Dr. Yofe, speaking in 1922 for the physicians' association, complains that Hadassah sends American doctors to treat the middle class for little pay, and to alienate them from local physicians so that immigrant physicians find no work and the employment of veteran ones is reduced, especially in Jerusalem. From the moment the Hadassah physicians arrived and started working he complains also that the foreign experts are inexperienced in local conditions but do not involve or seek advice from veterans, and that they are incompetent, inefficient and mendacious (Yofe 1971:363, 366, 381). Some part of the resentment toward the HMO may also be attributed to antagonism between socialist Zionists who had immigrated to Palestine (mostly from Eastern Europe) and American Zionists (led by immigrants from Germany). Even though the founders of Hadassah and of the other active American philanthropic organization, the AJDC (H. Szold and Y.L. Magnes, respectively), had immigrated to Palestine, the agencies' support, administration and expertise remained representative of American free enterprise.

Despite the HMO's declared intentions to transfer its facilities to the control of the local Jewish community following the recommendation in 1927 by an invited committee of experts that HMO activities devolve upon local communities (Rosenau and Wilinski 1928), and even when urban clinics and hospitals began to be operated in cooperation with the municipalities as of the 1930s, the conflict did not abate. On the contrary, after the formation of the Israel Workers Party (Mapai) in 1930 the HSF became identified as a Mapai institution; with the increasing activity of the General Zionists as the party associated with private enterprise and claiming to represent a majority of the passive middle class, the Hadassah Organization became more and more identified with the General Zionists (Halevi 1961). The issue of who should be the provider of health services for the Jewish population was politicized: the General Zionists majority faction in the WZO emphasized national unity and disvalued class conscious activity, and so argued against political-party association with education and health—i.e. against the HSF as an institution receiving favored official support. In this context the conjunction of HMO facilities with civic municipal services was also a political act.

Municipalities participated, as of 1931, in financing HMO outpatient and hospital facilities, and subsidized medical treatment of the poor; the Hadassah hospital in Tel Aviv was transferred to the city's control. The HMO in 1946 employed 44 physicians, 127 nurses, 41 public health nurses and 200 lay staff, a smaller personnel by far than that of he HSF (ESCO 1947:388-393). On the other hand its urban clinics, operating on the basis of fees per visit rather than on the basis of membership, were open to a wider section of the population. They were attended especially by the poor receiving public assistance, members of the middle class when they did not see private physicians, and anyone whose budget included occasional medical care rather than regular insurance. And HMO hospitals served almost everyone, including HSF insurees who were members of urban communities (Tel Aviv and Haifa, however, operated their own municipal hospitals). Members of kibbutzim, on the other hand, who neither belonged to the municipalities nor were insured through the HMO, did not have the resources for paying fees at these hospitals or for private care, and were therefore hospitalized in government hospitals more often than other Jews.

Not surprisingly, presented with American physicians, affinities and technology, American professional evaluators tended to be more impressed with the HMO than the HSF, in 1927 recommending that the HSF be absorbed in the HMO in order to rationalize duplication and waste, and in 1946 stating that it carried the main responsibility for supplying health services for the Jewish section of the population (Rosenau and Wilinski 1928:679ff, ESCO 1947:353). But given the competition and lack of effective coordination, in a growing situation of shortage of health care in the face of the needs of continuing waves of immigration, the various health care institutions soon supplemented each other to the benefit of the Jewish population. In 1948 there were a total of 120 mother and child health centers of which 90 were of the HMO, a few of the Tel Aviv municipality, and the rest of the HSF. In 1946 the HSF had a school health service including dental care, eyecare and treatment for ringworm in 50 schools, the HMO in 40. Each of the agencies had about 50 rural curative clinics (Grushka 1959). HMO physicians examined new immigrants on arrival, while HSF physicians treated them during (at least) the first period of their absorption. Immigrant health professionals were thus usually able to find work in their field.

With regard to the Arab population, the HMO (and the AJDC in the anti-tuberculosis program it operated from 1922-1931), influenced by the outspoken binationalist commitment of Y.L. Magnes, the beliefs of its founder H. Szold and of its first major benefactor N. Strauss, and congruent with the values of its American supporters, upheld a pluralist policy consistent with a political commitment to ethnic equality in Palestine (Halevi 1961). A nondiscriminatory policy was well suited to the liberal requirements of the American members of Hadassah, themselves an object of actual or potential discrimination in the USA. Clinics supported by Strauss explicitly maintained a pluralist policy, and this policy continued to be affirmed with the expansion of services.

At first the HMO offered some children's services for Arabs—school examinations in Arab schools, and two mother and child welfare centers opened in the 1920s in Arab neighborhoods in Jerusalem—but soon withdrew so as not to compete with the American Colony Aid Association which began to sponsor these activities (ESCO 1947:584-585). Two Strauss welfare and health centers 'for all races and creeds' opened in Jerusalem and Tel Aviv in 1927, but the one in Jerusalem became less effective in this regard after the hostilities of 1928-1929, while the center in Tel Aviv never did serve the Arabs significantly (Assaf 1970:95). After 1927, attending to the recommendation that HMO work should be controlled by local communities and that ancillary care such as infant welfare and schools should be taken over by the government, the government did indeed take over and develop these services, for the Arabs but not for the Jews.

Between 1918 and 1938, 2,360 Muslims and 1,030 Christians were treated as inpatients in HMO hospitals (in 1929, 1% of hospitalizations in these hospitals). In the span of these 20 years, 123,000 Muslims who made 475,000 clinic visits, and 17,000 Christians who made 105,000 visits, were treated as outpatients in the clinics (8% of HMO clinic visits in 1929) (ESCO 1947:584-585). Although the hospitalization rate is a token one and the outpatient numbers indicate a low average rate of visits per patient, these numbers nevertheless show an average of 24,400 visits per year by Arab patients to HMO clinical facilities for 20 years—a significant contribution by the HMO to health care of the Arab population. Anti-malaria work conducted in three HMO expert-centers in Galilee also affected Arab residents of the region. In addition HMO physicians in the rural sector saw Arab patients privately.

At least for the beginning of its tenure in Palestine, the HMO thus made special efforts to provide medical care for Arabs—both as gestures of goodwill and as expressions of pluralism. However, as the Hadassah Organization became increasingly allied with the General Zionists its binationalist commitment was replaced by the prevailing nationalist perspective (Halevi 1961). During the years of increased strife in the late 1930s Arabs came less to be treated in HMO clinics (Wellesley 1937:231). But later again HMO facilities, especially in the mixed cities, were a place of positive contact between Arabs and Jews: The cooperation of HMO and municipalities meant more affordable care for those who were able to pay, and subsidized or free care for the Arab poor, more so as municipal welfare services developed. Although even at their most pluralistic, as in this case, Jewish health services remained identified with the Jewish community, the arena of medical care was one where some salutary social relations could still be expressed even at times of national hostilities.

Adding to the variety of Jewish health care institutions, a number of (anti-left) voluntary sick funds (in addition to the HMO's People's Sick Fund) were founded in the 1930s, expressing political factions and serving the nonsocialist identified urban workers, the middle classes and independent small farmers. They were the Sick Fund for National Workers (later the National Sick Fund) formed in 1933, which represented the National Labor Federation (the workers' organization of the right opposed to the Histadrut); the Center Sick Fund, founded by the General Zionists (1936), who had their own workers' organization; and the Maccabi Sick Fund (formed as a professional organization by unemployed immigrant physicians, whose affinity was to the same political group). Also available to the urban middle class were private insurance plans formed by physicians, Physicians' Fund (later Shiloah) in Tel Aviv and Assaf in Haifa (Halevi 1979, 1980).

Not only were the various medical insurance plans associated with different segments of the Jewish population, they also differed correspondingly in the mode of their engagement of physicians and in the freedom of choice given patients. Whereas HSF and HMO doctors, operating within a well-institutionalized framework, were salaried workers and were assigned to patients in the clinics (although a difference between the two agencies was that HSF physicians and patients were—in principle if not always in full practice—solidary members of the Histadrut), physicians associated with the other plans worked on the basis of fees received for treating patients who could to some extent choose between them, and most often treated patients in their private clinics. Although some public clinical or laboratory facilities were established by most of the small sick funds, their number did not approach the number and range of HSF facilities with whom they had to compete in the cities. Still, the area of medical care was an arena where an exception was made to the general lack of institutional concentration by the passive center majority and the divided right (Horowitz and Lissak 1977:143). Here some successes were achieved by these sectors, albeit minor as opposed to the major achievements and power of labor institutions. Unlike the HSF, the other sick funds did not represent organizations which had any Arab members. Their associated physicians sometimes treated such patients on a private basis in the cities; physicians of the rural People's Sick Fund saw some village patients.

Other voluntary agencies were also active during these years. The Women's International Zionist Organization (WIZO) operated several baby homes for care of Jewish infants, and programs for care of premature babies, nutrition, and hygiene. A first aid ambulance service and a blood bank were established in 1930 by the MDA (Magen David Adom). The AJDC in conjunction with the Jewish Agency established institutions for care of the chronically ill and the aged. In addition to the AJDC's anti-tuberculosis program, a voluntary physicians' association (the Anti-Tuberculosis League) was also active in this field (Grushka 1959:142-146).

2.C. Developments in the Arab Community

Having examined some of the circumstances for the development of voluntary Jewish and Christian health institutions, the question must now again be asked why, relative to their comparative circumstances, the Arabs—given their traditional reliance on the state for provision of services—did not begin to develop their own voluntary institutions until the very end of the period of the Mandate. Whatever hospitals, clinics and physicians were operated by the existing non-Arab agencies, they were insufficient for accommodating the Arab, especially Muslim, population which was mainly rural.

The extraordinary natural increase during this period in the Arab population of Palestine exacerbated the fact that health services—which would have had to have been much expanded to meet the needs of the growing population of Arab poor, peasants and urban—were barely existent. This population increase, due mostly to natural increase through a reduction in the rates of infant mortality, was augmented by labor immigration from the surrounding areas (Gilbar 1989; see also Chapter 5.B., below). All in all, the Arab population was doubled from 650,000 in 1919 to 1.3 million by 1948.

Compared with this increase, the professionalization of western-trained medical personnel, characteristic of British colonialism (Johnson 1973) proceeded at a slow rate among Arabs. The Jews, through the immigration of professional manpower (along with external financial support and national, communal, and cooperative investments), had been able to overcome the medical consequences of an even higher rate of population growth than that of the Arabs (although preponderately immigrant and smaller in absolute number: the number of Jews at the end of the First World War was less than 100,000, in 1930 165,000, and by end of the Mandate 650,000 [ESCO 1947:507]). In 1946 a survey by the Jewish Physicians Association of Palestine reported 2,520 licensed physicians in Palestine, of whom 2,257 were Jews, and only 85 Muslim Arabs, 125 Christian Arabs, and 53 European Christians (in Transjordan by comparison there were reportedly eight physicians for a population of 300,000; Kurland 1947:112). Twenty-five % of Arab physicians (53) were in government service, the rest were in the cities— according to this survey, quite possibly selective in this regard, no Arab physician was found in the villages (Kurland 1947:112-113). Jewish health professionals worked for the National Council, the HSF, Jewish hospitals, the HMO, some in British hospitals and very few in other branches of the GDH, some in association with the other sick funds. The Jewish sector was characterized by high employment in the health services (as in all the public services) including, in addition to medical personnel, a bureaucracy which gave employment and local power to clerks and functionaries. The relatively high supply of physicians and dentists—mostly absorbed as salaried workers in an expanding public service system eager to employ them for the benefit of a population needy of their services—determined their role as public servants as well as their relatively low wages. At the same time, the willingness to absorb these immigrants in their own professions spurred health service institutions to expand further (Ofer 1967). (The HSF's capacity, however, to absorb manpower was, in spite of its expansive intentions, limited; many immigrant physicians who were not absorbed in it half-heartedly were not absorbed at all).

In addition to the expansion of public service, 66 private Jewish hospitals were established—mostly between 1930-1936 with the immigration of a large number of Jewish physicians from Germany. Because of this supply of manpower, the medical problems brought about by the large wartime and post-war immigration of Jews could be overcome: In 1930 there was one physician per 1,300 for Jews, and in 1940, despite the massive immigration, one per 660 (*Survey* 1946:614).

The number of Arab physicians, on the other hand, rose from approximately (the statistics include some non-Arabs) 68 in 1921 to 220 in 1935. Elsewhere, 240 Arab physicians were reported in 1935 (M. al-Hussaini, cited in Assaf 1970:296), and 256 in 1942. The ratio of Jewish to Arab physicians in 1945 was 9/1. The GDH Annual Reports showed the following increase in the numbers of physicians (See Table 2.1):

Table 2.1.   Western Trained Medical Practitioners in Palestine

a. Licensed Physicians, 1920-1946

	Jews	Christians	Muslims
1920	58	16	19
1924	285	161	35
1946	2,625	187	104

(GDH 1924:38, 1946:31)

b. Licensed Medical Practitioners, 1944

	Muslims and Christians (mostly Arabs)	Jews
Physicians	272	2,521
Dentists	54	742
Pharmacists	126	496
Midwives	297	507

(*Survey* 1946:623,703)

Arab midwives included a small number of western-trained licensed midwives—nine in 1924, one for every 4,000 Arabs by 1939, and a total of 315 in 1946—and thousands of traditional midwives who continued to give advice on infant care and performed most deliveries (GDH 1946:31,40, Government Committee on Development and Welfare Services 1940:66). The government made some efforts to supervise the traditional midwives: 1,200 of them held annual permits in 1938 (GDH 1938:79). Nurses, most of them Christian, worked mainly in hospitals, and were particularly badly paid (Washitz 1947:199); pharmacists practiced in cities and towns.

Because of the lack of medical training in the country medical students continued to be trained abroad, especially in Egypt, Beirut, and London. In 1929, seven Palestinian Muslims began medical study at the American University in Beirut; in 1944 there were 18 graduates from Palestine (who assumedly must have been mostly Arab) in medicine and pharmacy there, and that same year the first Arab woman doctor was graduated in London. In 1945 22 medical students from Palestine were accepted to study in Cairo (Assaf 1970:269). Government training and employment of Arab nurses resulted in a relative surfeit, so that in 1931 the ratio of nurses to population was 1/644 among Arabs, a lower rate but higher absolute number than that indicated by the 1/522 ratio among Jews (GDS *Census* 1931:xv).

Arab physicians worked for the government, the Christian missions, and in private practice. Jewish institutions, oversupplied with Jewish physicians, did not employ Arab ones. In 1946, a majority of the 20 GDH medical officers were Palestinian Arabs, two replacing two of the four British GDH senior medical officers supervising the districts, others supervising most of the subdistricts (*Survey* 1946:616-17, Grushka 1959:4). Those who did not find work within the available institutional arenas (Muslims especially) did not create their own, but remained private practitioners only; until the end of the Mandate, only one Arab hospital was opened—Dr. Dajani's private hospital (with 50 beds) in Yafo for well-to-do Arab patients (Dr. Kamil Effendi Dajani was a member of the Palestine Arab Party and of the Arab Higher Committee; Assaf 1970:297, *Survey* 1946:952, Washitz 1947:199). The impediment was not the small number of physicians per se (a handful of Jewish physicians had pioneered the socially active Jewish Physicians' Association) but rather an absence—rooted in the traditional elite social origins and in the individualism of most—of sufficient social impetus toward concerted activity for the public welfare (Shim'oni 1947:198, Rosenfeld 1978). In the 1940s there was, however, a growing involvement in medical activities among Arabs, as more Palestinian Arabs were trained and practiced as physicians, nurses and midwives. Some began to come from the educated working class or upper echelon government employees rather than from the landowning merchant class (Shim'oni 1947:198). There had been local elite professional physicians' associations in various towns, led by graduates of Beirut; after the founding of the Arab League in 1943, national associations began to be set up. An Arab physicians' association, the Palestine Arab Medical Association, engaging in educational activities and publications, and a dentists' association were formed in 1944. There were also anti-tuberculosis leagues similar to those formed by Jewish doctors and public (TB was introduced into Palestine during the First World War), and a professional (elite) midwives' association (Assaf 1970:297-298, *Survey* 1946:613-14, Shim'oni 1947:350, Washitz 1947;199). The first congress of the Palestine Arab Medical Association in 1945 gave priority to instituting free health centers for the Arab poor in the five biggest cities (*Journal of the Palestinian Arab Medical Association* 1945:2, 1947:1). Although apparently conservative in the social views it expressed and tending toward a philanthropic approach to health care, the Association's planned program included the Arab population as a whole in its purview. Following on this approach the Pan-Arab Medical Congress, meeting in 1946, decided to concentrate on setting up 'modern Arab Health Centres and Institutions in Palestine' and established a first anti-tuberculosis clinic in Yafo (*Journal of the Palestinian Arab Medical Association* 1946:1,2).

As urban absentee landowners and rentiers, merchants and money-lenders, most leaders of national institutions and municipal officeholders were not much concerned with benefiting either peasants or laborers. Preferring to collect high rents and interest rather than to dispossess tenants completely, they made no investment in economic development in the rural sector, and their involvement in improving the physical welfare of peasants was virtually nonexistent (Carmi and Rosenfeld 1974).

The pan-Islamic movement, in which local leaders represented the area vis-à-vis the Arab world, was strongly traditionalist and a conjunction of religion and politics prevailed in it. Thus, while Zionism at this time had a modernizing secularizing momentum, the religious Muslim basis and conservative leadership of the Arab national movement continued to favor traditional forms of social assistance, i.e. charity based on the collection of *zaccah* funds and on the allocation of *waqf* income. While the Supreme Muslim Council, which derived many of its tasks and its source of financial power from jurisdiction over the *awqaf*, did concern itself with issues of social welfare, it did so primarily within the traditional charitable modes which, in the absence of a Muslim state, did not include hospital facilities. Even when administered by newly constituted 'Muslim commissions,' considered part of government administration, *awqaf* funds were mainly used to sponsor traditionally supported religious institutions—mosques, courts and schools. Health care remained largely outside of this realm and facilities were only barely initiated—three clinics sponsored by the SMC are referred to (Washitz 1947:199). Although the SMC allocated funds for treatment of poor Muslim patients in existing hospitals, in 1942-1944 this allocation accounted for less than 2% of SMC budget. Out of a total of 10% of the budget for welfare, another small amount was distributed in cash for subsistence needs, and the rest paid for foods provided in soup kitchens. As mentioned above, the SMC also funded some anti-malaria (marsh drainage) activities, and sponsored the voluntaristic activities of the upper-class midwives' association in establishing an infant welfare center in Jerusalem, but preponderately it had other priorities (Assaf 1970:180, 290, 297, 320).

Conjointly, the structure and goals of Arab political institutions did not encourage sponsorship of new medical services. The Arab Executive, a body appointed by the Arab Congresses (themselves elite meetings), dealt with national political issues and not with social welfare. When political parties emerged in the mid-1930s they were socially conservative, so that the two Higher Arab Councils which represented and coordinated joint action between them were unlikely to sponsor activities for the benefit of Arab workers and peasants (although they did not necessarily oppose such activities [Mansur 1937]).

The Arab leadership, rejecting the British National Home Policy toward the Jews, and thus all institutions based on its premise, refused the government's proposal for creation of the ethnically-based civil administrative institutions (i.e., a Legislative Council and Arab Agency). For the Jewish National Council (the general council of the Jewish community in Palestine formed to function as a central authority for the Jewish community) and for the Jewish Agency (which coordinated international activities as of 1929), creating and supporting institutions of education, welfare, and health was an indispensable part of the Jewish efforts to create a functional national framework. The National Council supervised health and social services through a Health Council. As ineffective and prone to the pressures of vested interests as this Council seems to have been at least in its early years, it provided some coordination between Jewish medical institutions, as well as the ability to make demands, negotiate and cooperate with the Government Department of Health (Rosenau and Wilinski 1928:679-81, *Survey* 1946). In the 1920s, WZO financed the HSF as well as isolation hospitals and immigration stations staffed by the HMO, and paid physicians to treat settlers in new agricultural settlements. The National Council continued to employ some physicians to examine and treat new immigrants, while the Jewish Agency paid the initial (HSF) medical insurance.

Meanwhile, the momentum of Arab leadership was defensive, most intensely concerned with arresting the erosion of Arab primacy in Palestine in the face of increasing Jewish immigration. Thus, while the Jewish Agency and National Council were engaged in establishing institutional requisites, including medical ones, for independence of the Jewish community in Palestine, the Supreme Muslim Council, the primary national religious-political body as of 1922 and no less an institutional creature of the Mandatory government, increasingly put its energy into oppositional activities in the cause of liberation.

In this context, the availability of medical services provided by government, Christian missions, and Jewish organizations and individuals, was palliative. The Christians, mostly urban and becoming more so, used the services provided by missions most easily. For the Muslim population, the government and the missions provided curative services. Arabs also sought treatment from Jews, and Jewish institutions—HMO urban outpatient clinics especially—also offered some medical aid to Arabs. With increasing residential and social segregation, economic boycotts and strikes and acts of violent hostility, medical care was an area of some mutual trust. Even the Mufti of Jerusalem, Haj Amin al-Hussaini, had in the 1920s as his personal physician the Jewish Dr. A. Ticho of Jerusalem (Assaf 1970:85).

Together with the absence of a central Arab organization interested in and capable of directing Arab communities, the political weakness of Arab municipalities was detrimental to health care. The WZO could and did require Jewish communities and municipalities to collect funds for health, education and welfare. Although of the municipalities only Tel Aviv and to a somewhat lesser extent Haifa—a 'mixed town'—engaged in actually providing medical services, other Jewish communities also participated in financing HMO facilities and subsidized medical treatment of the Jewish poor. In the 1940s, with increasing prosperity and municipal tax collection, and a new civic consciousness among Arab municipal leaders, some Arab municipalities and urban communities also started welfare activities (Survey 1946:689). Ramallah and Yafo were planning the construction of Arab hospitals financed by the municipality (Assaf 1970:297-298). Urban voluntary associations collected funds for health and a (very) few opened clinics: When the government's 1942 survey on nutrition showed the extent of nutritional deficiencies among the poor, 14 town-aid committees paid half of the cost of meals for schoolchildren while the government paid the other half (Assaf 1970:300); outpatient clinics were opened by the Eastern Neighborhood Council in Haifa, the Jerusalem Women's Association, and the Nablus Sport and Culture club (Washitz 1947:199-200).

In this respect too the situation in Arab villages was worse: Whereas municipal councils were established as of the 1920s, only in 1940s were local and village administrative ordinances passed to regulate village government, so that most rural communities during these years continued to operate along kinship lines. Nevertheless, a number of villages did share responsibility with the government for local health care by providing (in spite of a growing shortage of housing) facilities for clinics while the government employed the staff. Local communities also participated in setting up and maintaining some infant welfare centers, cooperating with the government in financing 18 infant welfare centers in cities and 20 in villages (Assaf 1970: 297). The involvement of local committees (e.g. Jiffne, Rame, Khan Yunis) is mentioned in this respect (GDH 1925:26). Some of the committees involved were bourgeois charitable societies such as the 'Committee of Ladies' in Yafo, but village committees supplied quarters and furniture and a few larger villages carried operating expenses and provided volunteers (centers were staffed by a midwife or nurse; GDH 1938:81; Government Committee on Development and Welfare Service 1940:68).

Arab villages were also continually active in the crucial area of environmental sanitation. Assuring a supply of potable water and waste-disposal systems were tasks of the local community, and in the rural areas both Arab and Jewish settlements made early progress in improving their water systems (GDH 1924:43, 1925:39, 1931:6, 1934:11). Local bodies could more easily mobilize the delimited cooperation needed to install a better water system than to organize and supervise a waste disposal program, and the poor sanitation in both Jewish and Arab villages was recurrently criticized.

Most significantly, both an autonomous state and a significant middle class were late to develop in Palestine. Labor activism was thus the most promising path to health insurance and attendant health care and differential unionization of Jews and Arabs determined differences in the extent of medical services provided upon it (cf. Navarro 1989, on the role of labor movements in motivating, public health programs and services). Because a massive Arab labor movement was slow to organize, the potential of workers' organizations for mutual aid, including cooperative health care institutions, was undeveloped.

Wage-workers, in spite of the great increase in their number during the Second World War, were a minority of the Arab working population. Peasants remained the majority, and numbered 850,000, while there were 60,000 wage-workers who constituted 23.5% of Arab main providers. By 1947 with the Arab population at 1.3 million, there were 150,000 wage-workers forming 38.5% of the main providers (Assaf 1970:229-231). Even taking into account the high percentage (up to 20%) of non-Palestinian workers from neighboring countries who may have been less inclined to committed union activity, the size of this group was not in itself insufficient for significant union activity and mutual aid. The lack of institutional achievements was rather a function of factors contributing to the low level and fragmentation of labor initiative, organization and success. These factors—the slow development of Arab industry and especially the form Arab labor took as most workers were hired on a temporary, seasonal, and migrant basis—were unfavorable to unionization (Carmi and Rosenfeld 1974).

The HSF had initially been supported by the WZO, but the fees which made its second, self-sufficient phase, possible were paid by members, and to a lesser degree by employers' participation. Arab workers were at a complete disadvantage in both these respects, not only because of their lower wages and because the development of industry by Arab capitalists was slow, but because they had no leverage, as temporary and replaceable workers, for eliciting employers' participation.

The Histadrut improved working conditions in industry through collective bargaining, mostly for Jews but also for some Arabs, but most Arab workers, hired without rights or security beyond the daily wage, were unaffected by such improvements. In places of common work Arabs had higher wages, but the emphasis on preferring Jewish labor led to increasing separation (Horowitz and Lissak 1977). Some permanent Arab workers in large companies or government institutions did have rights and security, but the predominant trend toward working in the towns as migrant laborers as of the 1920s meant that the proletarized Arab peasant, usually underemployed in seasonal and fluctuating labor for low wages computed on the basis of his replaceability by others like him, could afford only the bare minimum (Carmi and Rosenfeld 1974). The wages and security of working (usually young) women and of minors were even poorer. Most Arab women did not work outside the home, but those who did were paid the lowest wages (Washitz 1947:158). Compared to the Jews, Arab urban workers' families spent very little on health as well as on education and on taxes, a higher portion of their earnings being spent on food which was nevertheless less varied than that of Jewish families (Assaf 1970:228). But Arabs paid more for actual medical treatment when it was needed—for Jews it was covered as part of the Histadrut tax (Washitz 1947:127).

Until the 1940s Arab labor cooperatives had no resources and institutional achievements. The Palestine Arab Workers' Society (PAWS) was formed in 1925 in Haifa with branches in a number of towns and villages, but was barely active for most of the Mandate period (*Survey* 1946:763-766). Several other workers' associations, especially the Arab Labor Federation in Yafo, were active in the 1930s, but only during the Second World War, which brought an influx of laborers to the cities and army camps with many employed on government jobs, projects, and enterprises, did this began to change (Shim'oni 1947:366-369, Carmi and Rosenfeld 1974, Taqqu 1987). Effective organizations emerged both in opposition to and in cooperation with the Mandatory government. A wave of common workers' strikes were organized against the government, and the PAWS was reactivated. Among its new enterprises was the provision in the Haifa area, the center of most progressive labor activities, of medical care for members at lowered prices. Dr. Omar Halil, a Haifa doctor (the son of a railway clerk) who provided this aid, later briefly headed the association (Assaf 1970:221, *Survey* 1946:764).

The Arab Workers' Congress (AWC, or Federation of Arab Trade Unions and Labor Societies), a Communist organization, became the largest of the Arab unions (*Survey* 1946:763-764). Altogether, the Arab organized labor movement amounted in 1945 to only 20,000 (only a minority of which were dues-paying members) out of 150,000 Arab workers. A maximum of 10,000 more government workers participated in labor actions without being union members (Assaf 1970:222-224).

Although none of the Arab workers' organizations was a general encompassing one like the Histadrut, still it is evident that after some starts and stalls the Arab labor movement was gaining momentum in the 1940s, including some beginning in cooperative health care. The argument made here is that as the unionization of Arab workers lagged behind that of Jews, Arab cooperative health care was during these years at its nascent stage, permeated with the forces of political activities, but at best informal, local, and only partially effective.

For the Jews, the HSF served both urban workers and agricultural workers in the Jewish rural settlements established as egalitarian cooperatives. Meanwhile, the Arab village was rather becoming less egalitarian than it had been, with its traditional cooperative basis slowly undermined. The privatization of communal land begun in the last decades of the 19th century led to increasing heterogeneity between peasants, who now ranged from the better-off to the landless, as did the differences in family wealth engendered by members' wage labor in the cities (*Survey* 1946:233-37, Assaf 1970:190-1, 211). Such inequalities necessarily affected nutrition, housing and access to private medical care. The majority of peasants, heavily in debt and uncertain of their subsistence, could barely afford any additional expenses. Although most owned land, for 70% their land was inadequate (Carmi and Rosenfeld 1974).

Peasant cooperatives, introduced in 1933, which may have had the potential for initiating mutual aid for health, did not develop as general institutions but rather served the wealthiest villagers. Only 5% of the peasants in 1937 were members of such cooperatives (Assaf 1970:186). In the 1940s when the British government, interested in insuring production essential for the war effort, encouraged the activity of both rural and urban cooperatives, most cooperatives included only the more affluent villagers and skilled urban workers. One such association in the Haifa area, however, the Society for Arab Village Revival, was involved in the construction of curative clinics in some of the large villages (Assaf 1970:219). For reasons mentioned, the Histadrut's half-hearted initiatives Arab medical cooperatives did not take root. Arab peasants were not organized or solvent enough as a rule for the possibility of developing health services themselves, labor unions which may have impelled them to widespread cooperative activity were only gathering, and assistance from above was not overly forthcoming.

2.D. The Distribution and Use of the Health Services

The amalgam, uncoordinated by central planning, of public (government and voluntary) and private provision of health care which was to become the framework for the development of the Israeli health system was already well in place before 1948. It included activities by the mandatory government, the Christian missions, Jewish and Arab national authorities, the HMO, the HSF and other voluntary sick funds, each of which linked to a political and ideological stance, some of the municipalities and local authorities, some Jewish, Christian and Arab voluntary charitable groups, private physicians and hospitals, and traditional practitioners. The development and distribution of all these activities was such that reasonably adequate care was available to Arabs only in towns. Although all the major providers of clinical care (government, missions, HSF and HMO) operated rural clinics, their scope in relation to needs ranged from inadequate to negligible, and Arab peasants were only minimally provided with health care and protection.

The overall utilization of health services was determined by the fact that the majority of Arabs was rural while the majority of Jews was urban. In 1944 about 70% of the Muslim population and 90% of the Druze were rural residents, while only 20% of the Christians and 25% of the Jews were rural. These figures reflected a ca. 5% rural increase among Jews and a similar urban increase among Muslims and Christians during the Mandatory period. The great absolute rural increase among Muslims was the primary condition.

The overload on medical institutions and practitioners were acute in both cities and countryside. In the towns, however, the concentration of services by and for Jews matched the concentration of the Jewish population (two-thirds of which lived in the four largest towns). Urban Arabs had access—however critically limited for the poor unable to afford it—to the given range of health care institutions and practitioners. But in the rural areas, where the small size of the Jewish population made communal provision of care feasible, the large and mainly Muslim peasant and migrant-peasant majority constituted a mass of many unmet medical needs.

Given the fact that, as shown above, the health services were designated for Jews and for Arabs along communal lines, the form that settlement took in Palestine determined a lack of integration in medical care as in other aspects of life. Residential segregation increased as many new Jewish settlements were formed, and Arab laborers no longer resided within and around the moshavot as they had done in the pre-Mandatory period, but arrived to do agricultural work as they did to work in the cities—i.e. as day laborers setting out each day from their own villages. Many Arab villages were small and unreachable, with no roads for transportation. Where Jews built new towns, some Arab villages encapsulated in expanding towns formed separate urban neighborhoods, and Arab immigrants from neighboring areas were concentrated in squatters neighborhoods in cities. In relation to medical services this meant that, with important exceptions in the large 'mixed' cities where there were both Jews and Arabs (ordinarily in separate neighborhoods), facilities were identified with a separate residential community of Jews or Arabs.

Jewish physicians were heavily concentrated in the cities. A survey of Histadrut members in Tel Aviv, Haifa, and Jerusalem in 1946 counted 1,969 physicians—highest among the free professions by far (Kurland 1947:96). There were a total of 2,257 Jews reported in the Physicians' Association survey of the country as a whole, so that it appears that only 288 of the Jewish physicians in Palestine in 1946 resided outside of the three largest cities. As to Arab physicians, at the beginning of the Mandate five of them lived in villages (GDH 1924:38-39), while toward its end still very few villages had resident private practitioners (Assaf 1970:281). Some were visited by government or mission clinic physicians once a week or once in two, and villagers close to Jewish settlements might be able to come to the HSF clinics in emergencies or otherwise for small pay, or else be treated privately by HSF or HMO physicians. These physicians, for the most part not local residents but rather visitors on circuit, were not always available beyond their assigned duties, although some were hired on a part time basis with the understanding that their incomes be completed through such private practice (Rosenau and Wilinski 1928; this was the situation at the beginning of the Mandatory period. With the increase in immigration and settlement it is likely that even more of their time was occupied with the needs of the Jewish populace). Rural nurses played an important but insufficient role.

The weight of the health services offered by and for the Jewish population was on ambulatory care, but in consequence of the shortage in government hospital beds, Jews began to develop their own hospitals which offered a total of 5,000 beds in 1946. They belonged to a variety of agencies: the HSF, the HMO and the municipalities in cooperation with the HMO, the Jewish community of Haifa, and the city of Tel Aviv which took over the HMO hospital in 1936, the National Council (in Tiberias), various philanthropic organizations in Jerusalem, and a large number of private hospitals with the heaviest concentration of beds in Tel Aviv and Jerusalem, and to a lesser degree in Haifa (see Table 2.2).

Table 2.2:   Hospital Beds According to Provider, 1944 (in %)

Mandatory Government	33
Missions	29
Jewish municipalities	13
Private (overwhelmingly Jewish)	10
HMO (with municipal participation)	9
HSF	6
	100

(*Survey* 1946:612-614)

Jews used government and mission hospitals much more than Arabs used Jewish hospitals. Thus in Haifa in 1934 34% of the patients in the government hospital were Jews, while only .7% of the patients in Jewish hospitals were Arabs. In Jerusalem, 23% of the patients in mission hospitals in that year were Jews (more than half hospitalized in Anglican Mission facilities), while only .3% of the patients in Jewish hospitals were non-Jews (Canaan 1949).

The relative weight of Jewish hospitals in the total number of beds, slightly more than a third, was not high enough to account for the large difference in hospital utilization rates between Arabs and Jews. In 1935 the rate of hospitalization of Jews in the population was twice as high as that of non-Jews, and this ratio rather increased in the next decade (GDH 1936-7:139). The 1946 GDH *Annual Report* (1946:57) gave the total raw number of hospital admissions of Jews as twice as high as that of Muslims, while the Muslim population was twice as large as the Jewish population.

The contrast between rural and urban hospitalization rates throws light on these differences. Jews from towns and from rural settlements were hospitalized at about an equal rate, while Muslims in towns had a hospitalization rate twice that of Muslims from villages. The hospitalization rate of rural Jews was three times that of rural Arabs, and that of urban Jews was one-and-a-half times the rate of urban Muslims (GDH 1943:4). Hospitalized Arab villagers were mostly residents of villages near the towns of Tiberias, Haifa, Tel Aviv/Yafo and Jerusalem (Washitz 1947:199).

Since these variations cannot be explained by differences in morbidity rates (see 2.E, below), it would seem that they were largely due to the lesser proximity and access of Arabs to hospitals, which were mostly located in towns (and were scarce or completely absent in some Arab towns). And despite the low fees, poverty would be a barrier to the use of mission hospitals by some of the rural population for whom other options were not available (GDH 1934:9). Resistance among peasants to what was perceived as a foreign and upper class medical culture must be considered of secondary importance only, since the evidence is that, wherever they were offered, 'western' medical options were sought after and used. It must be assumed that homeopathic medical practices were indeed prevalent among peasants, along with a medical pluralist and eclectic attitude. Traditional practice was evidently most persistent with regard to pregnancy and birth. The above figures include maternity hospital stays, and part of the difference may be due to delivery practices—about 2% of births among Muslims occurred in hospital, compared to 86% of births among Jews (GDH 1943:2).

Statistics on attendance at GDH outpatient clinics reveal an even greater disparity between Jews and Arabs. The Jews, who had other ambulatory care options as well, used the GDH outpatient clinics available to them much more often than Arabs, and the disparity in utilization was significantly greater for the rural populations: One out of 16 rural Muslims on the average visited a GDH clinic in 1942, in contrast to 3.3 visits per person among rural Jews (see Table 2.3).

For the Jews the outpatient rate, considered high, resulted as clinical care partially compensated for a shortage in hospital facilities. Ambulatory medical care may have been less efficient than adequate hospitalization would have been, but succeeded nevertheless in overcoming the significant health problems which accompanied immigration (Ofer 1967). The rate of visits to clinics by Arabs, relatively more deprived of both hospitals and private physicians, should on these terms have been even higher than that of Jews. It is clear rather that the very low rate among rural Muslims accounts for most of the difference between Arabs and Jews, and that it has as its first and sufficient reason the absence of clinics in rural areas.

Table 2.3:   Attendance at GDH Outpatient Clinics, 1942

Patients:	Muslims	Christians	Jews
Towns	277,611	50,638	811,259
Villages	43,840	1,543	396,238
Total	321,451	52,181	1 207,497
Estimated population:			
Towns	301,000	101,000	364,500
Villages	694,000	26,000	120,000
Total	995,000	127,000	484,500

(GDH 1942:10, GDH 1947:1,7,8)

2.E. Conditions of Health of the Arab Population

As of the early 1920s epidemic smallpox and cholera, controlled by vaccination and quarantine, were no longer scourges in Palestine. Malaria, the most important of the infectious diseases of wide prevalence, was submitting to control as a result marsh drainage and public health campaigns, although it continued to claim casualties among Arabs into the 1940s (Rosenau and Wilinski 1928, GDH 1926:15). The major communicable diseases were typhoid, dysentery, and the enteric diseases (all readily preventible but epidemic intestinal infections related to poor environmental sanitation), and measles. Also favored by unsanitary conditions were trachoma and other acute eye infections.

The diseases of underdevelopment—diseases based on nutritional deficiencies as well as infectious and parasitic diseases—had different sectors of the population at different risk. Given variations in the endemic foci of diseases, their prevalence and severity were affected by socioeconomic variations which determined nutrition and sanitation.

In the cities, unprepared for immigration and urbanization, and in some villages close to cities which attracted internal Arab migrants, there was severe overcrowding of both Jews and Arabs as well as inadequate infrastructure and sanitation. Slum housing was a growing problem (GDH 1932:10, Committee on Development and Welfare Services 1940:125, Mansur 1937, Assaf 1970:227). As late as 1932, three of the four largest cities did not have an adequate permanent water scheme (GDH 1932:6, Committee on Development and Welfare Services 1940:116-117). Neither Arabs nor Jews had a monopoly on sanitary problems or solutions. On the whole, towns and small cities were able to improve their water and sewage systems at a reasonable pace, while the large cities faced more complex technical problems, particularly regarding drainage (e.g. GDH 1929:12). Haifa, Jerusalem and Tel Aviv were still in the process of laying out sewage systems in 1940 (Committee on Development and Welfare Services 1940:116-121). Although 'mixed' municipalities could be arenas of Arab-Jewish conflict, the sanitary systems were no more than a marginal issue of contention (Committee on Village Administration and Responsibility 1947:18).

Inadequate water supply and sewage disposal became serious health hazards especially in those parts of the cities where Jewish immigrants lived in shacks and where Arab workers, many with their families, were crowded. Thus, while the plague was never out of control in this period, its appearance as late as 1942 led immediately to the demolition of shanty-towns in Haifa, Tel Aviv and Yafo. The consequences of unsanitary conditions and intolerable housing for the semi-migrant population were directly apparent in the pattern of enteric diseases, which had a low incidence as long as city populations were small and stable (GDH 1923:1). In the 1920s enteric diseases were chiefly endemic to urban Jews (GDH 1923:1, 1924:1, 1925:7, 1926:15). By 1925 they were on the rise (GDH 1925;14, GDH 1933;25). Reports of high incidence in the Arab population begin in the 1930s and increase into the 1940s; in 1937 most of the deaths from enteric diseases were among Arab villagers (GDH 1937:6, GDH 1942:18). From the reports it would seem that these diseases spread to Arabs in cities and through them to the surrounding villages (GDH 1932:20,34,13).

Typhoid, endemic among immigrant Jews in shantytowns, was concentrated in the cities, the four largest accounting for two-thirds of the cases in 1933 (GDH 1933:25, GDH 1935:34, Rosenau and Wilinski 1928:581). While its incidence was higher among Jews, the case fatality rate among Arabs was twice the rate among Jews (GDH 1938:47).

Measles also provided an example of unequal disease outcome. Epidemics were recurrent, accounting for at least one-third of the obligatorily reported communicable diseases (GDH 1923:17, GDH 1929:17, 1933:19, 1934:19, 1938:39). Both Arab and Jewish populations were susceptible; in 1938-1945 measles led the list of communicable diseases reported among Muslims and Jews. However, in that period it was responsible for only seven deaths of Jews, compared with 3,096 deaths of Muslims (GDS 1946:32-35). The high rate and pattern of infection reflected a lack of effective preventive methods, but the differences in outcome showed the relatively poorer health and nutrition of Arab children. Measles was only one, albeit important, of the causes of elevated rates of mortality among Muslim children.

Schistosomiasis (an infectious intestinal disease caused by parasitic flatworms transmitted by snails), leishmaniasis (skin ulcers contracted through sandflies), and hookworm (a severely debilitating disease which accompanied the development of citrus cultivation) were endemic in the Arab population and present in various subgroups of the Jewish population (Yekutiel 1979:976). Hookworm was localized particularly around the citrus groves in the area of Yafo, where its rate among Arabs was more than ten times as high as among Jews, reflecting the particularly poor sanitary conditions affecting Arab migrant laborers (GDH 1938:38, 56-57).

The incidence of trachoma was especially high. An early report found evidence in 97% of the populations of some regions, and widespread eye examinations in 1939 showed traces in a majority of Arabs examined (GDH 1923:2, GDH 1939:54). The HMO's program for treating trachoma succeeded in dramatically reducing the number of affected Jewish children (Rosenau and Wilinski 1928:597, HMO 1939: Chart 91a). Among Arab children in the schools high rates persisted up to the end of the Mandate in spite of the GDH's public health program (GDH 1946:5). Forty % of trachoma cases were estimated to occur in pre-school children, unlikely to receive early treatment (GDH 1939:13). Among school children in towns, trachoma was found in more than a half in 1924 and more than a third in 1938. In villages which had schools, three quarters of the children had trachoma in 1924, and more than a half in 1938. In villages without schools the rates were higher (GDH 1924:32, 1938:84).

In Jewish rural settlements living conditions were hardly luxurious, and faulty sewage was the norm in kibbutzim, but high awareness of sanitary needs and of dietary requirements, together with the Zionist effort at providing primary health care in every settlement, led to an increasing differentiation between the conditions of health of the Muslim peasant and proletarized-peasant majority and those of the Jewish agricultural minority. Undoubtedly the chief public health campaigns which reduced malaria and hookworm improved rural health proportionately more than urban health. Nevertheless, environmental conditions in Arab villages were inadequate, and in combination with agricultural poverty compounded by droughts, acted to make the health of rural Arabs on the average poorer than that of town-dwellers.

Whereas in urban areas deficient nutrition was found among a segment of the population—both Arab and Jewish—which was poor, in rural areas it affected almost everyone. A GDH nutritional survey conducted in 1942-3 found significant dietary deficiencies among most rural Arabs, resulting from insufficient consumption of fats and calcium (except among shepherds), animal protein, fruits and vegetables. The diets of affluent Arab villagers and of rural Jews were only mildly deficient (GDH 1944, *Survey* 1946:835-842).

Vitamin A deficiency, more prevalent in Arab rural locales than in towns, was linked not only to greater risk of ophthalmic disorders but inferentially (as an unfavorable influence on the lining of internal organs) to risk of pneumonial and enteric death (GDH 1944:60). Barely sufficient vitamin D, related to calcium inadequacies, was common among all groups. Dental caries, related to calcium and phosphorus inadequacies, was highly prevalent everywhere, including in the kibbutzim and moshavim where diets were otherwise adequate. The signs of vitamin D deficiency, rickets and stunting were confined to those not exposed to sunlight—generally Arab women and infants.

Among Jews, the fact that the rural sector was evidently in better health than those living in towns is demonstrated by the higher rates of infant mortality of Jews in towns than in rural settlements. Among Jews in the periods 1933-1937 and 1938-1945, urban births were 72-75% of all births, but urban infant deaths amounted to 80% of all infant deaths (computed from GDS 1947:18, 22, 59, 60, 63, 64).

The life expectancy at birth of Muslims rose during the period of the Mandate from an estimated 35 to 50 years, most of the increase attributable to the decline in infant mortality (Bachi 1945, Schmelz 1974, Eisenbach 1978). The rates among Christian Arabs were intermediate between those of Jews and of Muslims. In 1925 the infant mortality rate among Jews was reported as 131/1,000, among Christian Arabs 162/1,000 and among Muslims 200/1,000 (Rosenau and Wilinski 1928:574). Later comparison (necessarily rough because of gaps in rural reporting) shows a general decline in the rates of infant mortality among all groups during the Mandatory period. Because rural Arab reporting of deaths, particularly infant deaths, was erratic, more weight must be placed on case studies. Granquist in her census of the village of Artas in Judea around 1929 shows that for the period within memory about half of the children died by the age of 12 (Granquist 1931; similarly Eisenbach, 1977, based on reproductive-history interviews with a sample of Arab women). Mortality rates of Muslim children aged 1-5 were even more steeply greater than those of Christians and Jews (GDS 1946:26-27). The disparity in death rates between the groups was greatest in the early childhood years (see Table 2.4).

Table 2.4: Infant Mortality Rates and Life Expectancies

a. Infant Mortality Rates per 1000 Live Births, Palestine 1927-1945

	Muslims	Christians	Jews
1927-1932	174	133	71
1933-1938	132	126	71
1939-1945	123	90	50

b. Life Expectancies at Birth, 1944

Men	49	57	64
Women	50	60	66

(GDS 1947:76-78, GDS 1947:34).

Among listed causes of death, diarrheal and enteric infection in children under 2 appears regularly as a leading cause (GDH 1929:17, 19, 33, 1946:8 specifies in towns). It is safe to infer that the majority of deaths from measles were those of Arab children (GDH 1946:46, again specifies only town deaths). The high rates of death in infancy and early childhood among Arabs was linked, then, to poorer environmental conditions, to a greater extent of poverty affecting vulnerability to disease, and to the lesser penetration of health services. Hospitalization for birth, increasing among Jews, was still uncustomary among Arabs, as was prenatal care. The differences in the conditions of delivery of Jews and Arabs increased the difference in rates of early infant death.

The public health system, which made progress in controlling the subtropical infectious diseases especially through environmental campaigns, improved the chances of survival of children of all groups. But it is suggested here that the decline of mortality among Muslims during this period may in great part be attributed to a relaxation of modes of demographic control through infant and children's deaths, as rural families maximized their possibilities of subsistence in agricultural production for an expanding urban market and in wage labor (cf. Harris and Ross 1987, White 1976, Weil 1986; see also Chapter 6.C.).

Given the high birth rate and the high rate of mortality in infancy and early childhood among Arabs, the difference in the age-structure of the two populations gains in significance. Proportionately more Arabs than Jews were in the susceptible age groups and were at higher risk of death as well as of impairment. In contrast, the Jewish population grew by immigration; this meant a higher proportion of adults—not, in the circumstance of refuge from the Second World War, necessarily all in good health, but at some distance from the most susceptible years of infancy and for the most part from old age as well. The evidence that it was the young in rural settings who suffered particularly high health risks was of course of great importance in a population which was both young and largely rural.

Chapter 3

THE STATE AND THE STRUCTURE OF
THE PUBLIC HEALTH SYSTEM IN ISRAEL

After the creation of Israel, the state extended its responsibility for the health services through a partial national health service invested particularly in hospital construction and operation and in preventive services to pregnant women and children; through partial national health insurance applied within the national compulsory social insurance laws; as well as through undertaking a major funding role with regard to the voluntary sick funds.

The voluntary sick funds continued the pluralistic basis for membership initiated during the pre-state period, involving political affiliations in the provision of services and in medical insurance. The HSF primacy during the Mandate as the most general and comprehensive provider of ambulatory curative care (enhanced by its role in hospital service) was further extended, but the other sick funds succeeded in specializing in various niches of the emergent socio-political structure, among both Jews and Arabs.

3.A. The Development of Israel Health Ministry Functions

The creation of the state brought about, with regard to public responsibility for health, a struggle for dominance between the newly formed Israel Health Ministry (IMH) and the Histadrut's HSF, while other agencies previously active in this field—the other voluntary sick funds and charitable organizations—continued or transformed their activities in a secondary role. In this struggle, oppositions between the new national bureaucracy and the political parties, as well as between and within the parties themselves, were articulated and negotiated. To some degree jostling in this arena is still going on today, but by the mid-1970s the contest as a whole had been decided in favor of IMH control. However, accelerated deterioration for both economic and political reasons of welfare-state policies after 1977 has acutely curtailed the IMH's financial possibilities, never strong to begin with, so that its current directions are primarily characterized by a contraction in operating expenditures and a radical reduction in supportive budgets (Arian 1981, Baruch 1973, Doron 1975, Zalmanovitch 1983).

The fact that for a period of nearly 30 years IMH authority was far from determined has had definitive consequences—both negative and positive—for public health policies and services in Israel (Doron 1979, Halevi 1979, 1980, Palley et al. 1983, Tulchinski 1985, Yishai 1982). The particular outcome of the formative phase in health legislation (by 1951) and administration (by 1956) shaped the division of labor and distribution of power between agencies and with it the developmental trajectory of services and the scope of public responsibility for them.

The main issues under debate were whether the state would take over and nationalize the public health services developed by the pre-state Jewish community and how it would administer them, and whether and how medical insurance would become a state function. This dispute was part of a more comprehensive struggle between the political center and right on the one hand and the left on the other, with regard to statism as an alternative for and successor to the worker-identified institutions (Rosenfeld and Carmi 1976). In this struggle, the ruling Israel Workers' Party (Mapai) decided to side with the political center and right in favor of nationalization. What was to determine the character of the health services in Israel was that this alliance, effective in abolishing left-created defense and educational institutions and in nationalizing various of the Histadrut's social insurance plans, did not carry through in the area of health (Rosenfeld and Carmi 1976, Eisenstadt 1967, Doron 1975, Horowitz and Lissak 1977).

Comprehensive social insurance had been a major goal of the labor movement and of Zionist ideology (Kanev 1942). Demands for free hospitalization and government support of a national health service had already been presented to the Mandatory Government by the Jewish National Council as part of its proposal for equalizing conditions in Palestine with those being created in England. In 1948, a relatively state- oriented plan for the organization of health services in Israel presented by the Histadrut's Institute for Social Research reiterated—now vis-à-vis the still fought-for state—a proposed national health service which would provide elementary medical care, medications and hospitalization to all. The status of the HSF would be greatly altered, brought within significant government control as a part of national institutions. The government would become substantively responsible for financing the hospital and clinical system; it would take over the role of the Jewish National Council's Health Council in terms of collecting funds and budgeting, and transcend its weaknesses as a minor operating agency and a less-than-controlling national planning and overseeing one.

According to the plan all existing public general hospitals (including the HSF) would be transferred to the municipalities, so that a national system of state-supported municipal hospitals would be instituted and supplemented by special hospitals (e.g. mental; chronic) operated by the state. All residents regardless of political identification would be assured of hospital service. Local authorities and municipalities together with a proposed National Institute for Insurance for the social insurance of hired workers were to be responsible for operating the national health service, while the government and the local authorities would finance it. Elementary curative care for all would be provided in municipal clinics, but separate HSF clinics would continue to provide service for workers and members of agricultural cooperatives. Compulsory insurance would be legislated only for hired workers (and employers would be required to participate in insuring their workers) but others could join voluntarily. The system was to be national, but HSF independence on the level of clinics was to be maintained. In effect on this level a municipal and a HSF system were to function in a co-existence not much different from that which had existed heretofore between the HSF and the HMO. With respect to the Arab population, the majority view was that the same services should be extended to them (although an objection was made that funds collected in the diaspora for Jews should not equally be spent for Arabs). This was an issue of importance especially because Arabs were expected (on the basis of the UN plan for partition) to make up 40% of the population (Doron 1975).

Other opinions with regard to compulsory health insurance and ownership of the health services than that expressed in this plan were intensely pronounced. The political left supported continued complete independence of the HSF from state administration—because of ideological commitment to the continued success of the workers' movement, but also because transfer to the state meant direct control of these services by Mapai. Staunch support of Histadrut independence by Mapai's competitor for loyalties on the left, the United Workers Party (Mapam), made a change which appeared to supplant the Histadrut difficult for Mapai to defend. On the other hand the right and center were against any Histadrut ownership of health services and for their complete nationalization (Doron 1975).

The conflict begun during the Mandate between the General Zionists (liberals) and the Histadrut continued to be articulated through this controversy. The power and accomplishments of the Histadrut and the HSF created an ideological (though not a pragmatic) inconsistency in which nationalization of health services was opposed by leftist groups, while the center and right supported it (Eisenstadt 1967). The liberals did not have in mind central welfare-state responsibility for health, but rather intended to nationalize HSF services in order to decentralize them, operating local service through civic control in middle class interests. Municipal authorities, also representing middle class interests and responsible for more residents than those insured by the sick funds, supported a national health insurance for all and wanted ownership of a national health service to be transferred to themselves (Halevi 1979, 1980). Such transfer would eradicate the HSF and badly damage the Histadrut.

In 1947 the task of organizing a state health apparatus had been assigned to the Health Council of the Jewish National Council. Government ministries were established in 1948, and from then on a Health Ministry which took over the 'impartial' supervisory role of the Jewish Health Council, and which resembled the Mandatory Government Department of Health in structure and replicated its statutes, was in operation. Regional health bureaus and an epidemiological service like the GDH's were formed. The IMH inherited GDH formal structures and hospital facilities and some local personnel (Grushka 1959). It took over Mandatory governmental functions which superseded the HSF autonomous role, and was staffed and advised by former members of the Jewish National Council's Health Council some of whom represented political and professional interests opposed to the HSF. This meant—given a continued withdrawal of the Hadassah Medical Organization from nationally-ranging activities in Israel—that the two newly competing local bureaucracies not only continued the inevitable tensions between government and voluntary agencies under its control, but also continued the struggle begun during the previous period between socialists and liberals for the status of main guardian of health in the Zionist enterprise.

Like a number of other ministries, the Health Ministry was placed in the charge of one of the small parties and as in the other ministries its bureaucracy and its minister had a growing potential for actions and for status independent of Mapai (for coalitionary purposes Mapai's Chief of the outgoing Health Council had been denied the ministry he sought). A second Mapai-sponsored 'inter-ministry committee' attempted to formulate comprehensive legislation which would be in the Histadrut's interests and which would prevent the ministries from initiating social welfare policies not necessarily congruent with those of the Histadrut (Doron 1975).

The second plan for social insurance legislation, presented by this group in 1950, made no mention of a free national health service, and saw a transfer of public facilities to the municipalities as a matter far-off in the future. Preventive medicine—at that time fairly limited to immunizations in Mother-and Child Health Care Stations (MCHS) and schools and to control of infectious diseases—was to be free and universal, as was dental care for children. Health insurance was extremely partial in scope. Only hospitalization was to be free—paid for by the municipalities (50%), the government, Jewish voluntary institutions such as the Jewish Agency, and workers' insurance programs. Other curative care was to be provided without charge only to the indigent. Medical insurance, as well as maternity and disability insurance, were to be legislated only for hired workers. As to the question of ownership, eventually all of the sick funds were to be integrated to one (i.e. basically the HSF, with its clinical form of care) which would provide care for the insured workers population, but in the meantime the various agencies were to continue under the status quo, with the proposed National Institute for Insurance collecting the funds for them.

Instead of transforming it into part of a new national system, this plan would confer upon the HSF as it was the formal status of a national institution. Opposition from the right was understandable; nevertheless, the Histadrut itself did not contribute to this proposal supposedly made in its behalf and did not support it in spite of the financial advantage, inherent in compulsory insurance, of making employers' participation enforceable. The programmatic re-orientation between the first proposal and the second, as well as the Histadrut's lack of enthusiasm for it, resulted from political and demographic changes upon the establishment of the state (Doron 1975).

Post-state waves of immigration brought about financial problems which made real implementation of comprehensive service less and less immediately possible, but also made the argument about the reforms one of critical political salience, since with regard to immigrant groups especially the HSF was the Histadrut's major means of recruiting new members. In spite of the fact that a number of party leaders (including ostensibly the prime minister, Ben-Gurion) spoke for changing the HSF status in accordance with the statist alternative, a determining majority within Mapai saw as threatening even a partial distinction between the HSF and the Histadrut (such as would happen even on the terms most favorable to the HSF, which posited one united sick fund—i.e the HSF—as the agency providing national service). As a structurally defined instrument of the state, for which the government would do the service of collecting insurance, the HSF would no longer be completely controlled by the Histadrut. Mapai's self-identification with the state was such that in political terms, the argument in the party was essentially about the appropriate tactics for control of medical services—through the state or through the Histadrut.

With the elections of 1949, which initiated the long-term predominance of Mapai as the ruling party, the question of ownership of health services and of instituting compulsory insurance had become a ground of political tension and bargaining. While the left and the right both attacked Mapai's position, coalitionary considerations also contributed to defeating the nationalizing option (Arian 1981; Doron 1975; Zalmanovitch 1983). Mapai's alliance with the religious Workers' Party was in part based on allocating to the latter a portion of Histadrut members' fees; on the promise of considerable patronage appointments within the HSF's extensive bureaucracy; and on allowing the religious party's members to join the HSF without becoming Histadrut members while paying at a reduced rate (Arian 1981). Before the elections of 1951, toward final formulation of the range of the social insurance laws which were to represent a statist achievement, a coalitionary objection by the Progressive Party left health altogether outside of the proposed legislation. The Progressives, a middle class party with a significant physicians' constituency, represented the Israel Medical Association's position. The physicians' association supported a national health insurance plan which would assure them of fees, but only through the National Institute for Insurance and not through the HSF. They opposed the proposed national service through the HSF for fear it would limit the number of physicians' employed and control the conditions of public employment as the HSF already did (Doron 1975).

In fact legislation fell through because the Histadrut wanted no change in the status quo. Mapai was not interested in free hospitalization which would undercut the advantage of HSF insurees as members of an institution which had already developed (and intended to further build) independent hospitals, and was afraid of the loss of HSF independence from government inherent in national health insurance. The process of creating a welfare state failed to be completed in two crucial realms—health care and pensions (Horowitz and Lissak 1977).

The same compromise which led to the exemption of religious schools from nationalization and left them in the control of the religious parties, left the HSF and the Histadrut' pension funds within

Histadrut and Mapai control. The reason for both exemptions was the same—with the massive post-state immigration, each of these institutions was the most powerful agency for a politically decisive recruitment of new members to the party it represented (Arian 1981). These institutions were also central in attracting and attaching the middle class (Rosenfeld and Carmi 1976).

Mapai controlled the Histadrut, and the Histadrut used the HSF as a means of binding to it those sectors—both the new working class and the expanding middle class—which were not necessarily its ideological allies. In this, it operated always on two levels—the ideological motivation of identifying itself with the working class within the Zionist enterprise; and the economically and politically pragmatic one of allying itself with the middle class within nation-building terms which masked class differences. With the increase of means in the public sector after the creation of the state, Mapai and the liberals (including the General Zionists) competed for the middle class constituency. Benefiting from this competition, the middle class did not finance the welfare state but rather gained from it, receiving health services cheaply, advancing within the new bureaucracies, and prospering through the 'privatization of public means' afforded by Mapai (Rosenfeld and Carmi 1976).

Israel became characterized by a partial national health insurance—a limited compulsory social insurance, and wide state-subsidized voluntary insurance. The partial compulsory state insurance was augmented by the negotiation by the Labor Ministry for employers participation, as part of collective agreements, through a quasi-compulsory employers tax which entitles insurees to hospitalization and diagnostics. State support of the sick funds, and especially subsidies for hospitalization, may also be considered as incentives to insurance (Halevi 1979). In a realm of activity more directly subject to policy and not necessarily requiring legislation, conflict and cooperation emergent from the interaction between the IMH and the HSF in the first phase resulted in the creation of a partial state service: state hospitals and preventive service (family health stations and centers, school-service, supervision of sanitation and other public health measures) by the IMH, complemented by ambulatory, hospital, and preventive service by the first-among-equals state-supported public voluntary agency, the HSF.

The lack of legislation on health, and the weakening of the IMH, paid the HSF back for its usefulness to the party (Doron 1975, Arian 1981, Zalmanovitch 1983). As a consequence, the structure of responsibility for health care in Israel continued with no basic changes from that which had existed before the establishment of the state.

Only government hospitals were to give free service, and only for the needy, through the social welfare laws (and to patients with communicable diseases under continued Mandatory statutes). The set of social security laws which finally took effect in 1954 legislated medical insurance only for maternity, disability, old age, and dependent survivors (widows and children). Expansion of the social insurance laws in the area of health never happened, but proposed comprehensive insurance was kept in the forefront of public attention by being revived and reshaped, with various motivations but similar outcome, before, during and after elections. The *Outline of Government Policy* in 1953 (paragraph 52) proposed in principle the adoption of compulsory health insurance as part of the social security laws, on the HSF formula, and the Knesset approved this principle in 1955. Another committee was appointed in 1957, and presented the results of its discussions in 1959: While supporting national health insurance, with regard to a state service the HSF was in opposition, although its policy-makers granted that sometime in an unseen future Israel may become sufficiently rich and unpressed by more urgent matters to undertake such a plan (Israel Government Committee for Planning General Health Insurance 1959). Ben-Gurion and his associates in the statist Israel Workers' List (Rafi),.which had split off from Mapai, made national health insurance a part of their program for election in the early 1960s, but were heavily defeated (Eisenstadt 1967). The winning Labor Alignment prepared a proposal for compulsory health insurance and the regulation of state budgets to health services, put forth in 1973 during Mapam's Health Ministry (Knesset 1973). This bill, on the Histadrut's terms, attempted to arrogate to the Labor Ministry many health service functions, and its initial opponents included the Histadrut (opposed to collection of fees through the National Institute for Insurance instead of through its own tax offices and afraid the law would increase HSF autonomy), the other sick funds (Doron 1975), and the Independent Liberals who attempted to separate the HSF from the Histadrut altogether. The 1973 proposal was detained in the Knesset's Labor and Welfare Committee, while questions of jurisdiction were hammered out, until 1976—and soon afterward the Alignment lost power.

A bill put forth in 1977 by the newly appointed Liberal Health Ministry as part of their alliance (Likud) with Herut, proposed organizational unification and administrative regionalization of health services (Knesset 1981). While it spoke not of nationalization but rather only of decentralization through a residential principle for use of the services, it would abolish the whole principle of sick fund membership (Halevi 1979, 1980). The 1977 proposal was put to vote in

1981 and similarly detained in committee, opposed by the National Religious Party, which while now a member of the Likud, retained its allegiance to the HSF affiliation of its (Religious Workers) members. Neither proposal reached voting. Within the existing legislation, in 1982 the IMH took over health insurance for the needy from the National Insurance Institute, and in 1985 a nursing insurance addition to health insurance for the elderly was passed, which has not yet been activated for budgetary reasons (*IGY* 1983-86). Thus although in principle there has been constant public agreement between parties of the left, right and center on the value in principle of compulsory health insurance for all, the fact that there has been no legislative outcome in this issue reflects the Histadrut's power vis-à-vis the state, (the smaller sick funds have been no less against nationalization than the HSF, but have not been as powerful), and a virtual standoff between political economic and bureaucratic vested interests (Arian 1981).

With no changes in the structure of health-care provision achieved in the formative period through legislation, the IMH which emerged was a hybrid of roles and structures, combining the Health Council's weaknesses as a central planning and coordinating agency and the Mandatory British Government Department of Health's structure as a provider of preventive and hospital care—not badly designed for these delimited activities but highly inappropriate for planning and coordination in the wider sphere. Its realm more or less excluded not only provision of service in the crucial area of ambulatory care, but also extensive surveillance of these services (major state involvement in ambulatory care eventually re-emerged through the growing importance of outpatient consultative clinics centered in state hospitals). Notwithstanding its budgeting role, most financing for the HSF expanding network of clinics did not come from the IMH anyway, but from Histadrut members' fees, from other ministries, and from the Jewish Agency (Baruch 1973).

The voluntary sick funds continued after the creation of the state the political basis for affiliation and the substantial autonomy which they had had during the Mandate. In 1950 criteria for allocating direct IMH support to the voluntary sick funds were first defined (they have been under frequent debate and rephrasing since then). In order to be eligible for such funding and for allocations for treatment of cases under the (then projected) insurance bill, sick funds were defined as those which give service instead of the state to populations of which a needy sector could not supply services for itself, and were required to keep branches in all parts of the country. Only the HSF and the Le'umit Sick Fund, which served a working class population as well as a middle class one, qualified under these criteria at the time. The goal of such phrasing was to exclude the middle class voluntary organizations (Mercazit, Amamit, Maccabi, Assaf) from state support (Doron 1975, Arian 1981, Halevi 1979). Consequently these sick funds did establish branches in new places, and were approved.

The path of IMH sponsoring statist policies with regard to hospitals and preventive care, and leaving to the HSF primacy in ambulatory curative care, determined the distribution of health services in Israel. Without a clear-cut supremacy of the IMH apparatus, the HSF took on the status of a quasi-state agency with a near monopoly in health insurance and in the provision of primary curative care. The IMH on the other hand remained a ministry of secondary (and poor) status, half of whose direct budget (and indirectly more) went to the sick funds (Arian 1981). The opposition and competition primarily between these two major operating agencies meant, as it had during the Mandatory period, considerable duplication—each agency providing both clinical and preventive service, sometimes in the same locality (*IGY* 1954-1957, Palley et al. 1983).

The HSF at this time was still offering what it had succeeded in developing through the years—a comprehensive health service, ambulatory, preventive (albeit to a limited extent), and hospitals (though in this last it depended on government facilities to a large extent). With immigration, however, its facilities in the towns began to be overloaded, and did not recover the atmosphere of concentrated (and perhaps, in its own solidary way, exclusive) personal attention which appears to have characterized its 'Golden Age' during the Mandate. Moreover, the state's alliance with the HSF, first achieved at the expense of a strong IMH, eventually was to result in a weakened HSF.

In the post state period the HSF undertook major construction of hospitals and clinics with the help of government support and loans, and expanded as the most important provider of curative and rehabilitative health care in Israel. In the 1950s 40% of the Histadrut's income went to the HSF, so that the Histadrut's involvement also released the government from extensive responsibility for ambulatory care, as the Jewish Agency's and Jewish National Fund's activities released it from a major part of investment in settlement including in the infra-structure of the social services (Arian 1981). This was so at least to the extent that the Histadrut brought a fundraising potential overseas which might not have been available directly to the state, and that some of its local fees were paid for functions other than medical insurance (insurance fees and government budgets would after all have been transferable from the HSF to the state under nationalization).

The kinship between the ruling Labor Party and the Histadrut implied that the HSF acted as an agent performing state-building tasks such as constructing and operating clinics and hospitals, and received in return financial support and a free hand in its operations. These medical services brought in turn a voting payoff to the Labor Party. At the same time, the relation between the state's health bureaucracy and the voluntary sick fund has always to a smaller or greater degree been competitive as well as cooperative (Zalmanovitch 1983).

Under these conditions the IMH began its part in shaping health care operations away from the center of budgetary and political power; as a weakened domain it was all the more suitable to be further entrusted to Mapai's future coalitionary partners. From its inception, the policies and accomplishments of the IMH have been conditioned by the fact that in the coalitionary governments which have governed Israel the Health Ministry was invariably (except during a period of transition in 1955, and again in 1984-1986) entrusted to the secondary partners in the coalition. In forty years there have been eight cabinet Ministers of Health from four political parties (two from the National Religious Party [for two periods of four years each, 1948-1952 and 1961-1965], one from the General Zionists [for three years, 1952-1955], two from Mapam [for a total period of 15 years—11 of them consecutive under two ministers—1956-1961, 1966-1977], and three from the Labor Party [one transitional in 1956, and two from 1984-1987]). Each of these parties brought to the office its own political priorities, and different attitudes to the relation between the state and the voluntary agencies. The professional level as well has gone through successive reorganizations and re-formulations of goals (*IGY* 1949-1986).

Bureaucratic re-organization in the ministry was frequent from 1948-1952. Adaptive improvisation was in part a response to the constant crises brought about by immigration and by the creation of the state, in part reflected a lack of intensive planning by the first two Health Ministers for whom this office was not necessarily the primary concern (one of them was simultaneously also Minister of Immigration and of the Interior). But most importantly the state of flux reflected lack of resolution in the struggle for authority over the various domains of health care in the country.

After their success in the 1951 elections the General Zionists demanded, in exchange for their membership in the coalition, that the health services be nationalized. Mapai refused, but allotted the Health Ministry to them (Doron 1975). In a government constituted by Mapai's Prime Minister Ben-Gurion, the alliance with the center was based on a core of ideological agreement promoting an encompassing Jewish nationalism at the expense of class consciousness. With regard to health care, there was basic agreement that state responsibility for children included as a first priority the provision of preventive health care for infants and children in MCHS and in schools. From the time the General Zionists joined the coalition in 1952 and until they left the government in 1955, they were unable to make basic changes in the extent of HSF power or in legislation, but attempted from this position to gain ground for statist policies through administrative decisions. The period from 1952 to 1955, critical for the shaping and expansion of health services following the initial takeover of GDH structures, saw especially intensive attempts (only partially successful) to assert and widen IMH control and activities within those areas of authority allowed it (e.g. IGA IMH G4223, G4245, *IGY* 1953-55). But attempts by the IMH during these years to diminish HSF status (e.g. by denying it proportional representation in advisory and administrative groups, such as a convened health council which included representatives of the various agencies on an equal basis and professional experts unrepresentative of HSF predominance, and by the ministry's alliance with a cadre of physicians whose views—typical of those of the professional association [Israel Medical Association]—were frequently unsympathetic to the HSF) only stressed further the basic fact that what had emerged was a dual structure, not radically different from that which existed during the Mandate. Two Health Ministries were in operation—the state's and the Histadrut's (Arian 1981).

The tension between middle class and working class interests, which in the pre-state period was expressed through the HMO's competition with the HSF, was continued as the Health Ministry in its formative period adopted the HMO's public health policies. There was nothing particularly socialist in the form of the emergent health services provided by the welfare state in its first few years through the IMH; on the contrary, state public health policy was based on the political center's preference for local government frameworks obfuscating class distinctions.

In their stand against the HSF, the General Zionists were aided by their association and accord with the Hadassah Medical Organization (Halevi 1980). Both the HMO and the General Zionists were essentially for management of medical services by the affluent civic elite on a municipal basis, and for philanthropic treatment of the poor. The HMO, after its evacuation from the Mt. Scopus hospital site as a result of the War necessitated intensive re-investment in new hospital facilities, was interested in reducing the range of its activities and concentrating them in research, teaching and practice in the

Jerusalem area. Indeed, its medical activities in Israel after its new facilities in Jerusalem were built have focussed on their maintenance and development as a center for curative care and for medical and public health education and research. Most HMO curative facilities in the towns had already during the Mandate been transferred to the municipalities. The HMO's clinics in the rural sector had been transformed into the Amamit Sick Fund. The HMO's standing principle of transferring facilities to local hands when possible, and its previously announced intention to do so upon the creation of the state, complemented the IMH's eagerness to take over the country-wide network of MCHS and school-service. In 1950 the HMO announced its intention to transfer its preventive stations to the state; meanwhile the IMH financed new HMO stations. With the General Zionists' entry into office in 1952 the HMO signed the contract for transfer to the IMH, which was completed by 1955 (a few years later Hadassah transferred its preventive services in the Jerusalem Corridor to the state and it urban MCHS to the city). The IMH thus became responsible for this aspect of health care—for which it already had the appropriate bureaucratic structure inherited from the GDH. Its offers (provocative, in the context of tense relations with the HSF) to similarly take over the HSF preventive facilities (especially in the kibbutzim and moshavim) were rebuffed (IGY 1953-1955, IGA IMH G4245).

In addition to this takeover, the new policies which the administration initiated toward the end of its office in 1954 also expressed the General Zionists' persisting promotion of a centrally-planned but operationally decentralized national health service. These views represented as well the social and professional ideas of most of the IMH's bureaucracy, related to those enacted by the HMO. They were intended to show that the state could compete with the HSF, and encompassed the major areas of IMH activity:

1. Within the IMH's primary sphere of hospital operations, the plan was to transfer existing government hospitals to the municipalities, and then to build three central government hospitals in the north, center and south. Hospitalization in state (and municipal) hospitals was on a residential basis. (The hospitals in Tel Aviv and Haifa were so transferred, but in the 1970s were transferred back by the municipalities to the state. Eventually the IMH did build a hospital in the north in Zefat [completed in 1972] and renovated the Mandatory government hospital in the center [Tel Ha-shomer], while the HSF built a hospital in Beer Sheva which served everyone in the Negev by agreement with the IMH).

2. Within the IMH's preventive sphere, operations were decentralized, giving more power to the regional health bureaus.

3. Within the parameters of ambulatory curative care provided by the IMH—i.e. in those sectors (among arriving immigrants and among Arabs) where it had established a claim on state service—it planned to initiate several 'experimental' health centers which would represent its vision of how a national health service should function on the local level.   These facilities, on an American model of community medicine, would be comprehensive. They would integrate preventive and curative service, and in areas far from hospitals also include a few hospital beds—general, pediatric and maternal (*IGY* 1955).

Four new centers were planned at this initial point (five were added later) of which three were in the newest Jewish development areas in the south and north, and one in the Triangle. There, the IMH already had curative clinics; the new center was intended to represent a model of IMH support of local municipal participation in health care. For this purpose the IMH chose an established local authority (Tira), within the administrative regional health bureau (Netanya) which was designated as the showcase for innovation in increasingly autonomous health bureau operations.   Not to be outdone in his own locality, Mapai's Arab Member of Knesset from Baqa al-Gharbiyye in the Northern Triangle (within the Hadera health bureau region), F. Hamdan, used his influence (including an exceptional elicitation from the Prime Minister's Office of *waqf* funds for construction on land sold by Hamdan for this purpose) to prompt the IMH to soon add a center in the village (*IGY* 1954-57, IGA IMH G4264). Centers were also added in new Jewish immigrant locations, Qiryat Yovel in Jerusalem (operated by the HMO), the Adulam rural region, and Bet Shean. Upon Mapam's entry into office in 1956 a state curative and preventive clinic was opened—again with *waqf* funds with Hamdan's assistance— in Taiybe (and soon after in Qalansawe, Jatt and Umm al-Fahm, where they operated as subcenters of the two full-fledged family health centers.

By the time that the centers were actually built and opened, the General Zionists were out of office, but the IMH bureaucracy took some pride in maintaining them. Sooner or later, however, they were transferred to the HSF in whole or in part (in Qiriat Shemona operations were jointly coordinated from the beginning and continue to be so).   In the Arab centers in the Triangle, the original concept combining state-support and municipal responsibility continued and thrived the longest, mainly because—as part of a conjunction of favorable factors—in these centers municipal involvement was genuine. Some of the original centers, their transfer or phasing-out incomplete, remain in vestigial form.

In 1955 the General Zionists left the government, and from 1956 until 1977 the IMH was in the hands of Mapam or of the National Religious Party (1961-1965). During these years the two major health agencies, while bureaucratically and politically in competition, nevertheless operated in relative agreement. Both of these political parties' allegiances to the HSF, reinforced by their delimited role within the Mapai-defined room to maneuver, meant that HSF interests were protected, its areas of dominance preserved, and its growth financially aided and promoted. Even so, competition continued, a function of bureaucratic tensions as well as political rivalries. The two major areas of IMH activities continued to be hospitals and MCHS, with the former receiving increases in budgets and the latter becoming more concentrated in IMH hands.

The IMH reports at the beginning of Mapam's first term in the Health Ministry (1956-1961) cite the improved coordination with the HSF, the need for improving preventive services and integrating it with curative ones (supposedly made realizable through this new cooperation), and the lag in development in Arab areas, where there was no pre-existing basis (*IGY* 1957, 1958). Direct ministry involvement in regional bureau activity and planning was reconstituted and direct involvement in hospital operations increased.

In the Health Ministry Mapam was in a paradoxical position, impaled on the horns of a dilemma which characterized its political status. To begin with, its attempts to implement statist policies from the ministry contradicted, where they competed with the HSF, its own stated line which favored HSF autonomy and supremacy, so that objection to HSF expansion at IMH expense was impossible on an ideological basis as well as on practical coalitionary grounds. As a consequence, not only were its powers in the Health Ministry limited, but Mapam was forced to support policies in opposition to its pragmatic interests as well as ideological preferences. Since Mapai had annexed the HSF, Mapam's identification with HSF expansion was compromised by the HSF status, as its rival's HSF primacy (to which Mapam was ideologically committed) worked against Mapam's political interests. Mapam's hopes for approaching the condition of a socialist welfare state through the Health Ministry were handicapped by financial restrictions. Its egalitarian ambitions within the supposedly consensual statist realm of free preventive service—where it was also given less than full reign—could not be completed within these limitations. After 1970, however, a new forthcoming attitude toward hospital building and expansion by Finance Minister Sapir led to new cooperation with Health Minister Shemtov, which resulted in large scale hospital building by the IMH funded by donations by Jews overseas.

In negotiating with Mapai a version of the welfare state, however compromised, which nevertheless succeeded in making access to medical care widely available to the working class, Mapam at least had the Arabs in view. The liberals' stance toward the Arabs was one of nominal integration through local responsibility, amounting nationally (notwithstanding occasional endeavors) to benign neglect. Israel government guidelines have continuously specified a commitment to integration and equality, but under Mapai's ideological and even more so budgetary umbrella investments in Arab communities—even after Histadrut and HSF activities began to encompass it in the 1950s—were made at a relative rate which considered second class citizenship for Arabs to be legitimate within a Jewish national consensus. The economic and physical underdevelopment of Arab villages—maintained by the state through insufficient allocation of resources (land, water, money)—had consequences in the area of health as in others (Rosenfeld 1964, 1978). Mapam, motivated by egalitarian and electoral programs, named special problems and made special efforts among Arabs. In its closest constituency, the kibbutzim, HSF service was exclusive; Mapam's efforts were focussed on its next two potential constituencies and working-class foci: The towns, where it could claim a part in construction of hospitals as well as in preventive service; and the Arab population.

The division of labor between the two health agencies, had the consequence of nationally increasing separation between preventive and curative care as the state withdrew from operating curative clinics (except for those dealing with mental health): For the most part, Mapai built and maintained HSF clinics, and Mapam built and maintained MCHS. (In 1959 the HSF agreed to transfer 36 of its MCHS in the Haifa area and 66 school health service points to the state; *IGY* 1960). There was some joint construction and operation of facilities in which the operating division of labor was upheld, but on the level of local services competition between the IMH and the HSF was often expressed in the opening, most intensively during pre-election periods, of clinics and MCHS without sufficient consideration as to their quality.

In the mid-1970s, i.e., only at the end of Mapam's tenure, the balance of power between the two agencies changed, bringing about considerable potential state authority through the IMH (the state through its powerful Mapai ministries, Finance and Labor, had always controlled the HSF; Doron 1975, Zalmanovitch 1983). This happened essentially through the IMH's development of hospitals and its control of public hospitalization while hospitals were becoming the intensive, and expensive, centers of health care on which the sick funds including the HSF were dependent. It was due directly to the cumulative weight of greater government financial resources derived from increasing budgets, and to Ministry of Finance administrative decisions which increased IMH financial control of the sick funds—of the HSF more than the others since its greater size made it the most dependent. Much of this control was due to the fact that in the public sector in Israel, including the HSF, the Ministry of Finance is the major employer and subsidizer (Baruch 1973).

Since the establishment of the Health Ministry, government support of the HSF came only in part from it: The IMH was often bypassed, and funding proceeded instead directly from the Ministry of Finance, which unlike the 'social' ministries was always held by Mapai. Indirect IMH funding was often more substantial than direct funding, and the HSF expanded through subsidized and unlinked loans for construction (Halevi 1979, Palley et al. 1983). During the Mandate 30% of capital imports reached the public sector; after the establishment of the state 75% of capital imports did, and were instrumental in the Histadrut's aggrandizement (Ofer 1967). While in 1945 the Mandatory government's health budget was twice as high as that spent by the Jewish (voluntary) health services, in 1961 one third of total health expenditures were by the IMH. Proportionately to the voluntary services, then, government health service budgets were higher during the Mandatory period than in Israel. This indicates the greater means available to the HSF than to the IMH, into the 1970s (Baruch 1973).

For most of its history, the IMH was too weak to control the HSF but this does not mean that the HSF was autonomous. Not only was it controlled by Mapai's powerful ministries, but structural tensions between it and the Histadrut were and are also material, with the Histadrut, too, interested in limiting the HSF independence (Zalmanovitch 1983). In this sense the direct alliance between the Histadrut and Mapai furthered the same purpose.

In the 1960s Mapai pressured the Histadrut to not raise dues, in order not to cause a rise in the consumers' price index which would require a pay-raise to all public employees, and funded the HSF directly from the Ministry of Finance in return. Mapai preferred the sick fund over the Histadrut: Its share in the Histadrut tax rose from 40% in the mid-1950s to 60% at the end of the 1960s, and 67% at the end of the 1970s. The Histadrut meanwhile also preferred to allocate to it an increasing percentage of members' tax rather than to increase fees and along with them autonomy. All of the sick funds counted on the IMH to pay their debts; the HSF being the biggest also had more debts, suffered more from bad investments (and inflation), and had less profits. All of the sick funds received subsidies—from the national institutions before the state and afterward from the IMH; the main subsidy was the reduction of hospital fees in government hospitals. In 1976 the manner of Ministry of Finance payments to state and state-supported hospitals was changed to their disadvantage—since then full fees are charged, but the IMH helps pay them. Effectively, hospital subsidies to the sick funds were stopped, and the IMH given potential power, especially over the HSF (Halevi 1979).

In 1975, in the face of deficits caused by rising medical costs, the sick funds demanded to raise taxes but the Ministry of Finance, acting in its role as the major public employer, again refused to allow this and preferred to allocate support through the IMH (Halevi 1979). IMH control thus was achieved because of Ministry of Finance resistance to raising fees, which made the HSF especially more and more dependent on the Health Ministry. Because of this situation the HSF evidently became prepared thereafter to accept state supervision against budgetary support, but since 1977 under the Likud the state, i.e., IMH, Finance and Labor Ministries, have cut HSF budgets radically (Zalmanovitch 1983). Government supervision was increased partly because misappropriation of funds linked to the Labor Party was discovered, but mostly because the IMH in the period from 1977 to 1984 carried out the Liberals' and Herut's policy of opposing public institutions—i.e. Histadrut enterprises—and promoting private enterprise. If under Mapai the objective had been to control the HSF and use it, under the Likud the goal became to deplete it. The Ministry of Finance under the Likud has used HSF dependency as leverage against it. The HSF bureaucracy, for its own part, conducts wage policy in defiance of the IMH, and has refused to submit epidemiological and budgetary statistics to the IMH since 1977.

The new Liberal Party administration proposed again to combine family health stations (MCHS) and the HSF, through a reorganization of the public health service which would combine curative and preventive care—obliterating the HSF through proposed integrated service areas. A public health law (1980) governing hospitalization, passed during this period, re-instituted hospital care according to region of residence, replacing the more fluid 'on duty' regional assignment by day of the week which was instituted during Mapam's administration (as a means of integrating HSF and state hospitals into a nationwide network while maintaining maximum HSF discretionary powers over its own facilities). Through this complete regionalization the HSF advantage is reduced, and government jurisdiction is imposed on what had been a more autonomous administration. On the basis of this law, the HSF recent attempts to fight its competition by disqualifying HSF insurees from using HSF outpatient clinics have been legally rejected. In addition to the failed attempt in 1981 to pass a national health service and insurance law, this center-right policy was implemented through decreasing government budgeting of the HSF, and through 'compensatory' actions (e.g. tax rebates) favoring the interests of the other voluntary agencies, thus undermining the HSF autonomy and hegemony through its inability to function with economic success.

The IMH concentrated on hospital expansion both because the HSF was from its beginning unable to provide sufficient hospitals for its insurees, and because the government's inheritance of British hospitals gave it the basis to take primacy in this area. Currently there are nine IMH general hospitals, two municipal, eight HSF, 12 owned by other public agencies (Jewish charitable organizations and Christian missions) and five private. Hospital beds are owned half by the government, one-third by the HSF, and one-sixth by others (Arian 1981). Attempts to rationalize hospital access have been common to all administrations. Several recent hospitalization statutes make access to hospitals and medical examination therein increasingly assured to seekers so that since 1981 HSF hospitals ceased to be exclusive to members (*IGY* 1983-1986).

The development of government hospital facilities led to dissociation between ambulatory services (usually provided by one of the sick funds) and hospital care (provided, through various coordinative arrangements, by the IMH, by only the HSF among the sick funds, by several other public nonprofit agencies especially in Jerusalem and Nazareth, and by some private operators). The pluralist public health services system in Israel is characterized by fragmentation, duplication and inefficiency (Palley et al. 1983), but also by competition which can motivate improvement. As the state developed its hospital system, its outpatient clinics (and emergency rooms) became more and more important so that it has become a major provider of ambulatory as well as of hospital care (*ISCAR* 1984).

The various sick funds pay for services given in state hospitals and clinics to their insurees; thus while on the primary curative level and on the secondary (specialist) level other than hospital-linked clinics, the insurer in most cases is also the provider (even those sick funds which operate to a large degree through individual agreements with treating physicians attempt to make these agreements exclusive), on the increasingly important level of outpatient clinics this is much less the case than used to be. The HSF advantage, based on the crucial direct institutional linkage—albeit for the patient often circuitous and inconvenient—between primary, secondary, and tertiary care all within the HSF framework, has been at least temporarily drastically reduced.

The 1980s have brought a crisis in the major public health services in Israel—both IMH and HSF—due to Ministry of Finance budget cuts, to increasing costs of medical care, inflation, and with regard to the HSF also to poor management of its substantial assets (Kopp 1985; Ofer 1985). National expenditures on medical care, higher on clinical and preventive medicine in the 1960s, became higher for hospitals and research as of 1970-1971 (*SAI* 1985:668). There were large increases in the late 1970s in hospital costs (due to the expansion of high-technology medicine and of facilities for the old and the chronically ill), and government expenditures was contained through maintaining low wages of medical workers (Ofer 1985). After 1978, and increasingly from 1982 there has been not only a decline in IMH support of the sick funds but a also in total government expenditures on health (Kopp 1985). The elimination of Jewish Agency support (from 20% to 0%) from health budgets contributed to these cuts. The consequences were refracted throughout the system; in the ambulatory clinics and family health stations they are reflected in high case load and pressure. A Ministry of Finance review of the HSF has made recommendations for increasing economic efficiency which are currently being undertaken (*IGY* 1983-1986). Government support of the HSF has decreased from nearly 30% of the HSF budget in 1976-7 to 5% in 1986-7. The financial crisis affects hospitals no less than clinics, and state facilities no less than the HSF, in general hospitals as well as in geriatric and mental facilities.

Under the National Unity Government between the Likud and the Labor Party which came into being in 1984, the Health Ministry was again allocated to the Labor Party, and some new plans and policies favoring the HSF have been proposed and instituted, although major budgetary increases are not in IMH control. For example, an administrative proposal by a Health Minister highly identified with the HSF, to transfer all preventive health stations to the HSF regular clinics, is a counter-move in the debate around the integration of health services. While re-aggrandizing the HSF, it would also in principle solve problems of discontinuity. But under present conditions of overburdened HSF bureaucracy this moves threatens to destroy the achievements in service to mothers, infants and the elderly provided by the IMH's public health nurses.

The HSF co-optation by Mapai, achieved by 1951, denatured it. It resulted in a dependency on the state harmful to the sick fund's character as an activist mutual aid organization, in addition to its organizational dependency in the Histadrut. At the same time it led to the gradual loss of HSF's integrative aspect (whether achieved or only attempted), increasingly separating between preventive and curative, ambulatory and hospital care. This became more so the more this dependency increased in the 1960s, 1970s, and 1980s. On the other hand, the IMH was not given the legal and financial means to develop its own comprehensive service, although there is no reason to believe that a formally instituted national health service would have provided better curative care than the HSF.

What has emerged in Israel is an extensive preventive system for children, especially infants and toddlers, but a severely underdeveloped one for adults. As a consequence of the 1950 compulsory education law, children in state kindergartens and primary schools are supposed to receive free preventive care with IMH support. State involvement in personal preventive services since then for infants and children includes immunization, instruction, and diagnoses until the age of three in the family health stations (MCHS), and supervision, periodic and special examinations, hearing and sight tests, and some dental service between the ages of 5 and 14 in the kindergartens and schools.

After the state took upon itself the responsibility for personal preventive care, the HSF own activities in this field were greatly reduced. It did not altogether withdraw, maintaining total services in kibbutzim, in many moshavim, in some towns and in schools, but it soon was surpassed by the IMH. In addition to those places where the HSF provides both services, there are others where they are provided in common facilities with IMH family health stations (FHS). But whereas during the Mandate both the HMO and the HSF generally provided both personal preventive and curative care to their members and patients, affording some continuity of care by the same agency (in those realms of preventive care which were offered), the new division of labor resulted in a disjunction which corroded whatever integration of services there was, except where the HSF or the IMH maintained both. In Arab communities as a whole and especially in the Galilee, although there are some exceptions where there is coordination between the two agencies in this area, this division is ubiquitous and its repercussions in terms of a lack of continuity are pervasive.

This divided pattern was set by 1956. But it was precisely the possibility of coordination on the local level between the IMH and the HSF, which was intended to further minimize IMH control over the HSF while nevertheless allowing Mapam and the IMH an agreed-upon area of accomplishment of the welfare state, which finally succeeded—in most urban areas, in some Jewish rural settlements, and in most Arab villages—in throwing out the baby of (only partially realized) comprehensive personal service along with the bathwater of inefficiency and duplication.

Personal preventive services are currently provided by the state in family health stations and centers (formerly MCHS) for the benefit of pregnant women and infants, and in schools for the older children. Home assistance for the elderly is also within the scope of activities of the centers' public health nurses. In addition, the state continues to operate hospitals. Patients are charged for hospitalization and outpatient care through their insurance programs: The elderly, as well as non-working pregnant women and recent (within a three-months period) mothers, are insured through the National Institute for Insurance which pays their monthly sick fund fees (generally to the HSF). The Welfare Ministry, which has insured its clients through the HSF as well, has transferred this function to the IMH. Maternity, work accidents and old age insurance are now administered through the National Institute for Insurance—previously there were still some municipal welfare services. Most of the aged and the needy are insured by agreement with the HSF; those previously insured by another sick fund may continue in it.

A number of state-supported voluntary agencies (sick funds), in addition to the HSF and some charitable organizations, religious (Jewish orthodox and Christian missionary) and secular (Hadassah) provide and mediate for ambulatory care. All of the sick funds are nominally independent but actually subject to extensive IMH control through budgeting, collection procedures, and policy-making, and are sensitive to political trends. They act according to political and economic interests but the state does control access to public medical care, both in hospital service and locally. With regard to hospitalization it assures all patients of admission and treatment in state and state-supported hospitals according to the relatively universalistic criterion of region of residence. With regard to ambulatory care it requires the sick funds to disperse their services in order to benefit from funding under the social security laws (in fact, only the HSF had done so throughout the country before 1977, and benefited accordingly; two of the other sick funds, Maccabi and Le'umit, have significantly increased their geographic—but not necessarily their sociological—range since then). In hospitals, the IMH also increasingly controls quality. With regard to ambulatory care, in the absence of legal or formal criteria qualitative improvements nevertheless come about through competition between the sick funds.

In 1960, a WHO evaluation of the public health service system in Israel invited by the state saw the lack of community involvement in care, along with a lack of IMH control over the multiple agencies, as its major weaknesses (Evang 1960). IMH Control has increased, but communal involvement has not. The policies of the public health agencies are imposed from Jerusalem (the IMH) or Tel Aviv (the sick funds).

Tel Aviv and Jerusalem maintain some preventive stations, but this is the exception. In 1976 Haifa transferred municipal clinics which served the poor to the HSF, and in exchange the HSF transferred its MCHS in Haifa to the state. Municipal involvement with hospitals was never comprehensive, and in the 1970s Tel Aviv and Haifa ceded control of their hospitals (which the Hadassah Medical Organization had transferred to them) to the IMH. Local authorities do participate in funding preventive service in schools and in the FHS, but overall communal involvement, not to mention control, of personal health care is barely existent.

As elsewhere in the west, curative care has taken priority over preventive and environmental medicine, and advances in technology have given hospitals budgetary primacy over primary care (e.g., Navarro 1973, Waitzkin 1983, Nudelman 1986). This occurs in the nexus of trends in the social organization of western medical care, themselves reflecting political as well as professional priorities—toward high technology and increased specialization. And professional interests and demands for profit stress curative care at the expense of development of truly preventive public health approaches.

3.B.   Israel Health Ministry's Services to the Arab Population

With the establishment of Israel the remaining Arab population, greatly reduced and traumatized by the events and the effects of the war, outside and away from the center of development, and outside the designated scope of funding by the Zionist settling organizations, became completely dependent for health services on a government with whom it was in a relation of mutual suspicion and fear (Kayman 1984).

The Arab population within the new borders, reduced to a quarter of its former size, was concentrated in three regions close to the new northern, eastern and southern borders in which it formed the majority and was put under military administration. Of the 165,000 Arabs in Israel more than half were in the Galilee, one-fifth in the Triangle, and one-tenth in the Negev.   Another tenth resided in the 'mixed' cities—Haifa and Jerusalem and their environs, Yafo, Lud and Ramle—where they were under civil administration. The proportions of Arab urban and rural residents did not change: one-fifth were urban and four-fifths rural, including Bedouin (more than a tenth) in the north and south. As before, two-thirds of the Arab population were Muslim, a fifth Christian and less than a tenth Druze. Although the Arabs after the war constituted only one-sixth of the total population, they were an overwhelming majority in the three main areas in which most of them were settled (IGA IFM HZ 2402/23).

The immediate consequences, with regard to the health services, of the creation of Israel were interdependent disruptions for Jews and for Arabs. Arabs, who had depended more than the Jews on the health services of the GDH and the Christian missions, were more affected by the cessation of British activities and the reduction in missions' facilities. In Israel, a Ministry of Minorities was in charge of all government activities among Arabs during the first year after the war. Thereafter, the various ministries functioned along with the military administration through a Coordinating Bureau for Arabs in the Prime Minister's Office.

For the Jews, the challenge of creating a state health service was simultaneous with the challenge of providing health care for the waves of immigration which doubled the Jewish population of the state within four years of its establishment. In addition to the problem of organizing services for the population in general, the new IMH was faced with two groups which required special administration—new immigrants, and the Arabs who had remained within the new borders. From the point of view of the receiving veteran establishment, both populations were anomalous. The two national priorities—immigrant absorption leading to national growth on the one hand, and military security on the other— elicited concentrated attention and control albeit of different character. The new immigrants, officially perceived as undergoing transition from living as a persecuted minority to becoming part of the majority through absorption in the Israeli 'melting pot', were considered both a national challenge and a social risk. The Arabs, transformed from being a majority in Palestine to becoming a minority in the Jewish state, were seen as a security risk in view of the unfinished war, and as socially alien. In the IMH, two special services were set up—a Medical Service for New Immigrants in the immigrant camps, and a Medical Service for Minorities in the regions in which Arabs were encapsulated (*IGY* 1949-1952).

In addition to representing epidemiologically to the establishment 'alien' loci of communicable disease, the two anomalous populations were not encompassed by the existing structure of health services. New immigrants were not yet settled in permanent residences where they would be covered by the Jewish voluntary sick funds. Arabs in the Galilee, the Triangle and the Negev never had been more than tangentially touched by these agencies and had not developed their own; whatever services had been provided by the British stopped with their withdrawal, and while Christian organizations remained active, with hospitals and clinics in Nazareth, Yafo, Haifa Jerusalem and Tiberias, most mission hospitals were not within the new state borders, and the mission hospitals which continued to serve were inadequate to rural needs. Whatever Jewish services has been provided to Arabs in rural areas before 1948 were disrupted. Within Arab communities the HSF maintained only a couple of clinics, one of them in Nazareth (Landau 1969). Also, the structures of preventive care in Jewish communities were continued whereas in Arab communities they were not (Grushka 1959). The starts made in the 1940s through Arab communal initiative were discontinued as well.

Health services in Arab communities collapsed not only because of British withdrawal, diminished interaction in rural locations with individual professionals, and the insufficiency of the missions, but also because—as a result of the flight and expulsion of the Arab elite during the war and of Israeli refusal to re-admit Arab refugees—there were hardly any Arab professionals left. In 1949 a census of physicians found 20 'non-Jewish' physicians in the country. In 1953 the number of Arab physicians in Israel was officially counted as 10-15 (IGA IMH G4264, IFM HZ 2402/23b 1953).

The IMH clinical services were intended as temporary measures. For the Jews they were designed to last through the stage of permanent settlement, to be replaced by the voluntary agencies. With regard to the Arabs the officially expressed policy was to 'equalize' them with Jews by rather sooner than later making them responsible for their own ambulatory care—eventually as insurees of the voluntary sick funds which the IMH expected to become active among Arabs, and meanwhile through local taxes (IGY 1950, 1952).

While the services to new immigrants and to the Arabs were established along a formally parallel line, they were unequal in quality. By 1950 the Medical Service for New Immigrants operated 31 clinics and 14 dental clinics in transient camps. In addition to operating curative and preventive stations itself, the IMH also supported the HSF and HMO. When immigrants left the camps to live in permanent settlements where the HSF provided clinical care, the IMH paid their medical expenses until they were settled in work and insured. It also paid a major part of HSF and HMO budgets in new immigrants' urban places of residence (*IGY* 1951). Jewish Agency funding for immigrant health care, a national commitment and identification with the goal of immigrant absorption, and a large corpus of professional health personnel and government instructors highly motivated by this commitment, combined to provide intensive service in the camps.

In 1950 the IMH started a course for Arab public health nurses, and officially declared Arab schools under medical supervision (*IGY* 1951). In effect, the public health service to Arabs in these years at its best generally meant—as it did during the Mandate—anti-malarial activities, extension of immunizations and vaccinations, and campaigns against trachoma, ringworm and tuberculosis. In the early 1950s there were a total of eight physicians, four Arabs and four Jews, in the Medical Service to the Minorities, half of them working in urban locations and half in the villages. The Jewish physicians had before 1948 practiced privately among Arabs and were hired by the state to resume their activities on a salaried basis. In 1950 this service also employed 12 nurses and six sanitary inspectors. There were 28 clinics (i.e. points of service, doubled since 1949), eight in towns and the rest in villages, which were visited on a regular or occasional basis by physician and nurse. There were also visiting units for the villages around Nazareth (which were poorly attended) in the Western Galilee, and in the Negev, but the state of the latter service was such that when one of the two Jewish physicians serving the Bedouin was called to army reserves, medical services were interrupted. Ten additional IMH preventive MCHS in Arab locations provided a total number of immunizations in 1955 of 800-900 (IGA IMH G4264, *IGY* 1950-1951).

Service in state clinics was without charge and patients with dangerous epidemically communicable diseases were hospitalized at government expense (IGA IMH G4264). As to the rest, in municipalities local welfare paid for the poor, and in the 'mixed' towns Arabs had, in addition to the urban IMH clinics, access to municipal clinics (IGA IMH G4264); no-one covered the rural poor.

IMH activities in Arab communities were usually undertaken in cooperation with military administrators and often at their behest. Throughout the early years of the state, its official rejection of former Arab residents attempting to return across the borders and its definition of them as illegal infiltrators made Arab unwillingness to report communicable diseases and to allow registering of deaths by the epidemiological service acute and inevitable (IGA IMH G4264). The poor record-keeping and steep under-reporting of vital statistics and disease which make precise data on health in this period unattainable represent a conjunction of medical neglect and active resistance to registration.

In the area of sanitation—water quality, sewage removal and food control--the IMH's role was for the most part supervisory and instructional.   The number of Arab sanitary supervisors was inadequate so that most villages were unattended. Actual sanitation work was often done by the army (*IGY* 1950-1951).

All in all IMH work among Arabs during this period was an anomaly; the IMH, itself a secondary ministry, offered minimal service in an area which had become residual to its activities, to a population at the margins of national development. Moreover, while the IMH's direct expenditures for primary service for Jews were minimal and expected to dissolve, in Arab locations the ministry had to budget the cost of personnel as well as of rental of space for local clinics.

From 1952-1955 the IMH under the General Zionists phased out direct service, under the principle of transferring financial and operative responsibility for local clinics to municipal authorities. In Arab communities there were only a few such, but the number of clinics was also small, and the few which could not be transferred were continued provisionally. In the supposedly transitional phase until Arab local authorities were achieved, two planned state comprehensive health centers in the Triangle, in Tira and Baqa al-Gharbiyye, exhausted the IMH's investment in Arab communities. These centers were initially planned as showpieces of a supposed 'separate but equal' state attitude to Arabs—which under the circumstances of country-wide weakness or absence of Arab local authorities constituted no more than a token.

By 1954 the state's Service for Immigrants was reduced, to two temporary camps. Immigrants arriving in 1954-1956 were dispersed directly to permanent points of settlement, where local state and HSF services reached them—not necessarily immediately but always within a few years. The Service to Immigrants was discontinued, as was the administrative aspect of the Service to Minorities: Equality to the IMH administration in 1954 meant providing no IMH direct curative service to Arabs, as it did not provide it for Jews (*IGY* 1954-1955). But whereas in Jewish communities the ministry was released from responsibility by the public voluntary agencies, in the Arab communities it was not. And ministry attempts to make Arab municipalities responsible for health expenditures were hampered by the lag in municipal status; as it turned out, attempts to make Jewish municipal authorities responsible for IMH-established health services also largely failed.

However, the IMH increased its involvement in Arab communities with the termination of Mapai's coalition with the General Zionists, and the re-allocation of the ministry to other coalitionary partners. Upon Mapam's entry into the IMH in 1956, and during the National Religious

Party's tenure in the IMH from 1961-1964, new local clinics in Arab villages were opened (or were re-opened after having been previously phased out) as signs of party patronage.

In 1956 there were clinics in 16 Arab communities in the Western Galilee, Yizra'el Valley, the Northern and the Southern Triangle, and in Beer Sheva and the south (IGA IMH G4264). Physicians visiting these clinics also reached other villages, and the HSF had some local services in others, but in 1958 the IMH reported that in the majority (58) of Arab villages no physician attended at all, under any auspices.

From 1956-1961 the IMH under Mapam opened more than 20 new (or re-established old) clinics and MCHS and upgraded some others, including four clinical and preventive facilities designated to grow into additional comprehensive centers (*IGY* 1961). During the NRP administration from 1961-1965 four new clinics and five new MCHS were opened. In the Akko region of the Western Galilee there were four village IMH stations in 1958, established between 1950 and 1956. Between 1958 and 1965 ten clinics were added. Similarly after 1956, when compulsory service for Bedouin and Druze in the Army was instituted, a central IMH station for Bedouin was opened in Beer Sheva.

The lifting of the military administration in 1966 brought increasing mobility of Arabs for hired employment in Jewish locations, and with a new unrestricted eligibility for full rights in the Histadrut Arab workers in the early 1960s were joining the Histadrut in great numbers, supporting Mapai in elections. In 1962-1967 the state undertook a national five-year plan for development of Arab and Druze village to provide essential infrastructure in village roads, water sources and sanitation. The expansion of health facilities to Arab communities in those years took place in this context, and the State Comptroller's reports for 1963, 1964 and 1967 included evaluations of IMH performance in Arab communities (*IGY* 1961-1967, *ISCAR* 1963-1967).

In 1963 and 1964, after these reports noted much duplication of health services, the IMH and HSF agreed to coordinate activities in order reduce redundancies. The Comptrollers' review counted in 1964 a total of 54 clinics in Arab communities, 32 of them HSF and the rest mostly the IMH's. In the Akko as well as in the Hadera region there were no physicians' or nurses' visits of any kind, but in some other places there were two or three clinics per village—IMH, HSF, and another sick fund's. Consequently, the two major agencies agreed that the HSF would open clinics only where the IMH did not have them, and that it would undertake to serve the uninsured in these villages as well as the insured.

The Comptroller's report of 1964 signalled increasing investment by health agencies in local services in Arab communities (*ISCAR* 1967, #18). By 1971 there were some kind of curative clinics in two Arab towns (Nazareth and Shefar'am) and in 70 villages as well as in Bedouin locations in the Negev (*IGY* 1972)—in almost two-thirds of the recognized Arab settlements (see Chapter 5.A). Nevertheless there were still dozens of villages, not to mention Bedouin settlements, with no regular service of any kind.

Thus into the 1970s—for a number of years after the cessation of the IMH's operating role in delivering primary care to Jewish communities—the IMH continued to maintain direct curative service to Arabs (as well as to widen the network of MCHS). Only in the 1970s did it relinquish curative activities there altogether to the sick funds, as it had in Jewish communities. As the HSF began to develop its own comprehensive rural health centers for groupings of small immigrant moshavim, the IMH also transferred to it the curative aspect (or all of the aspects) of the 'experimental' integrative family health centers established in the 1950s. Among the centers which it gave up operating were the ones in the Triangle. While intended as token showpieces, within a few years they had indeed implemented programs of family-oriented and environmental community medicine, in their heyday throughout the 1960s (Saeb and Kornfeld Keller 1962, Mani 1965, Grushka 1968). Municipal involvement included partial financing, and patients were charged a symbolic fee per visit. These fees were collected through the local councils in Tira and Taiybe, and through the center itself in Baqa al-Gharbiyye (*ISCAR* 1963 #14:138-141). The IMH General Manager and then Director of the IMH hospital in the Center region adopted the Triangle as an area of practice and study, sent young physicians to practice there and recruited experts for consultation and research. There were connections as well with the HSF teaching hospital in the region. Comprehensive regional planning, to be established and expanded through the local authorities, was on the agenda and a regional guiding committee was active in proposing development plans and budgets for IMH participation. The IMH supported these developments.

But in the process of ceding curative activities to the HSF in the 1970s the IMH closed these centers on the grounds that HSF clinics in these villages already included a family health station. In fact the centers and subcenters, successful as they were although they were still dependent on physicians in training assigned form outside, did not fit the emergent HSF hegemony over curative primary care. The IMH concentrated on preventive activities. In the veteran labor-identified kibbutzim and moshavim and in some urban areas the HSF continued to provide integrated service, but among Arabs, preventive health service was overwhelmingly an IMH responsibility.

The first MCHS operated directly by the state had been opened in Arab communities: In Nazareth and in Rame in 1948-1949, and in Yafo in cooperation with the HMO in 1949-50. In these places there had been Mandatory GDH clinics and MCHS, and Arab physicians remained after 1948, so that the curative services on which preventive work depended remained available. In 1954, when after the transfer of Hadassah MCHS to the state there were about 200 MCHS operated by the IMH in Jewish communities, the IMH operated only four MCHS in minorities' communities in the Galilee, and in two in the Triangle (IGA IMH G4262).

In the 1950s MCHS in the Jewish settlements became family oriented; beyond immunizations, a nurse dealt with feeding problems and made home visits, offering some continuity albeit limited. A survey in the 1950s found that in Jewish locations there were 18 visits on the average per child to the MCHS in the first year, in which a physician was seen three to four times, and in addition each child had four home visits by nurse. At ages of 1-4, children visited the MCHS three to four times per year (Grushka 1959:100). In the 45 Arab communities which had MCHS in 1964—except for the newly opened family centers in the Triangle where treatment was more extensive—immunizations were the sole service offered, and that not always: Follow-up was such that it was unknown whether immunizations were complete.

With regard to sanitation, out of 93 villages in the country which were checked, 38 had local authorities—but only six of these had sanitary inspectors (ISCAR 1963 #14: 138-141, 1964 #15). This was a failure of the IMH in under-budgeting the regional health bureaus which were supposed to control sanitation and to require local authorities to maintain adequate level. But since the IMH's role in the matter of sanitation was secondary, more basic was the state's failure to provide the conditions for health services—access roads, running water, and electricity—and to guarantee the fundamental environmental conditions of health in adequate water-sources and sewage facilities. The IMH itself saw a safe water supply as a first requirement and still a largely unmet need in 1958 and local authorities, who bore chief responsibility for the water system, gave that problem priority (IMH 1968).

Arab local authorities also shared in the provision of school health care which, given the small number and poverty of the existing authorities, was neglected in most villages (Halevi 1962:860).

The commitment, interest and motivation of the public health service at all levels was undoubtedly lesser in relation to Arabs. The IMH in the 1960s had difficulties recruiting Jewish nurses to work in preventive stations in Arab villages; official disregard of the Israeli periphery was especially acute in the Galilee. The IMH county physician in the Akko area describes the situation of the public health service to Arab villages there in the late 1950s and early 1960s as: 'We were a province. Nobody cared.' Into the 1960s Arab villages had no running water. Transportation problems were a serious handicap to delivering health services as well as to seeking them. Conditions in the schools were poor and dependent on financing from the Ministry of the Interior which was not forthcoming. Routine examinations of school-children were introduced, but only a minority of the villages was reached. In the context of the general underdevelopment of Arab villages, where most villages in the Galilee had no access roads enabling automobile transportation in the 1960s, as well as no local authorities, electricity or running water (or telephones), stations (or clinics) were not ordinarily opened before these prerequisites.

The IMH under Mapam again from 1966-1977 attempted to improve preventive service in Arab locations by increasing the number of stations, and adding services beyond immunization. Twenty new MCHS were opened by the end of 1967, for a total of 72 MCHS—69 IMH, and three HSF. Services were constantly expanded. During its first term in office (1956-1961) Mapam had more than doubled the number of stations in Arab locations; from 1965-1967 the IMH increased MCHS again by one third. By 1967 there were IMH MCHS in Arab towns—Nazareth, Shefar'am (4) and in Akko—as well as in 56 villages, and several in the Negev. In 1961 the IMH had employed six Arab physicians, 63 nurses, seven sanitation officers, and four health educators; in 1967 it employed 44 physicians, 114 nurses, 21 sanitation officers, and three health officers (*IGY* 1961, 1968). With all that, just as the official statement in 1959 that 'Arabs enjoy existing services' (Grushka 1959) must be compared with the unofficial 'nobody cared' relating to the same period in the Galilee, the official claim in 1968 that every settlement of over 500 with an access road had local preventive service, and others mobile service for immunizations (Grushka 1968) must be put against the State Comptroller's finding in 1974 that in the north there were still a large number of communities of between 500-5,000 residents which had no preventive facilities (*ISCAR* 1974). In the Negev five MCHS continued to provide immunizations only.

Table 3.1: MCHS In Arab Localities, 1955-1986

Year	Number
1955	13
1958	32
1965	45
1968	75
1977	80
1986	90+

(*IGY* 1951-1970, Prime Minister's Office 1976, IMH 1979)

Since the mid-1960s, new national policy had added preventive service and home-visits for other family members (particularly the elderly and the chronically ill) to the duties of the MCHS, which were from then on called family health stations (FHS). Treatment of school-children was in some places added to the roster of the FHS nurse's duties. In the 1970s more developed versions, including more frequent obstetrician and gynecologists service, diagnostic service, family planning, physiotherapy, and a dental service were built, and called family health centers.

A new Mapam IMH administration, with Health Minister Shemtov assisted for a period by an Arab Deputy Health Minister, Member of Knesset Abd el-Aziz Zo'abi from Nazareth, expanded IMH activities further in the 1970s. Classes were opened to train several hundred Arab nurses to serve in village localities. Although in 1971-2 the ministry's stated goal for the Arab population was to complete opening stations in all villages, it succeeded in improving some facilities more than in greatly extending the number of locations. In addition to construction in Arab locations in cooperation with the municipality or alone, it undertook to begin, in cooperation with the HSF, construction of two new showpiece family health centers (proposed for several years) in Nazareth and Umm al-Fahm, declared to be equal to two centers planned for the Jewish development towns Qiriat Shemona and Ma'alot (*IGY* 1973-1974).

Beyond humanitarian and egalitarian ideals, the IMH's previous maintenance of its direct curative service to the Arabs, its eventual abdication, and its new active plans, all denoted competition within the cooperation between Mapam and Mapai—which was at this time establishing a network of HSF clinics in Arab villages. This competition took place in the context of Mapam's surrender, in effect, of most of its bargaining power vis-à-vis Mapai to the larger party, as a function of having joined with it for the 1965 elections to become the Labor Alignment.

The Arab population was rapidly increasing in absolute size: In 1973 there were 470,000 Arabs (14% of the total population) 70% of them born since 1948, half residing in Galilee (*IGY* 1974). As Arabs in Israel after 1967 were replaced in menial labor by workers from the West Bank and benefited from the market for export of agricultural products, their standard of living rose, along with political awareness and demands (Rosenfeld 1978). The improvement in their class situation after 1967 resulted in an even more accelerated joining of the Histadrut and the HSF, and continued electoral support of Mapai. A second five-year plan for development of Arab and Druze villages was initiated after the war in 1967. In 1970 the Ministry of Finance budgeted a large sum for a sanitation drive.

Along with construction of state hospitals which extended equality to Arabs by residence, preventive work by the IMH also represented achievable progress; new FHS construction, wide immunization success—against malaria, tuberculosis, polio, and cholera—and extension of services especially in the Galilee which was Mapam's bulwark, could be credited to it along with the renovation and opening of state hospitals (in Nahariyya in the Western Galilee a maternity department was added in 1968; a state hospital for the Upper Galilee in Zefat was opened in 1972).

New IMH MCHS/FHS construction, however, was impeded by the priority of hospital expansion. While in Jewish development areas the Housing Ministry, which was responsible for public building, received Jewish Agency funding for this purpose, such support was not available for Arabs. Construction and physical expansion of MCHS in Arab villages depended on allocations from government budgets; this was one of the reasons why local health stations were often in rented rather than specially built facilities (the other major and related reason is that land for building in Jewish development areas is also allocated by the Zionist settlement agencies, whereas in Arab locations it must be donated by the municipalities). Arab local authorities may however elicit some funds for construction of clinics and stations from the *waqf* as well as from the State Lottery (the latter is available to Jewish local authorities as well; for political reasons the State Lottery discontinued after 1977 its funding of HSF clinics).

Ambitions for achieving equal distribution of health resources in the realm of preventive personal care to Arab children, women, and the elderly were unattained. As of 1970-71 the limited IMH budget was weighted toward paying the increasing costs of hospitals at the expense of preventive service. At the same time, conditions of competition under divided responsibility between the HSF and the IMH sometimes made a score of mere presence of the points of service established—or, better still, constructed—by HSF and IMH the salient criterion for comparing Mapai's and Mapam's contributions, distracting both agencies from essential substantive improvements in quality of service.

Most fundamentally, IMH activities were constrained by the fact that in Arab communities health facilities were not planned and funded, as in most Jewish settlements, as part of a masterplan for settlement under the auspices of the settling agencies. They were contained within Mapai-controlled budgets which were inadequate to the task; and in addition they could be obstructed by hostile politicians from other parties. Thus construction of the center in Nazareth was arrested by the Ministry of Interior's regional officer in the Galilee.

As of now there is no fully developed HSF or IMH family health center in the largest of Arab towns (although there are several clinics and FHS). Construction of the center in Umm al-Fahm, begun in 1973 on land donated by the municipality, was stopped with the Likud's succession to the ministry in 1977. After a number of years of service under particularly backward conditions in this large community, a HSF clinic was finally opened in 1985, and currently services are being expanded. After 1977 there have been some additional facilities built where there were none before, but an official freeze on employment of public health nurses and of physicians affects FHS especially acutely in Arab villages where the number of small children has been constantly higher. The lack of local manpower was throughout the years cited as a major hindrance to the development of services; now that there are nurses, physicians, and other professionals available, there is insufficient funding allocated to employing a sufficient number in local health services.

In 1975 there were still 35 Arab settlements without local IMH preventive centers (Prime Minister's Office 1976). Since then the situation has improved; by 1986 eight new IMH family health stations have been opened in the Galilee alone where there was no preventive station previously, and some of the 22 HSF clinics opened throughout the country since 1978 also include preventive service. It is estimated that about 20 Arab villages are still without local preventive services. Residents of these villages are expected to seek care in a neighboring village or town facility. From the mountain villages of the Galilee and 'unofficial' Bedouin settlements which have no FHS, pregnant and nursing women would have to go a long way on foot even to a near community for non-emergency preventive service—and are unlikely to do so.

But even where there is a family health station, there is no physiotherapy, occupational therapy, psychologist and playroom in any Arab settlement (the IMH has started developing psychological services in the Triangle in Taiybe). Comparison of IMH FHS in large Jewish and Arab settlements in the Galilee shows a discriminatory nurse/per residents ratio of 1/1,470 for Jews, 1/2,121 for Arabs, while the proportional number of Arab infants and toddlers is much larger (IMH 1979). In the Galilee preventive service is provided for Arabs by the IMH, except for Akko where the HSF provides it, and for Jews by either the IMH or the HSF. According to a recent calculation, nurses in Arab communities treat on the average more than 400 families each, where the standard is 200 families per nurse—and Arab villages have proportionately more children of pre-school age than Jews (Kawar 1987).

There are presently still three 'FHS' in Arab villages without water, 15 without electricity, 53 without telephones, and four without toilets (Kawar 1987). Family health stations are staffed chiefly by public health nurses, supplemented by visiting physicians; in some villages a physician visits only once a month.

But local expectations from the IMH with regard to quality are undemanding: Many so-called FHS in Arab villages are not really familial, and do not offer the range of services given in the Jewish settlements. Some do offer clinic for high-risk and pregnant women and family-planning service. Nevertheless, in general some service is present; village women and elderly who are these stations' adult clientage are commonly unaware of what can be demanded from a station for family health, since such does not exist in any of the villages on this level and they have no occasion to use comparable facilities in Jewish localities. HSF curative services, on the other hand, are compared and criticized by users who must at some point, whether they want to or not, make contact with better facilities than the ones in their own village.

In the Galilee, 'nomadic' Bedouins, in some cases settled in a camping location for dozens of years if not longer, are supposed to be accommodated by clinics and centers closest to them (an IMH center in Zarzir, a sedentarized community with a population of more than 3,000, serves Bedouins in the Yizra'el Valley). In many of these 'non-settlement' locations, IMH officials may continue to administer only partial inoculations, if that, as a matter of 'good-will' in the absence of law requiring service. The HSF has until recently ignored and neglected these groups as well.

Beyond administering inoculations, the IMH administers sight and hearing tests in family health stations (for children until the age of three) and in state schools. Where there is no school nurse, this cannot be done. School nurses and visiting physicians are also able to supervise at least exceptional incidences of illness among children.

In the mid-1970s a State Comptroller's review found school-service in Arab communities deficient even in the larger schools of the Triangle, the best served of all Arab regions: in four out of 28 Arab schools there, no doctor or nurse visited during the year, and in five more schools there were one or two visits per year for a total of 2.5 hours per visit, per school (*ISCAR* 1974, 264; conditions in the Galilee and the Negev were worse). There has been no basic improvement in this situation. IMH budgets are, under present conditions, not commonly allocated for this purpose, and municipal budgets are most often insufficient to make this a top priority, (two-thirds of expenses are supposed to be carried by the IMH, and one-third by the municipality).

In 1977, while most Jewish settlements had a school physician and nurse, there was no school-service for Arabs in the Galilee, except in some of the smaller Arab communities where, in the absence of local or regional organization, the IMH had to assume more responsibility.

Since the budgets of Arab local councils are only a fraction of those of Jewish local councils, school health is not the highest priority. Currently a few local authorities do employ school-nurses on their own behalf—in the Hadera district where there is school-service in nine Arab settlements and one dental clinic; in the southern Triangle, where there are school nurses in three or four schools but no dental service, while Jewish schools in the area have school-service and three dental clinics; and in Shefar'am in the western Galilee.

The FHS range of assumed responsibility for prevention now includes children through school age, pregnant and recent mothers, the elderly, the chronically ill, and general health education. In practice budget limitations have not permitted more than an occasional new program in this range; the only area in which there has been more general albeit limited extension is school-service. IMH nurses now include schools on their schedules in many more places, Arab and Jewish. Jewish development towns have a school physician, dentist and nurse; Project Urban Renewal has expanded dental care in these towns. In moshavim a nurse visits schools one to three times a month; FHS nurses also visit more Arab schools, but only administer inoculations in most of the smaller schools. Arab villages over 3,000 (except Bedouin) usually are visited by nurses, but their schedule generally permits mostly screening of vision.

Dental service for children, offered by the IMH through many (but by no means all of) Jewish FHS and schools, is not offered in Arab communities—a serious deficiency especially because dental care is ordinarily not covered by sick fund insurance.

Since 1977 the Jewish Agency Plan for (urban) Neighborhood Renewal has undertaken renovation projects in poor urban neighborhoods (in 80 spots by 1986) in various scopes, some of which include family health center construction and expansion, enrichment of programs and additions to personnel. Project Urban Renewal is funded by Jewish communities overseas which donate funds and adopt specific local projects. Arab neighborhoods in the 'mixed cities'—or neighborhoods in the Arab towns—would be good candidates for such projects, but Arabs have been excluded from these developments: In 1984 there were no Arab locations out of 49 projects (*ISCAR* 1984 #35). Presently, however, there is a move within American Jewish communities to extend these activities to Arab communities and neighborhoods in the 'mixed cities' (Haifa and Yafo); this move, if it is carried through, is significant in that it represents an integrative pathway for overseas Zionist institutions (especially the Jewish Agency) instead of their traditional resistance to including Arabs within the scope of nation-building activities in Israel. It comes, regrettably, at a time when Jewish Agency budgets and possibilities are in decline.

Chapter 4

THE HISTADRUT SICK FUND AND
THE OTHER VOLUNTARY SICK FUNDS

4.A. Consequences of the HSF's Special Status

After 1948, the HSF built upon the Histadrut's hegemony and on its own previously achieved basis, on its commitment to national service, and on its instrumental value to the party in power for 30 years, to constantly expand its facilities and services. From 1948-1958 87% of new immigrants joined the Histadrut and thus entered this sick fund—a substantial proportion of them not for ideological reasons (Zalmanovitch 1983). At the same time the HSF continued to be, as it had been during the period of the Mandate, the means of binding the veteran and the new middle classes to the Histadrut.

All of the public sick funds thrived through state support and subsidies. The HSF, being the largest, has continued to dominate ambulatory care in Israel. In 1984 the HSF had 1,274 clinics, 297 MCHS, 370 schools supervised, and employed 5,071 physicians (HSF 1957, IMH 1968, HSF 1985, Histadrut *Report to the XV Conference* 1985). With regard to IMH support, its advantage was elicited largely because of its size: Although it received much more in absolute IMH budgets, in relative terms the smaller sick funds benefited more than the HSF both from hospital subsidies and per person support. But the HSF benefited more both relatively and absolutely from allocations for disability cases, maternity, and old age insurance by the Labor Ministry under the national social insurance laws, as well as from directly allocated development budgets given by the Ministry of Finance. Most importantly, the great expansion in its size was itself in large part a function of Histadrut power.

Its historic closeness to power was not, however, the only basis for the HSF success: It offered also advantages intrinsic to its conception and ideology, such as full coverage with no extra charges according to need, and a commitment, grounded in its history and ideology, to representing and providing for the more dependent populations and for non-urban areas throughout the country beyond what any other agency was willing and able to do (Kanev 1965). Its progressive fee structure has been advantageous to working class members, and special group-rates benefited collective Jewish agricultural settlements. At the same time it served well the interests of the highest-paid bureaucratic and professional levels by setting a limit on fees not proportional to income. The HSF has continuously competed with other sick funds for subscription of the professional and entrepreneurial urban middle class.

Indeed, because its identification and in some cases patronage over the public away from the urban centers was only minimally challenged, the real ground for competition between sick funds was, as it had been during the Mandatory period, the urban middle class. Although some of the other sick funds also had some working class constituency, most of their members were from the middle class, and each of these sick funds was particularly concentrated in Tel Aviv, Jerusalem or Haifa (Halevi 1979, Hett 1981). While the HSF has insured many more wage-workers than self-employed, all the others insured, at least until 1976, more members who were independent than hired.

The voluntary sick funds have had the potential, anchored in their origins, to act as consumers' interest groups vis-à-vis the state and other vested interests (Doron 1979). This potential has however only in part been fulfilled. Each organization developed a bureaucracy which acts in its own interests and profit, and each has consistently represented vested interests which have often been prior to, and not necessarily congruent with, the interests of its members. The HSF acted for the Histadrut and through it for the Labor parties; The Amamit and Mercazit Sick Funds eventually acted within their traditional affinity by uniting in 1974 to form the Meuhedet (United) Sick Fund, identified with the center-liberal parties; the Le'umit Sick Fund continues to represent the National Workers' Federation for the political right Herut Party; and Maccabi united with Assaf to some degree in the interest of the physicians who established these funds.

In 1948, HSF insured 81% of the insured, the Le'umit Sick Fund 10%, Amamit and Mercazit 2% and 3% respectively, and Maccabi and Assaf together 2% (Halevi 1979). In 1977 and 1981, the relative weight of the HSF in relation to the others remained the same, while among the smaller sick funds Maccabi expanded especially. Among Arabs, the HSF encompassed 90% of the insured, with the rest divided about equally between the three other sick funds (see Table 4.1).

Table 4.1: Total Insurance Rates (% of the Population Insured) and Voluntary Sick Fund Membership (% of the Insured)

		Jews*	Non-Jews**
1977	Total	97	71
	HSF	81	92
	Maccabi-Assaf	10	2
	Le'umit	5	4
	Meuhedet	4	1
1981	Total	98	74
	HSF	82	90
	Maccabi-Assaf	10	4
	Le'umit	4	4
	Meuhedet	4	3

* not including soldiers
**including East Jerusalem.

(CBS 1980 #639, 1983 #708)

In Israel, health care insurance, except that covered by the social insurance laws of 1954, remained voluntary in principle, but is in fact compulsory for full-time permanent hired workers in places of work under contract with the Histadrut, and voluntary for others. Contracts were for nearly 30 years achieved through the mediation of the Labor Ministry, held by the Labor Party. They require subscription of workers to a sick fund, not necessarily the Histadrut's, but overwhelmingly so since most workers are Histadrut members. Since 1977, it has been easier for new employers to operate without such contracts.

From its members the Histadrut collects a tax graded according to salary, out of which 67% are paid to the sick fund, 32% to union activities and 1% is for 'culture and education' activities. The percentage allocated to the HSF has increased several times over the years, a mark of the centrality of health services to the Histadrut. A parallel tax is collected from the employer. HSF insurance is (so far at least) an aspect of Histadrut membership, and vice versa.

Although the sick fund is formally autonomous in the Histadrut and most operating decisions are made by its own bureaucracy, it is nevertheless directly manipulable, through allocation of tax and other pressures, in matters of general policy as well as more local issues such as the placing of clinics. The Histadrut, in turn, was manipulable by Mapai and now by the Labor Party. So far, notwithstanding sharp increases in membership fees by all of the sick funds in response to drastic IMH budget cuts, the HSF financial considerations have taken a back-seat when it comes to political utility (Arian 1981, Zalmanovitch 1983). Members do not pay additional fees on treatment, and the Histadrut has resisted proposals to institute such charges (which the other insurers have) on the basis that this is incompatible with egalitarian principles and with what working class members can afford. On occasions in the past when the HSF proposed to raise taxes, it was prevented from doing so by the state in its role as the largest public employer as well as by the Histadrut, which preferred to allocate to the sick fund a greater percentage of the total membership tax rather than alienate members—even (or especially) those who could afford an increase. It was the state's refusal (on Finance Ministry considerations) to allow an increase of fees in 1975 which tipped the scales towards financial dependence on the IMH.

From its beginning the HSF was not simply a voluntary agency, but a publicly-oriented one global in its intentions toward the Jewish population, motivated by Zionist and socialist ideology as part of the Histadrut. Having been the state's agent and surrogate, it now is in a phase of diminishment and some disrepute, an institution fighting a defensive battle, for reasons both external and internal to itself. The HSF is one of the public services—some operated by the state and some by cooperatives—which expanded with state support until 1977. Since then, the government has undercut all of these services in the interest of maximizing private enterprises and dissolving public ones.

There was no government review of the HSF before the 1977 State Comptroller's Report; as of 1977 the Finance Ministry refused to cover its deficits (Arian 1981). During some tenure in the 1980s, in the context of 'National Unity Government' which has included a Labor Party Minister of Finance and Minister of Health, support of the HSF increased, but state commitment to it is precarious.

The HSF own independent stance vis-à-vis the state is expressed in its reporting procedures: It has often chosen to withhold requested information on the assumption (often correct) that the IMH is hostile to it. In 1979 an official freeze on manpower was declared (*ISCAR* #31, 1980); since then expansion of the HSF has been much slowed, and demands engendered by population pressure—acute in the fast-growing Arab communities even more than elsewhere—are unmet.

The HSF's reduced status and increasing dependency on the IMH have been determined not only by the IMH's growing power but also by the weakening of the Histadrut: Its economic weakening as result of the expansion of the private sector in the Israeli economy, as well as of high interest rates and institutional inefficiency; its social weakening as a function of the rise of the middle class and of antagonism raised by over-centralization and hegemony; and its ideological weakening resulting from the contradiction between its status as employer and as union (Zalmanovitch 1983). Its socialist ideology has also been affected by the cracking of the Histadrut monolith—at the occupational top through the increasing independence of the various occupational unions federated in it, and across the board through the emergence within it of an active competing minority Likud political faction. All in all, the Histadrut's hegemony was effective as long as it could credibly claim national leadership by virtue of representing and protecting workers' interests. Its ongoing discreditation in these areas affects the sick fund as well. The decline of the HSF is thus an aspect of a decline in the social significance of the Histadrut, and of its losses of economic power and political unity.

The Histadrut and the HSF were transformed— supposedly against their will but increasingly with their cooperation—from activist workers' institutions to ones significantly co-opted by state-controlled benefits. The ideology of the welfare state became, in the hands of a ruling bureaucratic elite both in the ministries and the Histadrut, an instrument for inducing dependent passivity in the working class while providing for them indispensable and extensive service, and for buying off the affluent while the unworking poor continued to be somehow provided for by national and municipal welfare benefits as well as by some charitable organizations.

Corrosion of the HSF charisma is part of the changes in the Histadrut as it became rooted in economic power based on the alliance with the state. This alliance and this power led it to directions of economic investment and of social management which are in contradiction to its working class identifications. In the HSF, this took the form of an increasing gap between the aspirations of the working class constituency for a personally-involved and considerately designed pattern of care, and the superimposed planning and executing by the bureaucratic and professional levels.

As a mutual aid organization motivated by socialist ideals, the HSF was characterized by most of its insured members' and at least some of its professional employees' identification with its goals. With post-state expansion it became an over-extended, bureaucratized and centralized institution increasingly required to deal with a growing alienation and dissatisfaction of both groups. Its status as a monopoly had an unhealthy influence on its character as a mutual aid organization concerned with members' demands for quality of service. On the one hand, it continued to serve well the economic interests of its members (and thus of the majority of the public) by subsidizing their care at the expense of the state and of its own physician employees, and expanded its provision of access to members of all classes and sectors throughout the country (Halevi 1979, Doron 1979). On the other hand, its potential for responsiveness remained latent during the period of hegemonious expansion: Growing into an 'empire,' the HSF treated much of its working class membership as a passive and to a large degree captive population. In turn this population, perhaps made passive by over-centralized bureaucracies not only in the domain of health, did not for a long time engage in activism in its own behalf. While a more affluent segment of the insured who could afford to do so supplemented HSF ambulatory care with private treatments, avoiding the inconvenience of public clinics altogether while reserving the benefits of subsidized hospitalization which is in any case the main motivation for medical insurance, working-class members could less well afford such expenses.

The HSF, patronizing and insensitive to local interests and problems, drew toward it much of the resentment which in 1977 displaced the ruling Labor Party from its dominance in Israeli politics. If in earlier years it was the establishment's agent of socialization among immigrant populations, it later absorbed much of the discontent of their children (and, by 1977, their grandchildren) on their way to becoming a demographic majority (Shapira 1980). The younger generations' political socialization through army service and awareness of their electoral power (both in the Knesset and in the Histadrut) enabled them to demand better service. The fact that the HSF has made efforts to answer these demands, by improving its services in the moshavim and development towns, showed a vulnerability to political pressure from membership (which, after all, may be considered a strength).

As a health empire owning facilities, employing a large personnel and controlling the terms of provision of services, the HSF like all Histadrut plants is caught in the structural contradiction between union-status and ownership of the means of production. While to many of its members it has become just another producer and seller of services, to its professional workers it is also, if not only, just another employer. The high employment share of services in the health field (so that most physicians were in the public sector) which began during the period of the Mandate increased with the formation of the state bureaucracy and its alliance with the Histadrut. It has led to a public clinical system characterized by a high number of physicians per person and 'low output' as measured by a high number of patients' visits to physicians per person (Ofer 1967, Shuval 1979). The high rate of visits to physicians enabled a substitution of available physicians for scarce hospital beds, and thus held back hospital expenses. At the same time, HSF clinics became overburdened (Ofer 1985). In its clinics, both general practitioners and expert consultants have been assigned rather than chosen. The queue system and referrals are formalized within the bureaucracy so that they include inefficiency, causing inconvenience and hardship. Public discontent is exacerbated by an awareness of the fact that in a bureaucracy such as the HSF, direct access to privileged service (by virtue of being sick fund employees, through personal contacts, or by being privileged members of related bureaucracies) favors the well-connected.

The conflicts between socialists and liberals which have characterized the debate about the character of health services in Israel continue to do so at present. With the ascendancy of the middle class and of the political center and right, the HSF's critical dependency on the state has become a pretext for increasingly directing toward it the rhetoric of social Darwinism. The ideology of private enterprise—whether expressed in public institutions or in private form—has transmuted the competing values of health service provision expressed during the Mandate by the HSF and the HMO, of mutual aid within a workers' movement on the one hand and of civic responsibility and public charity on the other. Within this ideology the HSF is seen by the new establishment as the undeserving serving the unworthy, while the prosperous are expected, against their will, to aid in support of the weak.

But antagonism between the IMH and the HSF (and between the various voluntary agencies—each representing a different agenda of social and professional priorities) is only a part of the story. Since the 1930s, and more so after 1948, physicians' professional interests—represented by the Israel Medical Association—have been in opposition to the HSF (and to the state when physicians are its employees in state hospitals, but in preferred cooperation with the state bureaucracy in the interest of private enterprise). The sick funds, as consumers' organizations, protect patients from domination by both. There is no reason to believe that State administration in health, in conjunction with the demands of the free market, would be particularly efficient or beneficent in Israel, and would serve patients better than the sick funds if these were reformed to better serve consumer interests (Doron 1979). This is especially so because professional medical interests in Israel as elsewhere in the West still favor development of high technology and high specialization, at the expense of environmental and personal prevention and of the effective treatment of routine and chronic illness.

Within the HSF itself this conflict is expressed in opposition between the bureaucracy and its physician employees (Yishai 1986). While the bureaucracy still (whether sincerely or insincerely) speaks the language of its working class constituency, physicians in the HSF as in the Israel Medical Association in general now speak mostly for their own professional interests. The willingness to absorb immigrant physicians in their own professions which spurred the development of Jewish health services brought about a constant surplus of physicians working for relatively low public employees' wages. With the rise in the standard of living many were unprepared to continue without private supplements. Many immigrant and Israel-born physicians who were channeled into a public-servant role against their will prefer, as do most physicians in the West, the role and profits of private enterprise here combined with the security of publicly salaried positions (Doron 1979). Moreover, the relatively low wages paid to physicians and other medical workers which enabled the HSF to contend with rising hospital costs in the 1970s and into the 1980s also increased employees' discontent. The organization is faced with their active dissatisfaction, as well as with the protest of nurses who are even more poorly paid. A similar conflict affects IMH medical employees. The patient-public meanwhile is further disappointed by strikes of disaffected personnel.

Beyond the HSF real achievements and the weakness of the institutional alternatives, its power was sustained by the Israeli majority's acceptance of it as a social fact of life delimited by economic possibilities which made private medicine for most an unaffordable luxury, and simultaneously by a public service attitude that bound most physicians, outwardly at least, to modest expectations of profit. The much discussed regression in services and status is to some degree and in some places absolute, but it is no less related to a new level of expectations and means.

By the 1960s the middle class was no longer small, its ranks widened by the veteran sector of bureaucrats and entrepreneurs enriched through the state (Rosenfeld and Carmi, 1976). Nevertheless, most of its members were still fairly modest in their habits of consumption—including of medical care—and constrained by the fact that there was no alternative institutional concentration of health services. Supplementary medical care by individual physicians was always—openly or under-the-table—available to this class.

Public salaries, in medicine as in other areas, do not reflect professional investment and expertise. Most publicly employed physicians were for a long period normatively governed by explicit

The Histadrut Sick Fund and Other Voluntary Sick Funds   99

employment codes which restrict private payments to state and to HSF employees. Although informal gifts accrued, in general they did so not openly and certainly not flagrantly. As medicine has kept pace with the changes in Israeli society toward increasing class differentiation, physicians continue to work within the public system but the system of unofficial 'black market' medicine has grown, benefiting those physicians who combine public salary and private practice, and encouraging patients covered by HSF insurance to increasingly add unofficial fees for medical services such as selected expert opinion, immediacy of elective hospitalization, and choice of surgeon. HSF and IMH employees need permission to practice privately; furthermore, at a high rate of taxation, unreported practice is highly profitable. To the extent that the role of private consultant—even practicing with permission and paying taxes—overlaps with physicians' gate-keeping roles in the bureaucracy (e.g. in expediting diagnostics and facilitating hospital admission), the possibility of corruption is involved. Pressure from physicians has led to the fact that in addition to private care as an option, HSF insurees often pay for private treatment which is optional in principle but less so in practice. A great part, if not most, of HSF specialists (and IMH hospital physicians) have active private clinics supplementing their hospital or clinic positions, and in practice private consultations previous to non-emergency hospitalization are often (unofficially) required rather than optional.

To a great extent such services institutionalize trends which have existed illicitly within and around the public system, offering outwardly private expert care and hospitalization as opposed to under the table payments to physicians. These trends are—not only in Israel—the consequences of an oversupply of physicians (Barer et al. 1989). In the 1980s public and private health services are in open conflict for the first time since the 1940s. Private commercial services accounted for one fifth of national health expenditure, with a rise in the 1980s (IMH *Bulletin* 1985:98). There was a rise of 8% in the per capita private consumption of medical service in the years 1980-1984 (Kopp 1985).

In the first round the public system in its expansive phase won, absorbing physicians on its own terms. There now is an increasing segment of the population which not only wants choice, convenience and immediacy, but is also able to pay for it. Such a segment exists among the Arab population as well. Within this group HSF insurance is now increasingly used primarily as hospitalization insurance, with ordinary, expert and emergency care often contracted on a private or partially private basis for maximum convenience. Private commercial services accounted for one fifth of national health expenditure, with a rise in the 1980s (IMH *Bulletin* 1985:98, Kopp 1985). In 1979, one third of the fully insured HSF members purchased private medical services as well (Machnes 1980). Some members of the Histadrut insured in the HSF choose to insure themselves in the Maccabi Sick Fund in addition; the interpretation of insurance trends must be affected by the fact that members of a household are not necessarily insured in the same fund, so that overlapping coverages of husbands, wives, and children in different sick funds may affect these rates. In the last few years, private medical groups and institutions have added to the medical alternatives available to those who can pay.

Private hospitals are a special threat to the HSF because it has always relied on its established basis of hospital facilities as its main competitive advantage. Since the other sick funds did not develop equivalent hospital facilities, the HSF hospital network has attracted members of the urban middle class who otherwise may have been more attracted by other sick funds' ambulatory care convenience, and who are unattached to the Histadrut in any way. Hospitalization according to region in HSF and IMH hospitals, instituted in 1981, has made these facilities equally open to members of all sick funds, and has in this sense operated to the harm of the HSF and to the benefit of its competitors; attempts to maintain at least outpatient clinics in HSF hospitals as the exclusive privilege of its insurees failed in court. If an alternative private hospital system develops which can bypass the bureaucratic delays and overlong waiting lists for surgery which characterize HSF and IMH operations at this time, it can be used by the other sick funds to drastically diminish the advantages of HSF membership.

Thus with the further growth of the middle class after the war of 1967 prosperity has flowed into the health services, resulting in the rise of the middle class sick fund (Maccabi) and in a proliferation of private services. This trend is usually presented by both opponents and proponents of the HSF as due to the failure of the public health system. Perhaps no less accurately, it may be considered to have been inevitable in the context of the increasing purchasing power and rising standard of living among the middle classes and of the abundant supply of physicians.

Maccabi contracts most of its physicians on an associative basis, i.e. on commission. Most of these physicians work in their own private clinics only, or combine such work with a public position such as work in government hospitals, practicing contractually and privately after-hours. Maccabi also has consultative clinics (where physicians work on salary), laboratories, and associated pharmacies in the towns; a recent expansion involves the establishment of clinics in Jewish development towns. In the Arab towns they are active in Nazareth and

Shefar'am; there are other branches in the mixed cities and a contracted physician in Rame (Maccabi 1986). Maccabi's main competitive advantages over the HSF are, first, the method of choice of physician and consultation by appointment arranged on an individual basis at the physician's home or clinic (a method which in response has also been instituted by the HSF in some locations, but not in general), and, secondly, its relatively uncumbersome bureaucracy which allows for a fairly direct process of specialist appointments, diagnosis and hospitalization—instead of the queue-bound, lengthy and often redundant process at the HSF.

In the 1980s a rising level of consumers' demands, means, and possibilities leads to a threat to the HSF from this sick fund especially. Competition is on a professional level of improved convenience and access, and tests the HSF adaptive capacities now also beyond the urban centers which had been the traditional locus of competition. Following the recent penetration of Maccabi to the development towns of the Negev, the HSF has initiated referrals to independent specialists in order to bring waiting for appointments down to one week (current average waiting time for HSF dermatologists has been two weeks to three months, for ophthalmologists two weeks to two months, etc.).

Competition between voluntary sick funds, and between private and public medicine, is of course beneficial to the extent that it motivates choice and improvements, but less so if it motivates them only for the benefit of the affluent. The HSF offers real and meaningful extensive equality to members regardless of class in the terms of insurance coverage and hospitalization, but requires improvement in the local and regional distribution of services which affect access and thus quality. The evidence is, however, that it lately concentrates its qualitative improvements in the areas of most rivalry—in the urban locales where it also contends for the middle class clientele with the Maccabi Sick Fund. Such features as clinic appointments by phone, individually scheduled appointments at the family physician's home, and referrals (guaranteeing repayment of fees) to a specialist of choice bypassing the queues to consultative clinics, have only been put in practice in towns.

Those Histadrut members who cannot afford additional spending on health are most affected by current trends. Dissatisfaction with existing ambulatory HSF services—or even more critically with their nonexistence—is more of a problem for those populations for whom HSF responsibility is not irrelevant or unnecessary, and for whom other alternatives are less open. But for the HSF itself, the most problematic arena is in those areas where it is most threatened by competition. The presence of alternatives intensifies public perception of relative deprivation and demands for improvement, but competition does not now benefit most of those who are in the most vulnerable positions—rural Arabs, and Jewish and Arab urban working class and poor. For example, the HSF has been instituting appointments by telephone, choice of physicians, and other innovative programs in the towns and in affluent neighborhoods where its competitors are most active; its major improvement in primary care—'the health team' consisting of nurse and physician—has barely reached rural Arab communities.

Current members' dissatisfaction and complaints about HSF services are so general across the country that they must be taken for granted (Histadrut Guiding Committee 1985). On the local level everywhere complaints center on the general (although not universal) lack of afternoon and night service; on absence of, or deficiency in, available specialists in most non-urban settlements; on the lack of dental service; on the requirement of seeing assigned general practitioners before consulting specialists and the overall inefficiency and inconvenience of the referral process, including long waiting lists for diagnostic and consultative procedures and results; on absence of prescribed medications in pharmacies (and the absence of specific medications from the 'prescribable' list); and on the insufficiency of preventive service and of education for health. Special mention is made of the need for regular checkups—of elderly patients in particular (Histadrut Guiding Committee 1985). A frequent complaint about HSF physicians is that they treat patients impersonally, even beyond the insufficient attention dictated by long waiting lines. Some of these charges may reflect changes in medical style with its bureaucratization: Veteran physicians may have visited once a month but appeared to know everyone.

Arab members add to this list demands for the opening of clinics in all Arab villages, for employment of Arab personnel—especially community residents—and for equality in services within the national average of what is provided. Special needs are for having a physician on duty in large communities, and for local pharmacies and diagnostics (e.g. blood tests for children) in the village. Access to specialist clinics is a serious problem in most small communities, especially given the HSF indirect pathway of referral and diagnostics, but some of the Arab communities without specialist service are quite large (over 15,000). Ambulance service is lacking, as are home visits. Explanatory and educational material in Arabic is insufficiently available. Arab members demand construction of clinics where they are now sometimes located in unsuitable rented facilities.

The current difficulties of public medicine, generally attributed to the rise in medical costs due to improvements in technology and to the concomitant rise in expenditures on hospitals as opposed to clinical and preventive care (Ofer 1985) are finally no less due to the accelerating trends which define the parameters of state policies and support: the slowing in economic growth as a function of economic dependency, high interest rates, shrinking of public budgets and low priority given to welfare activities and to development of public services. Because of its scope, these have affected the HSF more than the other sick funds.

Dissatisfactions with the present condition of HSF clinics must, however, be evaluated against the alternatives offered by the other sick funds and by private medicine. As it is, the HSF primarily among the sick funds has been the mainstay of curative ambulatory medicine in Israel: If any institution has served the needs of the public away from the urban centers, it has been this institution. For the working-class public as a whole, it has to a significant degree served as protector—however flawed—both from the demands of the private market and from total dependence on the state. If the HSF hegemony has led to typical problems, there is no reason to believe that a state-operated national health service would have done better. The real issue, given the specific dynamics and structural properties of the system as it evolved, is to what degree it has provided the egalitarian service which is the declared goal of both the state and the HSF, and how it can be improved. While a combination of Histadrut interests and state encouragement and constraints have determined a level of access which requires substantial improvements, motivation for such improvements is likely to come from the HSF (and the Histadrut) in trying to attract and keep members. The degree to which it succeeds in extending such improvements substantially will affect the status of medical insurance in Israel for everyone, and for the working class in particular.

In the degree of disappointment it elicits the HSF, in comparison both to the IMH and to the other sick funds, is to some degree also a victim of high expectations. IMH family health stations have reached more settlements than the HSF curative clinics and where they exist appear to be doing an adequate job in relation to their limited goals. But for curative care, by its nature, more immediacy and attributable responsibility are essential, and these set of pressures no less than criteria of distribution account for the fact that expressed dissatisfaction has centered on the HSF and not on the IMH. Another reason is that in Israel state responsibility for social services is often met by a wide-ranging agreement on other national priorities for the allocation of tax money, whereas when an agency whose sole responsibility is to their health does not meet their expectations HSF members feel cheated out of their dues. When it comes to the HSF, attribution of flaws falls directly on it and the Histadrut, rather than on the state which withholds its support. Similarly, the situation in state hospitals is no better than in the HSF; but public dissatisfaction with state hospitals centers on cuts in hospital budgets which are easily deflected onto Finance Ministry policies.

The HSF has been empowered through the membership of insurees covered by the Histadrut's negotiated contracts with the majority of employers, as well as through government policy and support. Its success as both insurer and provider, its special status as a quasi-state agency, and its own claims to national service, have made it much more than a voluntary sick fund or service-providing agency, and led to its being associated with the welfare state more than the state itself. However, no matter how expansive its view of its societal ambitions and responsibilities, as long as the HSF remains a voluntary sick fund which derives a main part of its income from members' dues, the official limit of its responsibility is to serve those it insures.   For this reason it can navigate at its interest between financial and political, business and social considerations.

The extent of the state's responsibility for providing health care is as problematic in Israel as it is elsewhere.   However, the state's responsibility for equitable distribution of those aspects of health care which it has undertaken to provide is implicit in the egalitarian commitments expressed by its governments. The HSF responsibility on the other hand is officially only to its insurees; nevertheless, demands that it act for the benefit of groups beyond this circuit can be made in light of its governmentally-favored position and its own ideological claims.

The HSF's competitive advantages over the other sick funds have been its well-established hospitals and consultative clinics, and the fact that it collects no fees beyond the monthly insurance fee whereas the Maccabi fund charges a small fee for patient visits. Both sick funds collect a partial payment for medications.   However, the HSF's main advantage and contribution to public health is that it provides services in the majority of smaller communities where no one else provides. Many of these communities are Arab. Whereas it has had extensive success in reaching and serving the great majority of moshavim, kibbutzim, and Arab villages where service is not necessarily profitable, the smaller sick funds for the most part (Le'umit is a partial exception) compete where service is most profitable—in the towns and among the affluent.

The other sick funds remained relatively small because the HSF was successful in recruiting and serving the middle class. Maccabi's recent expansion—often presented essentially as a symptom of dissatisfaction with the HSF—is probably inevitable in the context of an increasing socioeconomic polarization in Israel reflected in a new dominance of middle class consumer practices and ideology (Rosenfeld and Carmi 1976).

4.B. Expansion of the Sick Funds among the Arabs

Given the significance of Arab labor as well as the significance of Arab votes within the coalitionary system, all the sick funds have established themselves in the Arab communities along the lines of force created by socioeconomic affinities and by electoral politics, although the small sick funds have offered against the HSF a level of competition much less ambitious in its goals than that which had previously been attempted by the IMH.

Openings of HSF clinics, along with local party branches and Histadrut clubs, has been an integral part of Mapai's (and its successor, the Labor Party's) activities.   Clinics were offered as material benefits accruing to party members and as reasons for voting, established as election promises and rewards and as signs of the Party's ongoing involvement in the community.   While in Jewish settlements the instrumental aspect of the politics of HSF care was no less potent, it generally focussed on improvements in the quality of service rather than on its very presence. This is so because veteran Jewish settlements already had facilities, while new ones were planned by the Government and the Zionist settlement agencies to include health service, generally HSF (see Chapter 5.A). Only a small number of Jewish localities—moshavim within the Revisionist (Herut) Party planned with its associated Le'umit clinic only—did not include HSF facilities. The significant exception to this norm of planning occurred with the second post-state wave of immigration in 1954-1956, when a policy of dispersing new immigrants to peripheral regions upon arrival placed them in abandoned Arab villages in the Galilee and in some unbuilt locations in the south, without any provision of health care; Generally, however, service was introduced within a few years.

In Arab communities, the phase when mere presence of local services was something to be bestowed lasted at least 20 years longer, and to some degree goes on still today, although most communities have reached the stage where quality is improved or withheld, as prize or sanction by the government. Sanctions have been used against lack of political support. For example a HSF consultative center in Nazareth—where there is consistent communist voting in local and national elections—has not been re-started since its aborted beginning in 1973, despite the large number of Histadrut members in the city, although it has been under constant discussion. HSF full equal cooperation with the four Christian voluntary hospitals in Nazareth, which would significantly ameliorate conditions for the sick fund's insurees, is still only partial. The most rewards, however, did not necessarily go to the most dependable groups, but rather to the least dependent. Bedouin settlements and some small villages, perhaps the most loyal Mapai-voters among Arabs, nevertheless benefited, if at all, only last and least (cf. Landau 1969).

Soon after the establishment of the state, HSF services were provided in two Arab communities in the context of the Histadrut's Israel Labor League (formerly PLL) which, with its separate Arab section established in 1925, remained active until 1955. Competition with the Communist Workers' Congress in Nazareth, which operated its own sick fund, led the HSF to open its first Arab clinics in Nazareth and Rame. In these two locations, some Arab physicians (e.g. Dr. Seruji, Dr. Dib) remained and continued their practice established during the Mandate (Landau 1969, IGA IMH G4264).

Beginning in 1952, Arab workers began to be accepted into the Histadrut, which controlled the labor market. As of then, Workers' Congress activities were discontinued, and the Histadrut became the only permitted channel of workers organization among Arabs. By 1956-1959 Arabs were admitted to integrated professional associations. In 1959 there were nearly 15,000 Arab Histadrut members, mostly from the urban centers. As of 1960 Arab workers were accepted as full members with all social benefits including the HSF.

Since then, Histadrut membership and HSF services have been on the increase among Arabs, both in the 'mixed towns' and in the villages where most workers resided while working in towns (Landau 1969, Histadrut *Report to the XV Conference* 1985). The percentage of the Arab population insured in the HSF doubled from 1955 to 1968, and more than doubled again from 1968 to 1984. In 1984 there were 164,000 Arab members of the Histadrut, more than 10% of total Histadrut membership. Including their families, 438,000 were insured in the HSF, making up nearly 14% of its members (Histadrut *Report to the XV Conference* 1985:140). Of that number, 48,000 were in East Jerusalem; excluding East Jerusalem, the percentage of the Arab population insured in the HSF was thus about 70% (computed from *SAI* 1986, and from information cited by the HSF, Jerusalem Region. In East Jerusalem, whose Arab population was about 125,000 in 1984, about 40% were covered by the HSF; in 1987 the rate increased to 45%). Among the Bedouin of the Negev, only 55% were insured (Abu Rabi'a, 1987). Since the rate of HSF insurees in the Jewish population was reported as 79%, the Arab coverage rate is about 10% lower than that of Jews. In 1968, only one third of the Arab population was insured in the HSF. The high rate of Histadrut and HSF affiliation is a significant fact about the Arab population: It is determined by the emergence after 1967 of a large Arab working class employed on a permanent basis, and by the increase in the standard of living among most of the population, including the growing middle class—professional and entrepreneurial—many of whose members, especially after 1967, also joined the HSF.

But although Arabs are in fact Histadrut members with equal rights to social benefits, their rights do not include equal political representation. Specifically, Arabs have been held back from forming communal workers' councils similar to those which represent workers in Jewish settlements, out of the Histadrut's fear that such councils would be centers of communist or other non-Labor-Alignment party organization (as has been the case in Nazareth). Instead, integration within wider regional workers' councils is the current policy. Although the influence of workers' councils on the Histadrut's central bureaucracy is much less than such councils are expected to have in a democratic organization, they do provide an institutional channel for voicing communal demands for development and improvement of HSF service. Although local and regional HSF channels for individual claims and complaints (clinic councils) are available, the lack of local workers councils in Arab communities means that communal political pressures for improvement of services which may have effect on the HSF center are inhibited. While the HSF everywhere has been over-centralized, with its decisions imposed from Tel Aviv, HSF activities in the Arab sector have been even more insensitive to local communal demands than elsewhere.

After a comprehensive review of its activities in 1976, the Histadrut (the General Federation of Hebrew Workers) was renamed, to accommodate Arab members, the General Federation of Workers; the HSF was renamed the General Sick Fund. The Arab Department in the Histadrut—a symbol of special and discriminatory treatment (with an appointee in charge of relations with the HSF)—was renamed the Department for Integration in formal preparation for its abolishment, accomplished in 1986. Presently, out of 72 workers' councils only four are Arab—in Nazareth, Taiybe, Shefar'am, and among the Druze villages of the Central Galilee (Histadrut *Report to the XV Conference* 1985). These councils have been used to elicit better service: In Taiybe a well-equipped HSF clinic was built through pressures on the Histadrut applied by the workers' council; in Shefar'am, there is now also a clinic equipped with diagnostic facilities, and the HSF there has, exceptionally, a physician on duty in the evening hours.

Out of seven workers' committees with less than independent status in the Histadrut, five are Arab—two veteran ones prevented from becoming full councils (Umm al-Fahm and Sakhnin), and three new (Kafar Kana, Tamra and Rahat); in Umm al-Fahm after construction of the planned health center stopped in 1977, 7,000 HSF members were served for several years in a rented clinic with no laboratory or medical instruments, but in 1985 a well-equipped clinic was opened (Histadrut *Report to the XV Conference* 1985, Geraissy and Kana'aneh 1987). A reform in workers' councils in the 1980s, which promotes regional integration of workers into existing councils, is a gerrymandering policy evidently not necessarily aimed against Arabs but more generally against any serious political competition within the Histadrut, not least by the political right in Jewish locations. In spite of the small number of Arab independent and semi-independent worker-representative groups, on these new terms the Histadrut can claim that the great majority of Arab settlements are included in workers' councils, excluding only 20 small villages and 18 Bedouin tribes. One of the designated components of such integration is the development of regional medical services, and an exemplar consultative clinic has been established by the HSF in the Jewish town of Karmiel. Such centers are of course beneficial but no substitute for essential local care in Arab communities.

Local influence on the HSF center requires either a community representative doing his or her work quietly, or a high level of publicly audible demand backed by the threat of withdrawal of (political or membership) support, or both. Although compared to Jews few Arabs have reached national positions, the number of Arab office-holders in the Histadrut and the HSF is greater than in any other national bureaucracy or organization, and demands do get voiced by elected officials identified with the Labor Party and by other influentials within the Histadrut's local or national bureaucracy. But the full potential of unionization as the major channel for cooperative health care has been impeded. The political denial of non-Histadrut Arab workers' organizations foreclosed any other union organization around issues of health.

Analysis of data provided by the HSF (HSF *XI Conference* 1984) shows that while close to 14% of HSF members were Arabs (in the mixed cities Arabs made up 15% of the insured) professional and organizational representation as well as facilities were not proportional (Geraissy and Kana'aneh 1987). In HSF clinics 1,590 physicians were employed, of them 87 (5%) Arabs. Arab workers made up 3.8% of the number of HSF employees. Out of 160 delegates at the Conference, 7 (4.4%) were Arab. Out of 31 representative of HSF local supervisory committees, 30 members of central administration, and 10 members of the central acting committee, none were Arab. Arab representatives did make up 8% of the members of secondary committees. Out of 1,274 clinics, 94-101 (7-8%) were in Arab localities. There were no dental clinics in Arab communities, while there were 79 dental clinics in the Jewish sector

The fact that Arab villages have not been allowed to become part of the cooperative frameworks (e.g. marketing associations) which have governed agricultural production and distribution in Israel, also denies them the health services benefits of such affiliation. Since cooperative regional organizations in Israel are for the most part organized in each region according to social political alliances of kibbutzim and moshavim, Arab villages in close geographic proximity to Jewish communities do not belong to these organizations, and operate in separate orbits even in when they belong (as a minority of them do) to the same local government regional council.

The Histadrut's agreements with kibbutzim and moshavim specify special group-rates which take into account a discount based on the ease of collective collection. Kibbutzim pay through their movements, moshavim through the marketing association. This in effect has meant that the HSF often extends credit until such payments are made (with the recent collapse of some marketing organizations due to mismanagement and high interest rates, individual collection in moshavim is making an entry). In Arab villages, as in the urban sector in general, Histadrut membership taxes are individually collected based on income.

Regional cooperatives may share allocated medical manpower hours, so that HSF physicians may be employed on a circuit basis and be reachable beyond what would seem to be the case according to the hours allotted to each place. In more sparsely populated 'development areas' of planned post-state immigrant settlement in small moshavim, the HSF took over the rural centers built by the IMH in the 1950s and built supra-local rural health centers including some specialists and dentists, with a physician on duty most hours of the days. These centers serve 3-10 moshavim at one facility, with preventive care given either by the HSF or the IMH. Only a handful of the 87 moshavim which were served by such centers in 1977 had a population between 500-1,000, the rest being under 500 in size (IMH 1979). Regional services on the primary level are the exception in Israel, sporadic minor attempts for a small number of small settlements, while the vast majority of settlements are served by facilities within the community. Still, there are presently 21 such centers, none for Arabs.

Thus, after the establishment of Israel the Histadrut succeeded where it had failed in the pre-state period—in motivating Arabs, who were denied other avenues of organization, to become members on its terms. These were fraught with ambivalence between Jewish national state-building priorities on the one hand and representing all workers on the other, and Arabs workers' membership was considered a bestowed privilege as well as a right. The HSF's activities among Arabs have been only half-heartedly egalitarian; in this it reflects the Histadrut's general policy toward Arab workers and their communities, which constitutes the HSF context of action. Both the lesser development and its denial are part and parcel of a deep-set ambivalence which has characterized the Histadrut's attitude to Arabs from the beginning of its activities among them. However patronizing the Histadrut and the HSF were, initially, to the post-state Jewish immigrants, it is to their credit that they applied a pragmatic double-standard but not an ideological one toward that population. With regard to the Arabs, however, the double-standard was and has been ubiquitous, a function of the conflict between egalitarian ideals and exclusivist goals. Such conflict reproduces unfinished answers within the evolution of Zionist priorities toward bringing democracy fully to bear on the Arab citizens of Israel; within the range of political stances toward the Arabs in Israel, the best that can be said of this Labor Party/Histadrut line is that it is preferable to single-standard clearcut commitment to second-rate status for Arabs.

Its labor-union commitments and egalitarian ideology have brought about a consistent defensiveness by the HSF with regard to its relatively low rate of accomplishment in Arab communities. This defensiveness is expressed both explicitly and implicitly, in the wealth of HSF (Research Department and other) publications which, for example, supply no epidemiological data distinguishing between Jews and Arabs, and most often neglect to provide comparative analyses with regard to health or to the detailed dimensions of the provision and use of services (with regard to counts of services offered and to the rate of insured, the HSF advantage over its competitors is so outstanding that it may be presented forthrightly). Such lack of information and poverty of analysis amounts to a policy of denial rationalized as ideological commitment.

Within these limitations, the Histadrut has provided for its Arab members a primary organ for equality—however imperfect and improvable—within Israeli society. As an aspect of Histadrut membership, HSF coverage also established real equality in the extent of insurance available to Arab as to Jewish members and in the quality of care provided in central (specialists') clinics and in hospitals. However, the degree to which the HSF has provided local access to primary and secondary service within the Arab communities, while unsurpassed by that provided by any other agency, has consistently lagged behind HSF service in Jewish localities even though the Histadrut's constitution assures all members of medical care. While nowhere in this document is provision of local service assured, and neither does the HSF spell out qualitative criteria for local clinics, the Histadrut and the HSF are accountable for discrimination both because of their ideological claims to equality and because of the contractual nature of membership.

In the 1960s and 1970s, while in Jewish localities the HSF concentrated on building and operating consultative specialists' clinics, in Arab communities it was extending mainly primary service. The HSF has a Committee for Arab and Druze Affairs supervising activities in the Arab sector, and has made intensive efforts in this area especially since 1973 (Aharoni 1979, 1981), as the relative weight of Arabs in the Histadrut and their level of demand have been on the increase. In spite of this, in the 1980s this task is still incomplete. A total of 295 primary clinics were built from 1965-1985 (two-thirds in urban and one-third in rural areas, even though rural population decreased; 20-25% of these clinics were in built in Arab communities, accounting for much of the rural construction [HSF 1985]). Nevertheless there are still a significant number of Arab localities (about one-third of the full count of Arab settlements) without any sick fund service. A few of the Le'umit Sick Fund's stations are in localities which have no HSF service, but this does not change the picture significantly.

The HSF power to decide when to open—and when to close—clinics, is especially consequential when theirs is the only clinic in a settlement. In Arab communities, competition by the other sick funds and by local initiatives could act as a spur to improvement of HSF services. But the investment by the other sick funds in service in Arab communities is nowhere at the HSF level.

Table 4.2:   HSF Clinics in Arab Urban and Rural Localities, 1964-1984

Year	Number
1964	32
1968	42
1973	52
1984	94*

*Elsewhere, the HSF reports a current total of 103 or 101 HSF clinics (about 8% of the total) in Arab communities and for Arabs in the 'mixed cities' (Histadrut 1985, HSF 1984). The count of 94 may exclude the latter.

(HSF 1985, IMH 1968:130-140)

Of the Arab settlements which have no service, the HSF claims that most are small, or have few local Histadrut members. The first of these arguments is unconvincing since small Jewish settlements are not equally deprived, and the second is to some degree irrelevant in that the HSF has undertaken to treat the uninsured as well as the insured in Arab communities. Since the HSF has not defaulted in providing local service to regions in the periphery, the problem is special to Arabs. The Histadrut has announced an explicit priority of developing medical service in Bedouin communities in the Galilee, but these are still at the planning stage. For some of these small villages and Bedouin settlements, rural integrative centers might be the answer.

For others, especially in the mountains of the Galilee, local facilities are essential. Nowadays transportation is such that most patients from Arab villages could reach a private physician, an ambulatory clinic, or a hospital in emergencies. But where the topography is hilly, in villages without essential services where busses often do not enter the villages at which they stop, patients—women, children and the elderly especially—are unlikely to reach facilities outside the community to receive non-emergency care. A field study of health services in a northern sub-region in Akko County in 1979 showed that in this mountain area of difficult topography localization of health services is a crucial need (Davidov et al. 1981).

As a percentage of all HSF clinics, those in Arab villages and cities increased from 3% in 1963 to 4% in 1973 and 7% in 1984 (HSF *Institutions and Services* 1984). But Arab settlements of all sizes in all regions have local services lesser in range and in quantity, and thus in quality, than Jewish settlements of their size.

Some Arab localities still have no local curative service at all—whereas Jewish settlements of the same and much smaller size do have them. In 1976-1978 there were 56-60 Arab settlements without clinics; 11 of them had a population over 1,000 (Prime Minister's Office 1976; IMH 1979). From 1978 to 1986 the HSF Development Program accounts for 22 new clinics built in Arab locations. In 1984 38 Arab villages still lacked a HSF clinic (HSF *Institutions and Services* 1984). Many of the places without service are in the Akko and Yizra'el Valley regions.

Although a small number of villages may have obtained Le'umit Sick Fund clinics, well over 30 recognized villages have no local ambulatory service. In 1977, there were also several dozen Jewish settlements listed without local service, but the great majority were under 500 in population, and most were served in regional centers within a 3 km radius (IMH 1979). While several of these had declined in size by 1986, nevertheless a number of local clinics have been added in these communities since 1978.

With regard to all dimensions of local services beyond their mere absence or presence—dimensions such as frequency of medical presence and concentration of manpower, immediacy, quality, and continuity of treatment, and attention within this context to preventive care— dissatisfaction with the HSF is found on all levels, among both Jews and Arabs. But all of these factors are more objectively inadequate for the Arab population.

In Jaljulia, a village in the Triangle with a population approaching 4,000, the HSF clinic, open in the morning hours only, is visited by 60-70 patients per day in winter and summer. Only the most urgently ill can be seen, and patients at an early stage of illness receive no attention. Disputes between patients and personnel are frequent and add to the pressure. Patients who are accepted are seen by a general practitioner, and if they require diagnostic tests, specialist's attention, or hospitalization, they are sent to Petah Tiqwa, a Jewish town within close range. Medications for the chronically ill are also received in the town. While patients from a number of Arab villages in the Triangle are required to seek care in Petah Tiqwa, the neighboring Jewish community Rosh Ha-ayin has its own laboratory and diagnostic instruments, specialist clinics, and pharmacy. There is three times as much HSF service in Rosh Ha-ayin as in the neighboring Arab community of similar size Kafar Qasem, where the clinic, considered a good one, is nevertheless insufficient for the number of patients, and pressure reduces its quality.

In the Arab villages of the Yizra'el Valley, a pediatrician, gynecologist and obstetrician visit 1-3 times per month (Kawar 1987). In Rame (3,200 insured in 1984) the HSF clinic is in a rented place; medications are inadequate so that patients must go for provisions to the Jewish town Karmiel (to a pharmacy which serves a number of settlements, and has only one pharmacist). There is no laboratory in the village, and twice a week the nurse takes samples for analysis to the town of Akko. For X-rays patients must go to Haifa or Karmiel. In general, laboratories are lacking in the villages and medications are often not in stock. Because the nearest adequate HSF pharmacy is sometimes highly inaccessible, medications must often be purchased privately. Medical instruments are scarce or lacking. There is most often no nurse or physician in daily attendance. HSF clinics are closed at night; night service, jointly provided by the IMH, local municipalities, HSF and the MDA, is not provided in smaller settlements.

Lack of access to care means that allotment of working hours for travel and appointments is required—sometimes difficult for salaried workers, more so for the independently employed, and certainly no less a hardship for those of the chronically ill who are unemployed. The inevitable reaction of patients is to delay seeking of medical care and treatment.

The 'team unit' consisting of physician and nurse was first introduced in urban clinics in the 1960s; in 1984 over 70% of members were treated in HSF primary clinics in this way, which adds continuity to the treatment of individuals and families (HSF *XI Conference* 1984). There were 604 such units in Jewish rural communities; in Haifa and the Western Galilee there were 98 teams in 27 clinics and in the Negev 102 teams in 29 clinics. In Arab localities there were team units in a total of two clinics—one of them in the Golan Heights.

In the last 20 years the HSF has especially expanded its specialist clinic activities, but not in Arab localities. An 'independent physician' system introduced in the 1970s, which allows HSF physicians to schedule appointments outside of clinic hours and frees patients of the demands on clinic time and procedures, grew from 200 physicians to 560, and 250,000 in 1984 so treated—but not in Arab communities. Telephone appointments in some urban clinics were introduced (requiring a phone, often absent in any case in clinics in Arab locations).

None of the district specialist clinics are in Arab communities; there are eight clinics in Jewish localities in this category. According to a recent HSF listing of services (HSF *Institutions and Services* 1986) the only Arab urban specialist clinic is in Nazareth, serving also Arab villages around it. This means that only Nazareth has the local service of two or more specialists. There are no other local clinics in any Arab settlement which have more than one specialist on resident (not visiting) schedule—always a gynecologist. Eight Arab settlements have the service of one specialist, compared with 18 clinics in Jewish localities (for the purpose of this count, pediatricians are not counted as specialists).

Conditions in Nazareth are a particular focus of complaints. Comparison in 1985 of HSF services in Nazareth and the neighboring Jewish community Upper Nazareth showed Nazareth to receive less than one third of the quantity in most categories of service provided in Upper Nazareth, less than one fourth the rate of general practitioners per person, and no provision of rehabilitative, hypertension clinic, and mental health services given in the Jewish community (Geraissy and Kana'aneh 1987). In spite of the high number of insured, the HSF has not opened a planned central specialist clinic. Each of two existing clinics serves 22,000 members, three times the maximum rate for clinics in the Jewish sector. In addition there are disputes between the HSF, IMH, and the Christian mission hospitals which have long provided service with only partial state and HSF legitimation and support.

Comparison of large Jewish and Arab settlements in the north shows that the HSF and the state provide Arab communities with a much lower ratio of manpower to insured population and to total population (IMH 1979; each of these communities is also served by other sick fund[s]; see Table 4.3).

These ratios have worsened since 1977 as population increases, much greater in the Arab sector, have not been matched by increases in manpower. Within those services which are provided, too few physicians and nurses for a rapidly increasing population cause pressure on clinics; HSF personnel in Arab villages is more inadequate to the quantity of needs, and treatment is under more extreme pressure.

Another comparison of eight Arab villages with equivalent Jewish settlements of similar size showed that facilities in the Arab villages had half as many rooms, half as many nurses, two thirds the number of physicians, and one third the number of visits per person insured (Geraissy and Kana'aneh 1987). Jewish infants and children at ages 0-5 visited primary HSF clinics three times as often, per year, as Arabs (12-13 visits per year, compared with 4). Since Arab infants and children are generally not healthier than Jewish ones (see Chapter 6) this difference appears to reflect the lower availability of care.

Table 4.3: Rates of Manpower per Patient, 1977

a. In Large Settlements in the North

| | Population | Insured | Curative HSF | | Preventive | |
			Nurse	Physician	IMH Nurse	HSF Nurse
(J) Karmiel,	8,450	7,449	5	3		3
(J) Migdal ha-Emeq	12,400	11,255	6	7		8
(J) Shlomi	2,100	1,954	2	1		1
(J) Qiriat Shemona	15,600	13,364	13	13	12	
(A) Sakhnin	10,600	10,000	4	3	3	
(A) Arrabe	7,950	5,137	2	1	3	
(A) Shefar'am	14,210	12,924	5	4	3	
(A) Mughar	8,150	4,636	3	3	5	
(A) Tamra	11,100	8,884	3	3	4	
(J) Upper Nazareth	19,300	16,758	10	11	6	
(A) Nazareth	38,600	38,267	13	15	16	
(J) Ma'alot	3,550	3,335	4	2		2
(A) Tarshiha	2,200	2,108	2	1		1

b. Average Rates of Manpower per Insured in HSF Curative Clinics

	Nurse	Physician
Insured Jews	1/1369	1/1446
Insured Arabs	1/2665	1/2718

(IMH 1979)

(J) = Jewish, (A) = Arab

The utilization rates of ambulatory care in Israel have elsewhere been found to be much higher among Jews as among Arabs: three times as high among Jews at ages 0-14, five times at ages 15-24, and twice as high at ages over 25 (Ellencweig 1982). The main factor accounting for a high rate among Jews is said to be the availability of physicians, leading to the creation of demand for repeated visits by the physician and to a high level of referrals. On that basis the lower rate among Arabs would be due to the lesser availability of physicians (but see Chapter 5.C. below).

Perhaps reflecting pressures on the public health system resulting from budget cuts, from 1977-1981 yearly rates of visits by Jews to specialists (other than pediatricians and dentists) fell from 70 per 100 to 54 per 100; the lower rate of visits by Arabs increased slightly, from 18 to 20 per 100. The rate for medical treatments and diagnostic tests (X-rays, laboratory tests, physiotherapy, electrotherapy, dialysis, and radiation) for Jews was 71.6/1,000 and for Arab 14.5/1, 000 (CBS 1983 #708:xi). The fact that wide differences in test rates between Jews and Arabs were found at all age groups means that the differences do not express particular disease patterns, but rather a lower availability to Arabs of these medical services (CBS 1981:6).

There are now a large number of Arab physicians in private practice in the Galilee and the Triangle, to whom local residents can go to supplement HSF insurance (see Chapter 5.C). But availability of independent manpower is not in itself a solution, not simply because independent practitioners do not always own the essential technology for treating emergency cases, but more importantly because of rigidity in the HSF clinical system and in its structure of referrals, which makes patients' approach to independent practitioners problematic in more routine cases since they cannot refer patients for diagnostics, consultation and hospitalization within the insurance coverage. A patient who arrives without referral at a hospital for ambulatory care is charged for this service, although he or she may be eventually refunded. Referrals for further ambulatory care are more problematic.

Public hospitals all over the country are so overloaded by a crisis in over-use of hospital emergency rooms in the absence of alternatives (after regular clinic hours) and as a matter of patients' preference and convenience, that affiliating more local physicians to sick funds can be a partial solution (facilitating diagnostics, referral to consultants, and filling of prescriptions, and allaying anxieties which often drive patients directly to emergency rooms) but is no substitute for adequately equipped accessible secondary facilities.

Any of the sick funds which will be willing to widely employ local manpower would have an advantage in Arab communities. At the moment, several attempts by the other sick funds to work through contracted local physicians are not widely meaningful—both because they are few and because secondary support for them is poorly available.

Overall, although the rate of medical insurance among the Arab population is somewhat less than among the Jews, an overwhelming majority of the Arab population are members of sick funds—especially the HSF. The uninsured are concentrated in East Jerusalem and among the Bedouins. Altogether the percentage of both Arab and Jewish members in other sick funds is only a fraction of the membership in the HSF, and their clinical facilities are available in only a small number of Arab communities, but the circumstances of Arab membership in this context are of interest; these organizations are important as representatives of political traditions, and as medical care alternatives symptomatic of dissatisfaction with the HSF.

In 1950, after the state required the sick funds to provide wider service in order to be eligible for funding under social security, each of the smaller agencies marked out a particular niche within the Arab population, appropriate to its membership affinities and/or to its political goals, for development of services which often overlapped and competed with those provided by the HSF. Thus the penetration into Arab communities, beginning in the 1950s, of the other political parties which had an associated sick fund—the center's General Zionists and the right's Herut—was also accompanied by health care expansion. The General Zionists (later the Liberal Party) conducted election activities among the more affluent landowners and independent farmers in the large villages of the Triangle (Landau 1969). These activities were accompanied by opening of Amamit Sick Fund branches in Taiybe, Umm al-Fahm, Kafar Qara' and Ar'ara (IMH 1968:140). Amamit was the rural sick fund based on the HMO's rural clinics in the moshavot, historically identified with the General Zionists, and had an established presence in the Jewish moshavot west of the Triangle. The Amamit and the General Zionists' Mercazit Sick Fund which operated in the cities merged in 1974 to form the Meuhedet Sick Fund; in Arab communities it still offers services (in clinics in rented quarters) primarily in the Triangle and in Nazareth. In the five Arab communities which it served, it insured a total of 6,350. It also has branches in 'mixed cities' where some Arabs are members (Meuhedet Sick Fund reports to the IMH, 1987). All in all, the Meuhedet is a small fund, not offering a wide alternative to the HSF. According to the CBS study of sick funds membership based on 1976 statistics

(CBS 1981), Meuhedet had a high proportion of members among the Druze: if this is (or was) so, it can only be accounted for if a high Druze membership belong(ed) to branches in Nazareth, Haifa, Tiberias, Nahariyya and Hadera, in the period before the intensification of the Le'umit sick fund's activities among them (below).

Meanwhile, Herut opened Le'umit clinics in a number of Druze villages. The affinity between Herut and the Druze was based on the Druzes' special military and religious status relative to the Arab majority which enabled a mutual acceptability, as well as on the possibility of using the offered political alternative to the Labor Party in order to pressure for benefits from both parties (Landau 1969, Linenberg 1971, Ben-Dor 1979, Oppenheimer 1979). This alliance, intensified especially toward and after the elections of 1977, has resulted in the availability of both Le'umit and HSF clinics in many Druze villages and concentrations. About half of Le'umit's clinics in Arab communities are in Druze (or partly Druze) villages (and two-thirds of the total of Druze localities have such clinics). In the absence of sociological characterization, it is unknown whether memberships in the other half of the Arab communities where Le'umit has clinics and services mainly reflect political affiliations with the Likud and protest against the Labor Party, or a class-associated trend —or both.

Here again, while it appears that the portion of Arab heads of households to the total in this sick fund is about the same as (or not much less than) in the HSF (assuming an additional number in the cities), Le'umit's status among the Arab population compared to the HSF is minor (5%-10% according to the number of family heads and the number of family members per household head, difficult to estimate because of dependence on unavailable statistics about the stage in the life cycle in which new members have been joining the fund; in 1981 Le'umit's share of Arab insurees was only 4%). While it is rooted in the opportunities it provides for affiliated physicians to provide care in their own villages, it is interesting also as an alternative which has an ideological and political aspect. From the total number of insured cited by both sick fund and the IMH, there is indication that Le'umit's share of insurees in Israel as a whole is decreasing, in spite of the Likud's support of a construction drive since 1977. In Arab villages the number of clinics has nearly doubled in the last ten years, and Le'umit is still the second leading sick fund there. In Nazareth a branch started by a local physician now serves 13% of the population.

Table 4.4: **Reported Membership in Arab Communities:
Le'umit Sick Fund 1987***

Place	Population (Muslim, Christian, Druze; [B]=Bedouin)	Insured (Family heads)
North:		
Nazareth	MC	1,568
Mghar	DCM	584
Arrabe	M	583
Yarka	D	443
Bet Jann	D	424
Isifya	DMC	401
Daliat el Karmel	D	380
Dir Hanna	MC	359
Kisra	D	299
Julis	D	265
Peki'in	DCM	265
Abu Sinan	DMC	255
Kafar Sami'	D	248
Rame	MDC	183
Ilbun	CM	173
Fasuta	C	154
Ma'ilia	CM	150
Sejur	D	130
Majd al Kurum	M	109
Bir el Maxur	M[B]	199
Center:		
Wadi Salame	M[B]	97
Ein as-Sahala	M[B]	94
Baqa al-Gharbiyye	M	380
Jatt	M	175
Yama	M	130
Total		8,048

*Excluding in 'mixed cities'. Total number of family heads insured in Le'umit—105,211 including beyond the Green Line; total insured —about 250,000 (Le'umit report to the IMH for 1987).

Competition and the response to it have to a great degree been determined by the evolving class structure. The Jewish middle class which benefited from the achievements of public medicine in the 1950s and 1960s was enlarged further in the 1970s through the growth of the private economic sector in Israel following the 1967 War. Members in a segment whose adherence to the Histadrut was in the first place based primarily on HSF services, expressed their alienation and independence, along with their increasing consumers' awareness and power, by choosing to subscribe to one of the 'middle class' sick funds. They included members of the veteran middle class, some originating from the working class whose upward mobility led to independent occupations, lifestyles and aspirations, and some of the professionals who increasingly dissociated themselves from the Histadrut's mainstream within the occupational unions.   In this context enlargement of the Maccabi Sick Fund is notable; while the other small sick funds did not increase proportionately, Maccabi—the closest among them (along with Assaf, which it is in the process of assimilating) to a contractual insurance plan between physicians and patients—has been expanding.

The expansion of the Maccabi Sick Fund, which is not institutionally linked to a political party like the others, nevertheless also has a political aspect in that it has occurred among Arabs as elsewhere among a portion of the urban hired middle class some of whom were formerly in the HSF; for this population, joining Maccabi is a mark of their dissociation from the Histadrut, as well as of their preference for 'private medicine' style within a publicly recognized and government-supported agency. In the Arab population characteristics of Maccabi's membership—urban, well-off, and highly educated—predict a high membership rate among Christians especially. As of the 1970s there has been among the Muslims as well a significant increase in the middle class through professionalization and private enterprise, as Israeli Arabs were replaced in unskilled labor by Arabs from the occupied territories after the 1967 War. There is some indication that where sick-fund competition has been made available to this class Arabs join it as well as Jews (Maccabi serves Arabs in Nazareth, Akko, and Shefar'am, as well as in other mixed cities; it has an associated Arab physician accepting patients—without other local diagnostic or consultative facilities—in Rame).

In 1968 the Le'umit Sick Fund had branches in 9-10 Arab villages (especially Druze), serving 60,000 insured; since then it has more than doubled its clinics in Arab locations, and almost doubled the number of its Arab insurees. The Amamit Sick Fund had branches and 24,005 insured in Umm al-Fahm, Kafar Qara', Ar'ara, and Taiybe; since then

it has added a branch in Nazareth (Grushka 1968, IMH 1968). Maccabi
had clinics in Nazareth and Shefar'am (and in Akko). In Shefar'am in
1986 Maccabi had a memberships of 500, covering 2,000 insured. Even
assuming that a significant number of the 500 are unmarried, over-18
sons and daughters of Maccabi members so that significantly less than
500 households are represented, 10%-14% of Shefar'am's total of
3,500 households are insured by Maccabi. In Nazareth 6,000 insured
(13% of the population) are in Maccabi. Maccabi has added only the
associated physician in Rame to its small lists of Arab locations, but
it may be assumed that its Arab membership in the 'mixed towns' has
grown in absolute number.

Table 4.5:   Sick Fund Clinics in Arab Localities, 1967-1984*

	Total	IMH	HSF	Le'Umit	Amamit, after 1974 Meuhedet	Maccabi
1967	70	16	41	9	4	—
1984	131**	—	103**	23	5	3

*Some of Le'umit's, Meuhedet's and Maccabi's local presences are
private clinics of associated physicians
** Including in the 'mixed cities', East Jerusalem (4 clinics), and in
Druze localities in the Golan Heights; in some urban locations
including more than 1 clinic).

(IMH 1968,*ISCAR* 1968, HSF 1986)

The approximate number of HSF clinics in Arab localities not
including the 'mixed cities' is 90 (HSF 1985 lists 94 clinics in Arab rural
and urban localities in 1984). HSF thus provides local service in
60-80% of Arab communities, depending on whether
unofficially-recognized Bedouin settlements are or are not included.
The number of Arab localities served by the other sick funds (except
in the 'mixed cities') is:

Leu'mit	23 (including Nazareth)
Amamit	5 (including Nazareth)
Maccabi	3 (Shefar'am, Nazareth, Rame)
	‾‾
Total	29

A total of one-quarter of the officially recognized Arab localities, and none of the unrecognized Bedouin ones in the north and south, are served by the other sick funds (this proportion was also the highest extent of IMH curative service to Arab localities, when it existed). HSF serves 80% of the recognized Arab localities.

In 1977, 7% of the insured in the HSF were Arabs, 7% of the insured in Meuhedet, 2% of Maccabi, and 1% of Le'umit (CBS 1980). Since then there has been an impressive growth in the relative weight of Arab insurees in the HSF and the Leu'mit funds, and evidently of Maccabi as well. In 1984 10.6% of Histadrut members and up to 14% of HSF insurees were Arab. In 1987 8-10% of Le'umit's insurees were Arab. While some of this increase may be attributable to some reduction in the share of the Jewish population insured in these funds, joining of new Arab members and the increase in the Arab population are the primary factors. With regard to Maccabi, the doubling of its share in the population of Arabs insured from 1976 (2%) to 1981 (4%) also indicates an increased weight to Arabs in this fund (however much it has increased among Jews, it is unlikely that its share has been doubled to 20%). (No statistics are available with regard to the Meuhedet fund.) As the relative weight of Arabs in the voluntary sick funds increases further with population growth, inevitably pressures—political and economic—will be brought to bear for extension and improvement of services, especially in the HSF. In this respect as in others demography with democracy act in the Arabs' favor.

All in all the competition between the voluntary sick funds, and between the IMH and the HSF, has resulted in a widespread service which covers the great majority of communities and neighborhoods, including Arab ones. Most of the population, including the Arabs, is medically insured through the sick funds (another small number among the rich are covered through private insurance plans; soldiers in the Army are insured by the Ministry of Defense, with ambulatory care provided by the Army's medical service).

In 1984, an estimated 77-80% of the Arabs living in Israel within the Green Line were insured in the sick funds (already in 1977 and 1981 the percentage of Arabs insured was higher than that cited in the CBS survey, if the East Jerusalem population—where membership rate of Arabs in the HSF was only 40% in 1984—is not included). Another small number of Druze and Bedouin were insured through the Army. Approximately one-fifth of the Arabs in Israel are currently not covered by health insurance. This estimate is based on the calculation that 70% of all Arabs in Israel were in the HSF in 1984, that another 7%-10% were members of the other sick funds, and that changes in absolute numbers of memberships between 1984 and 1987 do not affect these sums fundamentally.

The high insurance coverage in Israel does not simply reflect voluntary investments according to individual planning; it is in large part the result of union-negotiated contracts covering a majority of full-time salaried workers and their dependents, as well as of government coverage of the pregnant, elderly, and the disabled at the HSF through the National Institute for Insurance and the Ministry of Welfare (these last have lately been transferred to the IMH). The uninsured, therefore, are those who do not fall within any of these categories —neither employed as full-time workers in places of work where they are required to be insured, nor receiving welfare or social security. They must be so financially pressed that the burden of elective payment is greater than the risk due to of lack of coverage. They are likely to be employed in places of work where workers are not unionized, or to be underemployed as part-time and unofficial workers, or to be marginally successful self-employed entrepreneurs.

Of the uninsured in 1976 48% were Jews, 39% Muslims, 10% Christian 3% Druze; the rate for Muslims is 3 times what would be projected relative to their number in the population, so that the number of uninsured in East Jerusalem does not account for this high rate. Young adults no longer covered through their parents nor through either army service or student status are more likely to be uninsured, though at the same time more likely to be fairly healthy (Hett 1981). Arab youths, who tend to start working earlier than Jews, and to be employed in temporary and underpaid jobs (such as in construction, garages, and restaurants) which are also more at risk for accidents, are especially vulnerable. The extremely low rates of visits to physicians by young Arabs may be related to lack of insurance.

In addition to those uninsured through neglect—especially among the young and unmarried—and to those who deliberately gamble on lapses and reinstatement, some make the choice not to enter the system or to withdraw from it. In case of extreme serious illness, they may become eligible for welfare or disability payments, and thus be eventually insured through the National Institute for Insurance. Medical needs including hospitalization will then be covered, but meanwhile (if and until this happens) the ongoing 'normal' medical expenses of adults and children must be paid. The risk is that essential treatments will be unsought or postponed, but in such cases the networks of familial support operative in Arab communities may also be called on for help (Weihl 1986). If a child's illness is seriously and chronically prolonged, he or she will also eventually be covered by disability insurance; essentially the existing welfare system is in the background both for those who choose not to be insured, and for those for whom paying fees is impossible.   Among those who actually choose, a decision to consult private practitioners at need instead of paying monthly insurance is more rational the more the available private medical care is of a higher quality and convenience than that provided by the public system. Among Arabs more than Jews this is now the case. The relatively low availability of public service in Arab communities is one side of this equation. The overabundance in many Arab communities of local practitioners who are readily and constantly available, are recently trained and eager to work, and can be expected to show toward their patients particular communal or familial concern as well as linguistic and cultural understanding, may facilitate such decisions. The impression of some Arab health workers that a large number of members are dropping out of the HSF duplicates the impression (reported in Israeli newspapers) that many are choosing other sick funds; the possible difference is that Arab drop-outs from the HSF may be more likely to give up health insurance altogether, where this is an option.

Table 4.6:   **Percentage of Health Expenditures Spent on Insurance, Dental Care and Other Medical Expenses, 1980**

	Health Insurance	Dental Care	Other
Total Population	42	29	29
Arabs	44	11	45
Jews from Africa and Asia	43	31	26
Jews from Europe and America	41	31	28

(CBS #691, 1979-80)

In 1979-1980 the medical expenditures of Arab families were only 63% as much as Jews from Europe or America and 73% as much as Jews from Asia or Africa. Arabs spent relatively less than Jews on dentistry, and relatively more than Jews on private care and medications (CBS 1981 #691).

Dental care is a particularly problematic area. There is no dental school-service for Arab children, and sick-fund insurance does not cover dental work (Fakhouri 1980). The level of care of Jews is also inadequate. According to the Israel Ministry of Health, 90% of the population of Israel has dental problems, but only 24% receive treatment (IMH Department of Dental Health, 1985). However, between 1977 and 1981 the rate of Arabs' visits to dentists was doubled (CBS 1983 #717:xi). This may reflect the conjunction of a rising number of available dentists (including across the Green Line) and increasing awareness of dental needs. The relatively high rate of among Arabs of spending for private medical care and medications evidently reflects spending by the higher percentage of uninsured Arabs, as well as by the insured. It is likely that the lower total average spending on medical expenditures by Arabs also reflects a lower average rate of HSF monthly insurance (a member's tax based on income) along with the lower spending on dental care. Given this lower average, it is also likely that the participation of insured persons in the high rate of spending for 'other' or private medical expenses reflects payments for emergency care not otherwise accessible.

Something very close to a national health insurance plan is thus in effect among the Jewish public—through a combination of voluntary and compulsory factors including individual, collective, and state responsibilities. While the vast majority of Arabs are also insured—voluntarily, through collective agreements, and through the social security laws—the uninsured in Israel are mostly Arabs. There has been no regional or sociological survey of this population (except that Muslims, especially in East Jerusalem, were highly uninsured in 1976, and that the Bedouins are most highly uninsured: Abu Rabi'a 1987). It is likely that their number is greater where local services are scarce or unavailable (or vice versa, that local services are scarcely provided where membership is low). In any case they must be presumed to be underemployed—working in menial part-time temporary and seasonal jobs, or working full-time in small Jewish and Arab businesses where there are no collective agreements and where they are poorly paid, or being among the marginally successful segment of the independently employed. The number of menial laborers and marginally subsisting small self-employed entrepreneurs is proportionately higher among Arabs. Average family income of urban Arab wage workers' families is two-thirds of the average income of Jewish families, and three-fourths of the average income of Jewish families originating in Asia/Africa, so that a budget for voluntary monthly health insurances is on the average less available (*SAI* 1985:283).   With regard to the full-time underemployed proletariat, given the fact that in Israel welfare eventually covers medical costs of those who qualify for it, it may be that some of the more poorly paid Jewish wage-workers would make similar economic decisions to risk exempting themselves from health insurance (on the calculation that in the case of major illness they will be covered by welfare), if they were not covered by collective agreements.   To the extent that compulsory health insurance has value exceeding the freedom to choose, Arabs have lost most because of its absence.

Chapter 5

CONDITIONS AND TRENDS IN THE ARAB POPULATION

5.A. The Inferior Status of Arab Communities

Most crucial in relation to the developing system of health services is the fact that in Israel residential segregation of Jews and Arabs in different communities has continued to be the norm. Thus, given the general national health policy of opening local preventive stations and primary curative clinics in most places of settlement, local services for Arabs were and are for the most part separate from those for Jews. More generally residential separation, along with the fact that Arab settlements are for the most part located within regional concentrations which have remained peripheral, has made possible a 'separate and unequal' development of Arab communities by the state at a rate slower than that of Jewish communities. Inequalities reflect a differential status of Jewish and Arab communities with regard to community planning and funding.

The expulsion and flight in 1947-1950 of the majority of the Arab population enabled the allocation by the state of areas of Arab village lands to Jewish agricultural communities. Jews were now concentrated in what were previously predominantly Arab towns and dispersed to abandoned or exiled villages, and in some areas established settlements in close proximity to Arab ones, including new urban centers next to Arab concentrations (Rosenfeld 1978). As the settling of immigrants in Arab cities in the 1950s resulted in the reduction of Arab-dominated urban localities, intensive planned Jewish settlement in the Galilee and Negev have achieved, more or less, demographic equality between Jews and Arabs in these regions as a whole. As an outcome of these settlement policies residential segregation does not as a rule imply geographic distance or low visibility. The Arab disadvantage in quantity and quality of health services compared to proximate Jewish communities is thus a constant and troubling center of local attention, even more than the relative deprivation compared to large towns where Arabs work or study, or to the national average which is evident to those who are most widely aware.

Most published government statistics on differentials between national groups are under the headings of 'Jews' and 'non-Jews.' While the latter category includes some European and other non-Arab Christians, as well as some Muslim but non-Arab minorities (e.g. Circassians) and a scattering of others (e.g. Buddhists, Bahai), it is overwhelmingly Arab. Presently, there are within the pre-1967 borders 870 'Jewish' settlements (i.e. with a Jewish majority or totality), and 126 'non-Jewish' ones, of which 122 are Arab, and the rest communities of Circassians (Muslim but not Arab) and European-based Christians (sources for this and the following discussion: CBS *Technical Publication #53*, 1986:1-13, 31-34, CBS *SAI #37*, 1986:30-55). Eight cities are significantly 'mixed'—having a Jewish majority but a substantial Arab population: Akko, Haifa, Ma'alot-Tarshiha (a municipal alliance between a Jewish town and the Arab village next to which it was built), Upper Nazareth (into which 3,000 Arabs have moved from overcrowded conditions in Nazareth), Tel Aviv-Yafo, Ramle, Lud, and Jerusalem. These are counted as both Jewish and Arab settlements. While there are thousands of Arab residents in each of these towns, their total Arab population (excluding East Jerusalem) is less than 10% of the Arab population in Israel. There is also one 'mixed' new rural community (Neve Shalom) highly atypical of the rest. Most other settlements are generally segregated.

The number of recognized Arab settlements (counting Tarshiha) is 114, and they include several communities of officially sedentarized Bedouins. About two-thirds of these are in the Galilee (half of them in the Western Galilee, and a majority of the rest in the Yizra'el Valley, with most of these concentrated near Nazareth; other villages are further north in the Galilee). Of about one-third not in this region, half are in the Haifa-Hadera area, about 12 in the Center (mostly in the Triangle), seven near Jerusalem, and four in the Negev.

Of the 'non-Jewish' settlements 71 are officially classified as 'urban,' formally defined as settlements with a population over 2,000. Under these criteria the overwhelming majority of Arabs in Israel are 'urban' although a great majority of the total number of Arab settlements are in fact expanded and overcrowded villages, economically underdeveloped and dependent on an urban center. Subtracting the eight 'mixed towns,' there are 63 Arab officially 'urban' settlements. Two of them (Nazareth and Umm al-Fahm) have a population between 20,000 and 50,000; eight are between 10,000 and 20,000 (Shefar'am, Sakhnin, Mughar, Tamra, Arrabe, Baqa al-Gharbiyye, Taiybe, and Rahat); and 53 (54 including

Ma'alot-Tarshiha) are between 2,000 and 10,000. Fifty-five 'non-Jewish' settlements are formally 'rural' (i.e. with a population of more than 2,000) and since the several 'non-Arab' and one 'mixed' communities mentioned above all fall within this category the number of Arab 'rural' settlements is 50.

Table 5.1: Arab Settlements, Israel 12/1985

Separate Arab Settlements

Population Size	Number of Settlements
less than 2,000	50
2,000-5,000	29
5,000-10,000	25
10,000-20,000	8
20,000-50,000	2
	114

Other Arab Localities

'mixed' cities (not including Ma'alot-Tarshiha)	7
Bedouin 'independent tribes'	36
	157

About 70% of the recognized Arab communities have a population below 5,000, and are rural by informal although not by official definition. Most of the others are expanded villages as well. In addition, 36 Bedouin groups with a total population of 37,000 (so that some of them are quite large) live outside of recognized settlements, are classified as 'independent tribes' and are not counted in the official sums.

Demographic pressures acting within the existing pattern of residence continuously exacerbate strains on the infrastructure and on local health services which were insufficient to begin with. In Israel, village land expropriations—by the state rather than as formerly by Arab landlords—continued to be partial so that communities which were not displaced were also not dispossessed; this, linked together with the employment of most Arab workers in the towns and the lack of public investment in the development of Arab communities, determined a dominant pattern of Arab men continuing to reside with their families within the village while working outside it. Since processes of village fission have been aborted by the state, the fast growth of population within communities which are encapsulated, overcrowded and further handicapped by the lack of public means for physical improvement, has meant that health services and the infrastructure of water supply and sanitation are increasingly inadequate for keeping up with the pace of expanded needs—everywhere but most so in larger settlements.

In the Galilee the Arab population has doubled in the last 20 years. About half of the Arab population in Israel lives in settlements of 10,000 to 20,000, fast-growing and overcrowded. In 1985 there were 35 Arab localities with a population more than 5,000; in all of these places, population has risen at a great pace (the 'mixed cities' except for Upper Nazareth and Ma'alot-Tarshiha also had Arab populations of that size) (see Table 5.2).

A major difference between Jewish and Arab rural settlement in Israel is that Jewish rural communities and development towns which were established from 1933 to 1978 were planned along particular models by the Jewish National Council and then the state, together with the Jewish Agency and the Jewish National Fund and in cooperation with the Zionist settling movements. Before 1933 there were only about 40 Jewish rural settlements (17 moshavot and the rest kibbutzim and moshavim), which the Zionist system of health services soon reached. In most of the more than 1,000 Jewish rural communities established after 1933 the physical masterplan—water, land, production quotas and facilities for services—was and is pre-planned. A crucial part of this planning is for health facilities and services. Immigrant moshavim of the Galilee which were established on sites of former Arab villages in the early 1950s were an exception to this rule, in that their infrastructure was effected only after they were populated. In any case, planning did not mitigate the austere beginnings of kibbutzim and moshavim, nor solve the later problems of Jewish settlements. Development towns, generally located in peripheral areas, have been held back by insufficient public investments in local industry. In the immigrants' moshavim (both pre-planned and not) a high birth rate and large family size along with insufficient land resulted in severe population pressure, in socioeconomic stratification within the communities, and in socioeconomic gaps between these communities on the one hand, and

Table 5.2: Population Increases 1972-1985 In Arab Settlements with Population of 5,000 or More

	1972	1980	1985	*Increment* 1972-1985
Abu-Sinan	3,600	5,300	6,600	3,000
Iksal	3,700	5,400	6,000	2,300
Umm al-Fahm	13,400	19,300	22,000	8,600
Ibillin	3,700	5,300	6,400	2,700
Baqa al-Gharbiyye	7,600	10,500	12,500	5,100
Bet Jann	3,800	5,200	6,000	2,200
Jisr az-Zarka	2,900	4,600	6,000	3,100
Jatt	3,400	4,000	5,100	1,700
Daliat al-Karmel	6,100	8,200	9,100	3,000
Taiybe	12,200	16,300	18,600	6,400
Tamra	8,500	12,300	14,400	5,900
Tur'an	3,900	5,400	6,200	2,300
Yafi'	4,900	7,000	8,500	3,600
Yirka	4,400	6,000	7,100	2,700
Kabul	3,100	4,500	5,200	2,100
Kafar Yasif	3,800	7,300	5,500	1,700
Kafar Manda	3,900	4,500	7,300	3,400
Kafar Qasem	4,900	7,100	8,300	3,400
Kafar Qara'	5,000	6,900	7,900	2,900
Mughar	6,500	9,200	11,300	4,800
Majd al-Kurum	4,400	6,000	6,700	2,300
Makr	2,400	3,600	5,300	2,900
Nahef	3,000	4,300	5,100	2,100
Nazareth	35,300	44,100	47,100	11,800
Sakhnin	8,300	11,800	14,000	5,700
Ein Mahel	3,500	4,900	5,600	2,100
Isifya	4,300	5,800	6,800	2,500
Arrabe	6,100	9,000	10,600	4,500
Ar'ara	4,000	5,600	6,100	2,100
Fureidis	3,400	4,800	5,800	2,400
Qalansawe	5,000	7,300	8,600	3,600
Rame	3,900	4,800	5,300	1,400
Rahat	—	6,000	14,400	—
Reine	4,100	5,600	7,400	3,300
Shefar'am	11,600	15,700	18,300	6,700

(*SAI* 1986:55-54)

the prospering veteran moshavim and the successful kibbutzim on the other. All of these factors had an effect—as the parallel factors did in Arab villages—on the adequacy of health services and on differential access to them. But at least in the Jewish settlements a basis of health facilities and care was established which made health service an integral part of the physical and social requirements of each community (in the Galilee, in part because of the difficult topography, no regional social and health services were proposed). Arab villages on the other hand—their number reduced rather than expanded—were not only unplanned (except for some Bedouin communities sedentarized by arrangement with the state) but are still as of now (in the Galilee especially) unplannable—since the state has denied them approved development plans.

In the Galilee (except in the Yizra'el Valley) most moshavim were established after 1952 (although there were some veteran moshavim); in the rest of the country they were established earlier, since the 1930s. In the Center and in (most of) the Yizra'el Valley moshavim have had large land allocations for small families, and are nearer to cities. In the Galilee most were far from the population centers because the few veteran ones and the kibbutzim took over large areas of land. In the early 1950s a few thousand Jews were so settled; until 1960 Jewish men were paid public assistance for work in the moshav or in public works, and some worked for Arabs and for kibbutzim. In addition to struggling with poverty they contended with institutional paternalism. Problems of transportation also affected them, no less than they did Arab villages. But the state sent agricultural and social instructors to these settlements, and the IMH sent public health nurses (until 1955 for inoculations only). In the first few years patients consulted mostly their own local curers. After 1956 the IMH began to send its physicians and nurses on monthly and weekly visits, and the HSF's ideological commitment to cooperative settlements began to assert itself in this form as well. In general, the Galilee had full institutional support only as of the 1960s. The beginning of Ministry of the Interior presence in the development town Ma'alot in the late 1960s started regular local ministry officials visits—and patronage—in these settlements. The Negev received governmental attention earlier, and its development towns and rural communities were invested with state interest, although living conditions in them were no less harsh, and most of the population poor. In the Center area, institutional interest and support were earliest and most constant.

Kibbutzim had medical service, at least a medic and nurse, from the beginning. Kibbutzim also received Ministry of Housing budgets for sick rooms and for physicians' residential quarters which could supplement the salaries of hired personnel. Even more importantly, the communal arrangement enabled them to send members to study nursing (and in a fewer number medicine), while the familial basis of the moshavim did not provide such backing. Both kibbutzim and moshavim were planned as small communities encompassing, even after expansion, a maximum of several hundred people. In the 1960s most moshavim had only 200-300 people; toward the end of the decade the expansion of population with the birth of the third generation began to have effects, and in the 1970s residents began to demand improvement in services at least to the level provided in neighboring kibbutzim.

Moshavim were not a powerful lobby until 1977; their influence in the 1977 and 1981 national elections was a pay-off of high birth rates. The active political weight of development towns also was felt then. Around the 1977 election especially, bribery was vast: The Ministry of the Interior has the authority to allocate land for public building, and the National Religious Party which held the ministry paid off in construction. In Likud-voting moshavim there are now new clinics, built with Ministry of the Interior and IMH approval and with State Lottery financing. Most Arabs, except for Druze, voted for losing sides; Labor voting localities were not paid off with government assistance, communist voting localities were 'punished' by having funds withheld, and Druze localities gained (Le'umit Sick Fund) clinics and social clubs. In the 1980s birth rates in the moshavim and family size has declined (to 4-5 persons per family), but a young population which has done army service demands the improvement of communal health services as a right. The Labor Party through the Histadrut and the HSF has attempted to maintain a hold on these votes through improvement of health facilities in moshavim and development towns toward the 1981 elections and following.

In Arab localities the decisive handicap caused by lack of access to state and extra-state financing was intensified by the lag, until recently, in municipal organization which could bring more active pressure to be instrumentally applied beyond the local level on the major health service agencies vulnerable to it, the state and the Histadrut. The more general failure in Israel to develop communal involvement and responsibility for health as for education (with the significant exception of the kibbutz movement and the orthodox religious sector, groups of high solidarity and consciousness in these areas) was even more pronounced in the majority of Arab communities, whose municipal organization was weak or lacking.

State budgets—both direct and hidden—are allocated through local government. The power to make organized demands and the ability to initiate independent activities in this regard, are major consequences of local government organization. The government has only slowly approved Arab municipal authorities. Although at present almost four-fifths of the recognized Arab settlements have some municipal status, there are 24 Arab villages without it. There are a number of Jewish settlements which also have no municipal status, but they tend to be recently established ones, or landed (e.g. educational) communal institutions. Thirty-three of the Bedouin 'tribes' are excluded from such status as well. Although lack of municipal status does not necessarily imply absence of local personal health services, in the absence of municipal status IMH officials have been able to rationalize state inactivity on the convenient basis of 'there is no-one to talk to.' In these cases, historically conditioned passivity combines with official deprivation of instituted political channels for making demands, to grossly diminish access to budgets and services and in other ways directly affect health. Conditions in such villages and locations tend to be especially poor, with no-one officially responsible for requesting and administering government resources.

Municipal involvement of Arab localities and sharing in health care was possible from the beginning in the Triangle, as it was not in most of the Galilee, because a number of local councils there were recognized in the early 1950s and because of distinctive over-all attitudes in the Israel Ministry of the Interior toward these two regions, center and periphery. In the Galilee the Ministry of the Interior had no local presence until the 1960s, and thereafter its regional officer there (Mr. Koenig) proved to be exceptionally malevolent toward Arabs (*Al Hamishmar* 1976, *Journal of Palestine Studies* 1976). On the other hand, the ministry's Regional Officer in the central region in the 1960s and 1970s was particularly interested in developing the villages of the Southern Triangle. Without development plans the municipalities in the Galilee could not allocate land for construction, and individuals whose land was generally already insufficient for familial use were reluctant to sell for public building. Consequently in the Southern Triangle local councils have been able to own clinics and share in their maintenance with the IMH, while in the Galilee the IMH has often rented rooms and maintained them.

Since Arab communities did not have plans which included housing for health care facilities, they have had to buy land for construction or alternatively find rooms to rent. This ordinarily requires persuading village residents to sell scarce private land for the public benefit, and for the most part is not possible where there is a weak local authority or none at all. For the IMH, dependent on local authorities for the site of clinics and stations and insistent on partial municipal participation in some of its operations, there was often no authority to deal with. While the HSF did not attempt to involve local authorities in maintenance and services, it also required land allocations and ministerial subsidies and loans for construction, and for these aspects was also dependent on the existence and functioning of local government.

Three Arab communities (Nazareth, Umm al-Fahm, and Shefar'am) are full municipalities. Nearly a half of the Arab communities (compared with less than one-tenth of the Jewish ones) have local community councils. Thirty-five smaller Arab villages and three of the 'independent' Bedouin groups—compared to 760 Jewish communities in the country— are governed within regional councils, this being the preferred mode of local political organization of Jewish settlements. The fact that the great majority of Jewish communities in Israel are so organized is a function of planned implementation by the state, the settlement movements, and the Jewish Agency, of settlement-types which have led to a proliferation of organizationally-linked, small communities. For example, there are currently within the 114 recognized Arab settlements 14 which are under 500 in size (one-eighth of the total of Arab settlements), but communities of that size make up about two-thirds of the Jewish settlements; 90% of Jewish settlements have a population under 2,000, whereas 45% of the counted Arab ones and less than 60% of a fuller list including Bedouins are of that size.

In spite of their small size, the overwhelming majority of Jewish settlements have been provided, as part of their planning and implementation by the state and the Jewish Agency, with public local primary health care facilities. And, members of regional councils are jointly responsible for activities such as garbage collection for which they receive Ministry of the Interior budgets—beyond those allocated per capita —for equipment and maintenance. Dental service for school-children, budgeted by the IMH, is offered through the joint schools operated by regional councils, and publicly financed MDA stations and ambulance service are also jointly maintained.

After 1977 the Likud has allowed some free enterprise settling, on an individual basis and by corporations and private groups not linked to movements. As of 1978 too, for the first time in the Zionist enterprise in the Galilee, new settlement types have been planned to be dependent on outside facilities, including health services. Their impetus was to continue—in conformance with reduced Jewish Agency budgets and the scarcity of interested Jewish settlers—Jewish settlement in 'strategic' points of this underdeveloped area of high

Arab concentration.   From 1978 to 1980, 54 'Lookout Points' were established, each planned for 15 families but some peopled by less—80% of them north of Haifa and a few in Wadi Ara—at the total cost of one ordinary settlement, with a temporary water-line, no schools and no clinics, a gravel access road and a small public building.   Some were planned to eventually become a moshav or kibbutz which would then have a clinic.   Another new type of community, non-agricultural in conception, is a 'communal settlement' consisting of large, medium and small subtypes the last of which (up to 50 family units, but again actually peopled by less) is dependent on outside services, while the others have been provided with local health facilities.   All of these settlements then are quite small, but for some of them in the Western Galilee the HSF has constructed a regional center.

Although a regional model for health care integrating preventive and curative service might be an alternative to local service for some small Arab villages which still have no facilities, and might beneficially be superimposed on a region where partial and divided health services exist (such as in the villages of the Western Galilee), except for one IMH preventive center for Bedouin no regional centers have been established for Arab communities.

The unplanned status of Arab communities affects environmental health conditions beyond clinical facilities, health stations, and manpower for the personal health services.   Thus according to the Mandatory laws adopted by the state, responsibility for sanitation and for garbage collection continues to be municipal responsibility, with the IMH in charge only of inspection through the regional bureaus. However, the different relation of the state and the Zionist funding agencies to Jewish and Arab communities determines a critical difference in the levels of development of the infrastructure of environmental sanitation.   Water mains and sewage plants are under various ministries' control (Housing, Agriculture, Interior), but in most Jewish communities their basis was in large part funded by the Jewish Agency and the Jewish National Fund, with moneys collected abroad for developing the Zionist enterprise.   The poor condition of Arab villages with regard to water-sources and watermains, sewage plants and housing, is a function of their not falling under the financial auspices of these Jewish settling and developing institutions—which are coordinated with the state but not part of it—so that in the Arab sector the state and the local authorities have had to make whatever investments were needed.

While local authorities, after cessation of direct IMH service, did not significantly participate in the personal health services, their responsibility was effectively extended in the area of environmental prevention and the creation and maintenance of the infrastructure for environmental sanitation. These functions were to be shared by the state and the municipalities, and in the case of Jewish settlements by the Zionist agencies. Although sanitation departments and garbage collection remained municipal concerns and problems, the state through the Ministries of the Interior and of Agriculture—and with Jewish Agency funding—took responsibility for the development of sewage and water plants and installations in Jewish localities. As a consequence Arab municipalities carry a heavier responsibility, and Arab communities have consistently lagged in development of the infrastructure for environmental health.

In the 1950s water pipes began to be extended to virtually every Jewish settlement, and within the following decade to most Arab settlements. Water and sewage lines were sometimes laid without comprehensive mapping. In hilly areas sewage flows into creeks and pollutes water supplies; maintenance is not always adequate, and not all the municipalities do the required testing. Examination of available data on water pollution shows, however, that contamination of the water supply is a more serious problem in Arab communities. The IMH samples water quality in supervised settlements throughout Israel; examination of the results of these samples shows that in 1985 27 localities had contaminated water to a degree signifying unreasonable risk, and in one other case (Tiberias, where the Lake of Tiberias constitutes a special problem) water quality was a serious health hazard. Of the 27, 17 (10 Jewish and 7 Arab) were in the north. It is common in the hills of the north to exploit small, difficult to monitor water sources, rather than to pay for more expensive water provided by the national water supplier. Small settlements face a higher per capita cost for water, and as a consequence they have a lower standard of water in the country as a whole. The 27 most badly contaminated settlements include 15 Jewish localities, two-thirds in the north, most of them tiny hill settlements numbering several dozen families. But the Arab localities with water-contamination problems were distributed along the geographic and size spectrum of Arab settlements. In 1985 seven were in the north, three in the Hadera district and one in the Negev. They were not small, distributed rather between middle range settlements of all sizes from over 10,000 to under 1,000. Contamination often results from sewage in quantity polluting the water supply. This is widespread occurrence in Jewish communities of the coastal plain, but a more widespread possibility in Arab settlements. Water drawn or piped from wells less than 30 meters deep is most vulnerable. These wells are found much more frequently in Arab than Jewish villages.

But more problematic and more common than contamination of the water source is infiltration of the water pipes by liquid wastes. In 1950 only three villages had a piped water supply, as Arab villages used local water sources. Water pipes were connected in most Arab villages as part of two development program in the 1960s and early 1970s. The increase in the population of these villages since then has brought about a great rise in water consumption. With no land available for public purposes, there is an overload in the centers of villages especially. While in some Jewish settlements water pipes were also often laid without mapping and without coordination with sewage arrangements, in Arab localities the problem has been complicated by the fact that when the policy of using plain steel pipes was re-evaluated during the 1960s and it was decided to switch to more durable materials such as cement-lined steel, plain steel continued to be used in Arab localities. As a result, corrosion and fissures of water pipes are found distributed across the range of Arab settlements, and the systems in all Arab localities will evidently have to be replaced within a decade (Farah 1987). Planning did not take into account the great population increase: Since heavier water use shortens the life of the steel pipes, it is the larger, faster growing localities that can be expected to suffer more ruptures, rusting, and instances of waste water infiltration. The danger is compounded in Arab localities by lack of central sewage systems or other community-wide arrangement for disposal of liquid wastes (Jewish settlements have either a combination of septic tank and seepage pit, or in the majority of places, piped sewage collection, treatment and disposal). In addition, water is not chlorinated in these water pipes.

Regulations governing the management or (until recently) the amount of water to be used did not place the local authorities under obligation to undertake tax-collection or other action. At the same time, planning and execution of environmental projects, while formally under local jurisdiction, require the agreement and/or direct help of governmental bodies such as the Ministries of the Interior and of Agriculture and the Water Commission; hostile officials have consistently withheld permission for planning.

Local authorities provide more than 90% of the budget and manpower for environmental control. Because of their lower budgets Arab communities are also deprived in development of central sewage systems. These plants are supposed to be financed by residents, with the National Sewage Project participating only in partial financing of purification plants and main collection sites. An additional problem is the lack of public land, and resistance of private owners to selling their land for public purposes (Finkel 1983).

In 1948 there were no central sewage systems except in the three largest cities.   After 1948 municipal sanitation departments were established but in the 1950s and 1960s in rural areas, Jewish as well as Arab, sewage arrangements were primitive. In the coastal Netanya region in the 1950s the United States Operations Mission under the Marshall Plan carried out a sanitation program which encompassed the Southern Triangle, but most Arab villages still have no adequate sewage systems, due to a lack of funding, unavailability of land, and operating problems, and cannot afford essential replacement of water lines. Inadequate arrangements support bacterial, viral and parasitic agents as well as mosquitoes, flies, and rats.

As of now, only one central sewage system is more or less complete in an Arab community, seven are in last stages of construction; and ten more have been started (Farah 1987). In Umm al-Fahm only 10% of the houses are connected to the central sewage system.   Government budget to the local authorities for health for Arabs has been calculated as 2.2% the sum for Jews, whereas Arabs make up 12% of the population governed by local authorities (R. Geraissy 1987). While the problem of concentrating and purchasing fragmented private lands for public purposes is a serious one, as is some local resistance to using liquid waste for agricultural irrigation (Finkel 1983), budgets are the main problem for the lag in development of central sewage systems which are expensive to build. The whole development budget of a village (local council) of 6,000 is not enough to lay 500 meters of sewage construction (Farah 1987). Under present conditions, solid waste (garbage) disposal accounts for most of the health and sanitation budget of each local authority.

Disposal of solid wastes is another problem which requires planning (Ghattas and Nahas 1987). Because garbage collection is the responsibility of local authorities, it is a function of settlement patterns which are especially problematic in the Galilee, where communities of various sizes, types, and municipal status are interposed. Local government in the Galilee is inefficiently conceived for rational provision of services—divided so that moshavim and kibbutzim are organized separately from the towns (Jewish and Arab) and the villages to which they are most proximate. In the Galilee Arab villages are generally not included in the regional councils to which kibbutzim and moshavim belong (with the exception of the Galilee Heights region where three Arab villages are so included).

This means that in Arab villages garbage is usually collected and disposed of by the local authority. While smaller settlements within regional councils may have the benefit of jointly using a truck bought with a special Ministry of the Interior budget, local authorities must use their per capita budget from the IMH to engage a tractor for this purpose. In the existing conditions, a small Arab village using a tractor achieves better sanitary conditions by disposing of garbage itself than a village which has to wait for its (weekly) turn, as do small settlements—Jewish and Arab—within regional councils in the Galilee. But the larger Arab villages, most overburdened by quantities of garbage, are deprived of an equal means by this Ministry of the Interior arrangement.

5.B.   The Class Situation of the Arabs in Israel

After 1948 the number of landless Arab villagers increased, because of the large size of families in relation to limited land further depleted by expropriation. Arab peasants—most without enough land for subsistence—continued to be proletarized, dependent on hired work outside the village, mostly unskilled or semiskilled in construction, simple services and agriculture with no security at work. At the end of the 1960s, although there were some rich and middle class Arabs, the overwhelming majority of Arabs were wage-workers, and about 80% of men aged 15-40 worked or sought work outside the village, mostly in menial temporary labor, rarely with fulltime permanence and thus without fully benefiting from Histadrut rights (Rosenfeld 1978).

After 1967, the entry into the Israeli labor market of manual workers from the occupied territories brought about the rise of a wide established permanent working class and of a new occupational level of contractors and administrators between the local working class and the longer-established land-owning and merchant middle class, as well as of a growing group of independent entrepreneurs, extremely sensitive to changes in the economy (Rosenfeld 1978, Semyonov and Epstein-Levin 1987). Some of them failed with the fluctuations in the economy in the early 1980s, while others succeeded. Increased investments of private wealth in Arab villages have resulted in the fact that in 1985 only one-half of the male working force and a somewhat lower proportion of working women worked outside their own communities, as in the 1970s and 1980s more affluent residents' capital investments in the industrial infrastructure of Arab villages began to be substantial, resulting in some industrialization (still insufficient) of Arab communities (Chimansky et al. 1984).

In spite of significant mobility and a general increase in the standard of living as Arabs have moved from unskilled proletariat toward fairly full employment in skilled and semi-skilled labor and toward the regeneration of a middle class, and although the Arab population participates in state benefits—child allowance, income completion and other social insurance payments—a considerable part of this population is poor. The re-stratification of the Arab population implies that the economic situation of many individuals and families is good, while communal development still lags in spite of advances, and while a significant stratum of menial workers and poor remains (e.g. Bar Yitzhak 1981). This class is small in the villages of the Southern Triangle, large in Umm al-Fahm where unemployment is rife and in some villages of the Northern Triangle; it is distributed in the Galilee in particular villages and as a stratum of most other villages and towns, and encompasses the Bedouin population; and it is general to the Bedouin of the Negev (the situation of unsedentarized Bedouins living outside of recognized settlements—29,000 in the Negev and 8,000 in the Galilee—is particularly poor). In the 'mixed towns' there is a stratum of poor along with the working class and middle class sectors.

Arabs are on the average poorer than Jews. The average income per 'standard person' among Arabs in 1978-1983 was less than one-half that of Jews (see Table 5.3). According to an index where 100.0 represented the income of a Jewish household of four whose head-of-household was born in Europe or the Americas, the average gross income per non-Jewish urban (i.e., resident of a community with a population of over 2,000) employee's household in 1984 was indexed 60.4, while the index for households whose head-of-household was born in Israel was 88.6, and in Asia or Africa 77.5 (SAI 1985:283). The larger average size of Arab households does not account for this difference.

Arabs, who made up 17.6% of the population in 1988, constituted 55% of the poor population, (defined as having an income below the 'poverty line' of 50% of the median income, taking into account National Institute of Insurance benefits, as well as taxes). While less than 10% of the Jewish population was in this category, more than one-half of the Arab population was considered poor according to this definition of relative deprivation. Moreover, poor Arabs are poorer than poor Jews. The 'poverty gap' measuring the difference between the 'poverty line' income and a family's actual income (taking into account social security benefits and taxes) was higher by 25% for poor Arab families then for Jewish ones. Arabs benefited less than Jews from state income maintenance programs (National Institute for Insurance 1988). Among both Jews and Arabs, the monthly average

Table 5.3:   Socioeconomic Characteristics of Population in
Local Authorities, Israel 1978-1983

	Jewish Communities	Arab Communities
Standard Age	26.8	16.7
Children per household	2.3	3.9
High school diploma at ages 15+	48.9%	18.0%
Employed	53.9%	39.1%
Employed in free, technical, or administrative occupations	30.2%	14.6%
Average income*	13.9	6.4

* monthly income (in old Israeli shekels) per standard person in a
household whose head is a wage-worker. 'Standard person' computes
a decreasing cost for each additional person as the number of persons
in a household rises.

(Dor et al. 1988)

income per person of the poorest (at the bottom 20% of local
authorities) was half as much in 1978-1983 as that of the more affluent
(at the top 20%); but the average income per person among
wage-workers in the more affluent Arab communities was about the
same as that of the poorest in Jewish communities, and the average
income of the poorest 20% of Arabs was less than one-half that of the
equivalent sub-stratum of Jews (Dor et al. 1988).

Government policies and publications have continued the British
(Mandatory) practice of classifying by religion in categories of
Christians and Muslims (both mostly Arab, the second more so than
the first), and Druze (Arabs). In spite of resultant evasions, all of these
categories may therefore be considered to be indicators of the status
of the Arab population. Muslims make up more than 75% of the Arab
population, Christians about 15% and Druze about 10%. Christians
are mostly urban, while Muslims and Druze are mostly rural. There
are major differences in income, occupational status attainment and
in education between Jews, Muslims and Christians as well as ethnic
domination of European-American born Jews over Jews born in Asia
and Africa (Smooha 1978, Kraus 1990, Swirski 1981). The Christian

population occupies an intermediate class position between Asian-African Jews and Muslims; for example, Asian-African Jews and Christian Arab males averaged in 1974 three years less of schooling than European-American Jews, and Muslim Arabs averaged five years less than the latter (Kraus 1990). There has been no change in the relative positions of these three groups following the entry into the Israeli job-market of Arabs from the occupied territories after 1973 (Semyonov and Epstein-Levin 1987). Arabs continue to be in effect excluded from employment and mobility in much of the public services, the military (except the Druze) and linked industrial sectors.

The transformations in the class situation of Arabs over the last two decades involve a decrease in family size, as well as increasing standards of living and education (Eisenbach 1989). An increase in total fertility rates among Arabs and until the mid 1960s evidently continued the increase in family size begun in the late 19th century (Gilbar 1989) in a population in which larger families were desirable and advantageous (see pages 34 and 53 above). This increase was followed by an accelerating process of decline since then (Eisenbach 1978, SAI 1985). Increasing permanent employment in the broader economy, improvement in the class situation of Israeli Arabs especially after 1967, and the opening of channels of mobility through education have led to a smaller desired family size. Fertility in urban locations (and among Christians especially) declined earlier and faster than in rural areas.

Total fertility is higher among Muslims and Druze than among Jews, and the Arab population is constituted of larger households. The average number of persons per household among non-Jews in Israel is 5.9 (Muslims 6.1, Christians 4.2, Druze and Others 5.9; average household size among Jews is currently 3.4; SAI 1987). Almost three-quarters of non-Jewish households have four or more children under 17 years old, compared with one-quarter of Jewish households (SAI 1987:85; one-half of non-Jewish households have 5 or more children under 17, compared to about 10% of Jewish households). The Arab population is thus an increasingly young one, more than half under 18 years old. While the absolute number of Arabs over the age of 65 was tripled from 1950 to 1980, their percentage declined from 5.4% to 3.1%, and is lower than among Jews, among whom 9.7% were over 65 in 1980 (Weihl 1986). In 1986 only 7% of Muslim males were over 45, compared with 23% of Jewish males, and only 14% of Muslim females were over 65, compared with 25% of Jewish females (SAI 1987:67).

Of the three areas of Arab residential concentration--the Galilee, the Triangle and the Negev— conditions in the Triangle are relatively best. Municipal organization, the level of education and standard of living are on the average better than elsewhere, as are environmental conditions (except for water quality). There are notable exceptions: In Umm al-Fahm environmental conditions—sanitation, access and housing—are catastrophic, there are a number of smaller villages which are still isolated and closed societies, and a stratum of poor in most communities. In the Jewish settlements of the coastal plain for the most part economic conditions and possibilities are better, and those who are poor—while they have a surfeit of medical problems—benefit, unlike Arabs, from good local medical services. Unlike poor populations in the Negev and the Galilee, both Jewish and Arab settlements in this region are at least close to medical centers and have easier access to the hospital emergency rooms which have become the favored method of seeking emergency care.

In the Galilee the economic situation of Arabs is on the average poorer than in the Triangle, and the underdevelopment of infrastructure and medical services also affects communities whose residents are economically more successful. 'Unrecognized' Bedouin settlements in some cases living in in tin huts and tents, receive minimal service. In the Negev, where most Bedouin reside, conditions are worst.

5.C.   The Re-emergence of Arab Professional Medical Manpower

The re-emergence of Arab medical manpower since the 1960s and its accelerating abundance is part of the re-establishment and growth of an Arab middle class, especially after 1967, through occupational mobility, education and private enterprise. On the basis of compulsory primary education, families' support of children's study as the major means to economic independence and mobility has led to an emphasis on formal education at all levels (still less, however, for women than for men).

Arab medical personnel have been been graduates of all programs of study in nursing and medical schools in Israel. But their admission to academic programs, their absorption in public health institutions including hospitals, and consequently their access to training in medical specializations, are significantly lower than those of Jews.   While the Arab population constituted 17% of the total population, only 6% of the registered nurses (RNs), and 11% of licensed practical nurses (LPNs) in Israel in 1986 were not Jews: In a profession whose workers are preponderantly women (94% of RNs), 67% of Muslim RNs were men, as compared to 25% of Christians and only 4% of Jews (CBS 1986b).   In the context of this low payed profession, the relatively high participation of Arab men marks class differences between Jews and Arabs which favor Jews in employment opportunities for the academically trained. Within this distinction Arab men are favored over Arab women: 94% of Muslim and 100% of Christian LPNs in 1986 were women. In 1988, 11% of the graduates of academic RN programs were Arabs; of them a majority (58%) were men.   Arab women made up the great majority of graduates of LPN programs (Ha-Ahot be-Israel 1988). Arab male nurses are absorbed especially in the more prestigious and better paying urban hospitals, while women tend to work in the community.

By 1971 only 40 Arab physicians had finished medical studies in Israel (IGY 1972).   As overall demand for study in Israeli medical schools has exceeded available places, the last decade has been characterized by the increasing importation of foreign-trained Israel-born MDs, Jewish and Arab. But only 10% of the more than 400 Arab medical students from the Galilee studying medicine in 1985 were being trained in Israel, most of the rest studying in Western and Eastern Europe (Awad and Kana'aneh 1987). A large number are returning to practice—privately or in combination with public position—in their own communities.

Young Arab physicians are relative latecomers to a system whose expansion has ceased, as are the newest Jewish physicians. As a larger percentage of Arab physicians are of current vintage, the proportion of them not employed in public service is larger. They are at an oversupply not only in relation to the public system, but also in particular communities. Out of 71 Arab communities in the Galilee 34 villages had more than five resident physicians, while 31 villages had none.   The preferred professional strategy of being both private employees and private entrepreneurs at the same time is less open to Arabs than to Jews. Proportionately half as many Arab MDs and Arab RNs as Jewish ones work in public clinics. While only 3% of the physicians in Israel were not Jewish, 25% of the dentists were in this category (CBS 1986b). This probably reflects a professional choice by Arabs of a field where practice is generally private and demand is high.

There is a scarcity of Arab mental health professionals, pharmacists, and paramedical specialists. In the field of mental health this has been especially problematic since the field is particularly vulnerable to gaps between patients and professionals' cultural assumptions, and to patients and families' mistrust of physicians not accessible through the Arabic language.   Jewish psychiatrists, psychologists and psychiatric social workers are not necessarily (or at all) trained to be keyed to Arab culture-specific systems of belief and action.   Some traditional healers are active and treat especially chronic illnesses, in coexistence with western specialists, as they do among Jews (e.g. Abu Rabi'a 1979, Greenberg 1982, Bilu 1980).

Since the Mandatory period, Israel as a whole has not suffered from lack of physicians but from their over- concentration in urban areas and scarcity in the periphery. In the early 1960s, the rate of physicians per person in urban areas was 3-4 times the rate in small towns and rural areas. In Jerusalem the rate was 1/243; in Jerusalem, Tel Aviv and Haifa 1/273; and in cities larger than 15,000 317/1. It was much lower in the north (1/931) and south (1/837) where Arabs were concentrated, and in these regions the situation among Arabs was much worse than the average indicates. In the rural Western Galilee (Akko) region, the rate was one physician per 6,280 residents (Smith 1964:37). The Arab town of Akko itself had been used to a high level of service by Arab physicians and the GDH during the Mandate; when they were replaced by Jewish physicians after 1948, suspicion and anger on the side of the Arab population along with anti-Arab sentiments of Jews settled in Akko resulted in poor health care for Arabs.

Well into the 1970s only a few Arab physicians from the Galilee came back to their villages to practice, because they were not employable in local public service.   The great majority of Arab physicians began to practice in the 1980s, and their number is expected to increase. While there are now a large number of Arab physicians in private practice in the Galilee and the Triangle, the extent of local Arabs practitioners' institutional affiliation is such that many of them are unable to provide to their patients the critical access to referral, diagnostics and hospitalization which are the major functions of medical insurance.   More HSF employment of local physicians is a central demand by Arab members of the Histadrut.

Strong urban concentration of physicians and higher level of medical care in the cities have continued to be the rule, but the overall ratio of physicians to population in Israel, with almost 12,000 physicians in practice in 1983, is a high 1/360. Arab physicians are no longer scarce in the Galilee and in the Triangle. If the chronic shortage of resident manpower in these regions was related both to difficult economic conditions and to the lack of public employment, the current abundance is testimony to the rise in the standard of living which is able to support both medical studies (of family members) and private practice (in the community). Although the Communist Party has continuously sent medical students to Eastern Europe, less than half of the students from the Galilee study there. The rest, it must be assumed, are financed mostly by their families.

The rate of Arab physicians per Arab population in the Galilee in 1980 was about 2/10,000. It reached about 10/10,000 in 1985, and was expected to rise, on the assumption that medical students from the Galilee return to the region upon graduation, to nearly 20/10,000 in 1990 (Awad and Kana'aneh 1987). A separatist calculation for the Galilee is, however, inaccurate as a rendering of medical services. Some—albeit a minority—of the Arab manpower is employed by the HSF and the IMH, not necessarily for Arab patients exclusively; Jewish physicians serve in this area both publicly and privately (there is a concentration of private Jewish physicians in Nahariyya); there is some cooperative private practice—Arab and Jewish physicians and dentists share rooms, for example, in Karmiel and Zefat; and there are Arab physicians treating Jewish patients also in Akko and Upper Nazareth.   Nevertheless, this calculation clearly demonstrates the quantity of Arab personnel now available, and stresses the need for their public employment as a priority in this region.

In the Negev, there is no such abundance; on the contrary, shortage of medical manpower is a general problem. In Dimona, a Jewish town of 27,000, there was in 1977 a ratio of one physician in the local HSF clinic per 2,000 residents (almost all town residents were insured in the HSF). In 1986 no physicians lived in the town, so that it remained without local medical care after clinic hours and at night. Transportation to the HSF hospital in Beer Sheva is however available, as it often is not for the Bedouins. In 1985 55% of the Bedouins in the Negev were HSF members; non-members are treated in HSF clinics for pay (Abu Rabi'a 1987). Settled Bedouins in Rahat and Tel Sheva have local (though insufficient) HSF and IMH services: The ratio of physicians to population in Rahat was 1/2,500. Five more service points in the Negev serve the Bedouin population, and more than half of the population was receiving HSF services in the seven locations, in which the average ratio of physicians to population was 1/2,600. The ratio of these HSF physicians to the full Bedouin population in the region which is nominally served (only) by them was 1/4400—a highly deficient ratio considering that there is scarcity of other physicians available for their benefit in this area.

Most Arab physicians, like most current Jewish ones, have not until recently been active in public leadership. General restriction to professional activities is no longer a function of elite class identifications, but rather, as among Jewish physicians, a function first of struggle with livelihood and concentration on personal and familial needs, and more globally of middle class and professional identifications aiming at economic mobility through private enterprise. In this sense young physicians trained with Communist Party support in Eastern Europe have not necessarily been more publicly dedicated than others. Nevertheless, there is, toward the end of the 1980s, an increasing public involvement of Arab physicians in the health care of Arabs.

5.D.   A New Activism

In the 1980s, as in the 1940s, the combination of economic prosperity of a middle class with political awareness has led to the rise of civic participation and activism in the area of health as in others. In all regions and all types of settlement, the great natural increase in population has raised the possibilities of increasingly using political and consumer pressures effectively to gain improvement in access to health care. At the same time, the growth in medical manpower in Arab communities in the 1980s has enabled the emergence of Arab voluntary associations active in providing improved medical services for the Arab population.

There are thus some new mutual aid and other voluntary associations—national, regional, and local—organized along political, religious, communal and professional lines. In part these are the result of the rise in education and in professional manpower, in part of the increase in civic activism and leadership; some actions occur in the context of religious revival; they may also be attributed to contact with Arabs from the West Bank and from East Jerusalem especially, where voluntary organizations have been a mainstay of medical care (there are many such voluntary associations, from the Red Crescent to Muslim women's organizations, and a number of clinics run by charitable organizations).

The possibility that these efforts may grow into a sectorial sub-system is latent, contingent on funding and on the success of achieving equality within the national system. Among the voluntarily half-separatist Jewish orthodox religious sector in Israel charitable institutions and fundraising channels were developed into a semi-separate network of services, a network which operates alongside a highly adept proficiency for using the best of the more widely available public and private services and manpower (within the country and outside it) through their institutional and personal cooperation. As Árab professional medical manpower develops along with national and international institutional connections, efforts in the public's behalf may be increasingly applied both to achieve national equality and to develop special services.

As of now, these new associations do not so much compete with as fill the gaps and correct some inadequacies in the institutionalized voluntary activities (especially HSF) initiated by established political parties, and in IMH services. Most party initiatives have concentrated on sick fund activities, although the Labor Party also supports Histadrut clubs and 'cultural activities' such as sports in addition to HSF branches (Lustick 1980). The Communist Party, most of whose constituency and investment are among Arabs, attempts, as part of its ongoing activities in most Arab villages, to organize in each village a group of volunteers for environmental improvement tasks. Some of these tasks involve investment in local facilities, schools particularly, with over-seas aid. A most important Party activity for many years has been funding of Arab students—including medical students—for study in Eastern Europe.

Christian mission hospitals, remaining in some of the towns, have on the whole played a minor role, except in Nazareth. In the context of insufficient HSF and IMH investment, the Nazareth Hospital, first established in 1861 and supported by church funds, is developing into a major voluntary institution active in serving Arabs in the Galilee. The Galilee Society for Health Research and Service, directed by Dr. H. Kana'aneh, engages in research and activist planning and lobbying aimed mainly at enabling Arab communities to initiate services as part of the national system, and thus to receive their share of national funding. It also conducted the first conference on the issue health of Arabs in Israel in 1986, and published the papers delivered in that conference (Kana'aneh et al.1987).

The Muslim Brothers concentrate on maintaining mosques, cemeteries, and nursery schools, but in Umm al-Fahm they also organized an association for the advancement of health and medical care, have opened an emergency clinic (including a small pharmacy where drugs are sold for small pay) and employ a physician afternoons and nights. The National Fund for the Advancement of Communal Activities and for Early Childhood, with the help of the German Mission in Yafo, funds and trains public health nurses to provide health education to needy families. Local associations for health and environmental improvement are active in Nazareth, Akko, Yafi', Ilbun, Daburiyye, Reine, Mashhad, Taiybe, Ar'ara, Kafar Qara', and Umm al-Fahm. Rahat is one of the few Arab towns with an MDA emergency service and an ambulance; the local council paid for the renovation of a building and pays the nightly salary of a local physician and other maintenance. In 1987 Nazareth and Shefar'am as well introduced emergency service under the municipality's aegis. Shefar'am is planning a complete school program. In Nazareth, where there is a large branch of the IMA, the Nazareth Academic Union has a forum for health and medicine; in Akko the Association for Improving the Conditions of Health in Akko and its Environs conducted some screening and lectures. The Majd al-Kurum local council arranged in 1986 for eight physicians to administer eye, teeth and heart examinations in schools. The Kafar Qara' health committee obtained the services of a dentist to screen school-children. While in the Jewish sector in general there have long been nonprofit voluntary associations concerned with health, they have for the most part been organized, nationally or regionally, around particular medical problems. These new developments in the Arab sector are particularly striking and positive in comparison with the lack of communal involvement on health in the Jewish sector (except in the kibbutzim and among the orthodox).

Municipalities have taken initiatives, with limitations, either within IMH and HSF (and other sick fund) frameworks, or on their own. Thus the decision of Shefar'am's Mayor Nimr Hussain to appoint a physician on the municipality's IMH budget was subsequently approved. In Kafar Qara' an association of 18 physicians, 6-7 nurses, social workers, pharmacists, ophthalmologists, physiotherapists and paramedical workers have carried out, with the local council chairman's assistance, special preventive campaigns—such as blood tests for thalassemia and anemia, blood pressure tests, and electro-cardiograms.

An area of health care where local authorities have traditionally been involved in Israel is dental care, in which sick funds have only lately become active (local councils maintain 175 dental chairs, the IMH has 210, the HSF 266, Le'umit 39, Meuhedet 37). Local dental societies active during the Mandate transferred their clinics to the HMO, which later transferred them to the state. The IMH provided some service for the needy and for inmates. Lately Project Urban Renewal has initiated services in development towns, but there has been very little progress in setting up dental health clinics in Arab communities (or in moshavim). Of 76 settlements in Israel 5,000-20,000 in size, 20—of which 19 are Arab (i.e more than half of these middle sized Arab communities) have no dental services at all. Four of these settlements have a population over 10,000 (Rahat, Tamra, Sakhnin, Mughar). There are no sick fund dental clinics in Arab settlements (IMH Department for Dental Health 1985). On the other hand, among the 102 local authorities which sponsor dental clinics for pupils and the needy are the following Arab communities: Baqa al-Gharbiyye, Taiybe,

Tarshiha, Nazareth, and Isfiya. Baqa al-Gharbiyye had an IMH clinic which lapsed when its dentist left; in 1986 the local council hired a dentist for school-children. In the local council's current initiative in Taiybe, the IMH is involved as well. The Kafar Qasem local council and the Daburiyye local council have also set aside funds for dental clinics.

Traditional forms of mutual and charitable aid also persist. In spite of the trend toward the nucleation of extended families, the patrilineage retains social and political importance, and Arab community and family support networks are still reliable and effective during times of illness (Rosenfeld 1976, Al-Haj 1986, Weihl 1986). One positive consequence of the maintenance of residence in villages is a communal solidarity which has been noted to be expressed during health campaigns (Kana'aneh et al. 1976), and has beneficial consequences at times of need. During Ramadan 2% of earnings are still contributed to charity, which Ramadan committees allocate to the local needy.   The Muslim Brothers have established their own charitable organization— a *zaccah* council—which also distributes such funds. Friday appeals for aid in the mosques elicit further aid for local purposes. While *waqf* property, administered by the Prime Minister's Office, is not directly controlled by the Arab community, allocations made from it for construction of IMH facilities since the 1970s do represent communal participation. The Supreme Muslim Council, still active in East Jerusalem, has recently initiated some distribution of funds the needy in Israel along with other activities.

Direct access to foreign sources for aid has become more available to the Arab community in Israel. While a compulsory tax paid by Palestinian workers in Arab countries finances PLO activities outside Israel, so that the Arab diaspora's contributions to national development are mostly targeted outside of the local center, a number of Western international sources from the United Nations to Christian charitable groups are increasingly open to health-related enterprises in the Arab community. Thus the World Bank has financed a national sewage project fund; before dealing with a local authority's request, they demand a general plan and specific solution. The regional health association in the Galilee employs a civil engineer for this purpose (it also grants loans for dental clinics, and conducts research activities); Shefar'am's Mayor Nimr Hussain recruited engineers to prepare plans for the project with no charge. Formation of lobbies, channels to local and international institutions, and advisory committees (such as a local authorities' committee for planning of services to advise not only international sources but also the State Lottery in its investments in the Arab sector) would further this cause considerably.

Arab leadership in the matter of improving health services provided by public institutions is only lately in the process of organizing and becoming vocal. Pressure based on electoral power within the Israeli system can be used as a leverage for improvements. Those communities with activist traditions and longest established municipal status— Shefar'am, Taiybe, Tira—are able to better use influence with the planning and budgeting institutions. For example 'Eshel' (the Association for the Planning and Development of Services for the Aged in Israel) was established by the JDC in 1969 (the JDC also maintains some hospitals for chronic illnesses and a research center [the Brookdale Institute]). Its activities are funded by the JDC, the government, the State Lottery, and the National Institute for Insurance. In 1987 it had 1,500 institutional places and 45 day centers for 3,000 persons; one of the day centers for the elderly was recently opened in an Arab community (Taiybe). Nazareth on the other hand, although long established and activist, is less able to elicit institutional support in a political constellation which has excluded the Communist Party from government coalitions.

As a consequence of the War of 1948, for the first 20 years of the state the political focus of Arabs in Israel—notwithstanding a high participation rate in Israeli elections—was on Palestinian and Arab centers outside of the country. After the wars of 1967 and 1973 a re-focus inward motivated by repeated Israeli military victories accompanied by economic advance has led to a new resolution to gain equality within Israeli society. Along with this resolution, in Israel during the second half of its existence the exigencies of democratic politics are such that the great rise in Arab population impels a rising level of demand for services along with the growing awareness of citizenship rights and political power.

The Arab public, disallowed independent political channels of organization, has not until recently been able to organize in its own cause (Lustick 1980, Zureik 1980). Thus, Arabs have had a low rate of political representation in the Knesset in spite of their high voting participation; there were six (out of 120) Arab Members of Knesset until 1955, seven until to 1973, and currently there are five. This representation is half of what it might be if votes were maximally used for leverage in Arab interests.

Finally, residential segregation of Arab and Jewish communities has made it possible to begin to use the municipal basis of the National Committee of Chairmen of Arab Local Authorities as the foundation for national Arab political organization. The emergence of this municipal basis led by an educated leadership is itself a function of the re-stratification of Arab society and of the re-emergence of an

Arab middle class. The Arab public has begun to see this Committee as a power-base and framework for advancement within the framework of Israeli local government, and health care, institutions (Rosenfeld and Al-Haj 1990). For the first time acting in unity beyond their political parties, the five present Arab Members of Knesset have now joined the National Committee of Chairmen of Arab Local Authorities in acting as a lobby for Arab interests; in the context of these initiatives, a Physicians' Supervisory Committee for Matters of Health in the Arab Sector was formed and the lobby has been vocal on the national level on matters including health.

Chapter 6

SOME INDICATORS OF THE HEALTH STATUS
OF THE ARAB POPULATION IN ISRAEL

In Israel, a conjunction of factors which define its historical situation places the Arab population at high medical risk with regard both to the infectious diseases characteristic of underdevelopment, and to the chronic degenerative diseases produced by the manufacture and marketing of convenience foods which have been replacing traditional cuisines, by industrial pollution and smoking, and by the psychosocial stresses which the economy brings about.

Substandard sanitary conditions in many Arab villages, together with the class situation of the Arabs and a transition from traditional to modern lifestyles, converge to affect the health of this population. On the one hand, infections carried by inadequate water sources and sewage disposal, and diseases and accidents caused by environmental hazards in unplanned and unfinished housing and roads maintain a grip; the overall rise in the standard of living and in health awareness of the majority on the individual and family levels is unmatched by environmental improvements on the communal level.

At the same time, diseases related to industrialization and to the conditions of working-class life—the chronic degenerative diseases as well as labor-related accidents and disabilities—have attained a solid foothold. Ischemic heart disease, cerebrovascular diseases, and cancer are produced by industrial class society through differential risk factors of habits of consumption, psychosocial stress, and environmental pollution. Lags in awareness of these factors, a fast rate of change, and a lack in health services offering early discovery and treatment greater in Arab than in Jewish communities, mean that among Arabs these diseases less often receive even corrective treatment (Rabi 1987).

The health of the Arabs in Israel is thus related to their structural position in Israeli society. Health status is primarily a product of environment and socioeconomic opportunities, and only secondarily a function of the distribution of the personal health services (e.g. Townsend and Davidson 1982). Nevertheless, the distribution of medical care can add to and amplify other factors which affect health.

The following discussion of health status is focussed on several indicators of health and disease comparing Arabs and Jews in Israel, and relies for its basis on national statistics collected by the Israel Central Bureau of Statistics. The discussion proceeds according to these topics: life expectancy and rates of mortality; mortality in infancy and early childhood; major causes of death, and data on hospitalization. It is supplemented with a review of particular case studies on topics of mortality and morbidity in infancy and early childhood, where a variety of these studies exists.

The reporting of death, its timing, and its diagnosis, may not be uniformly credible among all groups at all times. It is assumed, nevertheless, that reporting procedures have become more rather than less uniform with time.

An attempt to assess, on the basis of available data, the relative contribution to health status of class, ethnic origin, health-services availability and utilization, and other health-related behavior can proceed only on a general level of attribution and cannot in any case explain etiologies. Causal attribution beyond indicating the extent of problems requires research on social, nutritional, environmental, genetic, and cultural factors which has yet to be done among the Arab population.

Israel government publications on vital statistics generally include East Jerusalem (as of 1970) and the Golan Heights (after 1982) in the data for Israel, separately from the rest of the West Bank and Gaza. Statistics for East Jerusalem, whose population made up about one-sixth of the total Arab population reported for Israel in 1987, may affect some of the data on health. With regard to the Golan Heights (Arab population about 14,000), health information on Arabs is not available in these data and thus does not affect it.

6.A. National Statistics

Life Expectancy and Rates of Mortality
Changes in the life expectancies at birth of Jews and Arabs can be seen in Table 6.1. Among Jewish and Arab men and among Jewish women, the life expectancy at birth in the early 1980s was above the European average (67.2 for men and 74.8 for women; Rosen 1987, reporting the WHO's 'Quantitative Indicators for the European Region'). Arab women's life expectancy at birth in 1980-1984 was lower than that average, but rose to 75.8 by 1985. While improvements from 1970 to 1985 occurred among Jews and Arabs at approximately

the same rate, a 2-3% difference in the life expectancies of Jews and Arabs was maintained.

Table 6.1:   Life Expectancy at Birth, and at Ages 45 and 65, According to Sex and Population Group in Palestine and Israel, 1942-1987

	Non-Jews		Jews	
	Males	Females	Males	Females
Life Expectancy at Birth				
1942-44	[50]		64.1	65.9
1960-64			70.6	73.1
1970-74	68.8	72.2	70.5	73.6
1980-84	70.9	73.8	73.0	76.4
1987	73.2	75.8	73.9	77.3
Life Expectancy at Age 45				
1987	31.5	33.4	31.2	34.1
Life Expectancy at Age 60				
1987	19.5	20.0	18.5	20.7

(*SAI* 1985, 1987, 1989)

The improvement in life expectancy among Arabs is primarily attributable to a decline in infant mortality, and the difference between Jews and Arabs is due mostly to the fact that in spite of this decline the rate of infant mortality among Arabs has remained twice as high as that of Jews. The rise in Arabs' life expectancy over the period of the state does not necessarily reflect increased life expectancies at later ages; on the contrary, for Arab men over 45 and women aged 65-69 a comparison between the periods 1956-1962 and 1974-1977 showed rather a rise in age-specific mortality (Abramson and Gofin 1979).

Examination of differences in life expectancies in 1985 at age groups from 0 to 85 (at five-year intervals) shows a female advantage over males at all ages among both Jews and Arabs, and a slight advantage of Jews over Arabs among both males and females until the age of 55 (*SAI* 1987:131). In 1987, age-specific mortality rates (for one year only) were higher for Muslim than for Jewish females at all age-groups except 45-54, and at 80-84 (*SAI* 1989:140). Muslim males had higher mortality rates than Jews at all ages except at 70-74 and above 80. Differences between Jews and Arabs were highest by far during infancy and childhood (at ages until 14), when the rate among Arabs was more than double the rate for Jews.

Mortality in Infancy and Early Childhood

Infant mortality among Arabs in Israel has undergone a steady decline over the period of the state, but comparison with Jews is unfavorable. Among Jews, the rate rose sharply with the post-state entry of large African and Asian immigrant families, and declined with their permanent settlement and eventual transition to a low fertility, low mortality demographic regime (see section 6.C, below). While the infant mortality rate of Arabs declined, like that of the Jews, by more than 70% from 1956 to 1986, it has consistently remained about double the rate of Jews (see Table 6.2).

Deaths during the various phases of infancy. The breakdown of infant mortality rates into perinatal (through the first week) and neonatal (during the first month) on the one hand, and post-neonatal (one month to one year) on the other, distinguishes between factors influencing the newborn's health. In the perinatal and neonatal phases mortality is most often the result of congenital defects and immaturity, both of which are frequently related to the mother's poor health and to genetic factors, and both of which are also influenced by pre-natal screening and supervision as well as by delivery care. In the post-neonatal phase, infective environmental factors which affect the infant directly are primary, and the quality of nurturance of the infant, as well as the availability and use of preventive and curative care, play a role.

While infant mortality rates are higher for Arabs than for Jews both during the first month of life and from the ages of one-month to one-year, the difference has been, and remains, especially high in the latter phase (see Table 6.3). At this post-neonatal phase, the infant mortality rate is still more than three times as high among Arabs as among Jews, although its decline among Arabs has been steep (cf. Schmelz 1974, Davies 1979).

Table 6.2: **Infant Mortality Rates per 1,000 Live Births, According to Population Group, Israel 1949-1986***

Year	Non-Jews	Jews
1947	**	29.2
1949		51.7
1952	67.7	
1956	61.6	35.9
1969	40.3	18.9
1975	39.5	17.8
1984	20.4	10.3
1986	17.5***	9.6

* Until 1979, the rates for Jews are per 1,000 infants in the population including immigrants.
** See also Table 2.4a, page 52 above.
*** Official statistics since 1970 include the population of East Jerusalem. While it is probable that the average national rate was raised by statistics for East Jerusalem during the 1970s (at least), the infant mortality rate cited for non-Jews in the Jerusalem district in 1986 was 13.5/1,000, which was lower than the average for Israel. Its low rate of decline among non-Jews in the 1969-1975 interval might be due to the incorporation of data for East Jerusalem; however, the rate of decline among Jews during this interval is also particularly low.

(IGY 1957-1977, SAI 1986, 1988)

Table 6.3: **Infant Mortality Rates per 1,000 Live Births, According to Population Group and Age, Israel 1969-1984**

	Non-Jews		Jews	
	1st Month*	1 Month—1 Year	1st Month*	1 Month—1 Year
1969	14.7	25.6	13.1	5.8
1975	17.8**	21.7	12.3	5.5
1984	10.2	10.2	7.1	3.2

* perinatal and neonatal
** It is possible that the increase from 1969 to 1975 reflects the incorporation of data from East Jerusalem.

(SAI 1986)

Causes of infants' deaths. In spite of significant reductions in deaths from infectious diseases and perinatal causes, differences between Jews and non-Jews in infant mortality from all causes remain, as shown in Table 6.4. Given the fact that only one cause of death is listed for each infant, it must of course be noted that cause of death determinations may not be consistent among the two groups; thus, for example, the rate of deaths from 'other and unspecified causes' is almost three times as high among Arab as among Jewish infants.

The decline in deaths of non-Jews from infective causes (reduced by more than one-half from 1980-1985) as well as from perinatal and other unspecified causes (reduced by more than one-third during this period) is especially dramatic. Congenital mortality, reflecting both genetic and environmental factors, is persistently high among Arabs. In the prevalence of genetic diseases (not necessarily limited to mortality during the first year of life), genetic factors interact with cultural preferences in marriage. Patrilineal endogamy maintains a functional hold in Arab villages (Rosenfeld 1976, Freundlich and Hino 1984). At the same time, a current trend toward increasing openness in selecting marriage partners carries its own risks, since it brings gene carriers for these diseases into communities in which they have heretofore not been present.   Deficiencies in health education, counseling and prenatal care affect the discovery and management of genetic diseases.   State clinics for genetic counseling—generally affiliated with hospitals in the cities—are also not always adequate in their reach as long as individuals are unaware of risks.

Although congenital anomalies and perinatal causes accounted for the majority of infant deaths in 1985, and the rate of infant mortality from congenital defects remains two to three times as high for non-Jews than for Jews (cf. IMH 'Budget Proposal', 1982), infective causes, in spite of their decline, make up the largest difference between Arabs and Jews in the cause of death.

As to mothers' poor health in pregnancy, in 1977-1980 the mortality rate for infants of Jewish mothers over 35 was reduced to almost the same level as for those under 35, while the mortality rate of infants of the older Arab mothers remained high (Tzadka 1985:i-62). This, in a period when births in the highest risk over-40 category were declining, raises questions about the health and nutrition of the Arab mothers.   However, another indicator of maternal poor health—the extent of births at high-risk weights under 2,500 grams—does not present evidence in this direction. From 1977-1986 the percentage of low birthweight among non-Jews (and among Muslims specifically) was consistently lower than among Jews, with the exception of infants of Jewish mothers born in Africa, whose rate of low birthweight was particularly low (*SAI* 1987:127).

Table 6.4:   **Infant Mortality Rates per 1,000 Live Births, According to Population Group and Selected Cause of Death, Israel 1980 and 1985**

	Non-Jews	*Jews*
	1980	
Total:*	**25.6**	**12.4**
infections	**4.4**	**0.6**
intestinal	0.4	0.0
other	0.9	0.2
pneumonia	3.1	0.4
congenital anomalies	**4.2**	**2.8**
perinatal causes	**8.4**	**6.0**
birth trauma	0.2	0.1
other	8.2	5.9
external causes	**0.8**	**0.3**
other and unspecified	**7.8**	**2.7**
	1985	
Total:*	**18.3**	**9.8**
infections	**1.9**	**0.5**
intestinal	0.4	0.0
other	0.8	0.3
pneumonia	0.7	0.2
congenital anomalies	**5.4**	**2.4**
perinatal causes	**5.4**	**4.5**
birth trauma	0.1	0.0
other	5.3	4.5
external causes	**0.8**	**0.3**
other and unspecified	**5.0**	**2.0**

* Slight discrepancies in some cases between the total and its addenda are evidently due to the rounding of figures to the first decimal.

(*SAI* 1987:138-139)

Perinatal and neonatal mortality rates decreased after 1948 in part because confinement for birth was becoming almost universal with the availability of maternity wards and the universalistic application of maternity benefits (*SAI* 1985:677). Half the reduction in neonatal deaths in the population has been ascribed to the availability of neonatal units in hospitals (Tzadka 1985). Notwithstanding the high rate of confinement for birth, among Arabs there is a high number of stillbirths and of perinatal deaths.

Infant deaths in subgroups in the population. Variations between subgroups in infant and early childhood mortality rates conform to the socioeconomic ranking of these groups (see Table 6.5).

Table 6.5:   **Infant Mortality Rates per 1,000 Live Births and Mortality Rates of Children Aged 1-4 per 1,000 (Standardized), According to Population Group and Sex, Israel 1985**

	Muslims		Christians		Jews	
	Males	*Females*	*Males*	*Females*	*Males*	*Females*
Age 0-1	20.5		14.7		10.9	
		19.3		11.8		8.9
Age 1-4	1.1		(1.3)*		0.4	
		1.3				0.6

* combined rate for males and females

(*SAI* 1987:128).

Among the Arab subgroups, the death rates of Muslim infants are especially high. The rates of Christians are between those of Jews and of Muslims. Infant mortality among the Druze was highest among all groups in 1976 (Abramson and Gofin 1979); in 1985, it was 12.3/1,000 for males, and 13.9/1,000 for females—somewhat lower than that of Christian males, somewhat higher than that of Christian females (*SAI* 1987:128).

A study of the socioeconomic characteristics of settlements from 1978-1983 (Dor et al. 1988) showed that the correlation in Arab communities between average incomes and average infant mortality rates was consistent: As average income in a community increased, its infant mortality rates declined. Among both Jews and Arabs, the infant mortality rate in the top 20% of communities ranked according to socioeconomic status was two-thirds of that of the poorest. But the average infant mortality rate of Arabs was twice that of Jews. The income of the highest 20% of Arabs was similar to that of the poorest 20% of Jews, and infant mortality rates of the poorest of Jewish communities was lower than that of the highest among Arabs.

Infant mortality rates of males and females. Given a greater morbidity and mortality risks to male fetuses and infants (as well as at later ages), differences in the mortality rates of males and females, and in particular excess female mortality, provide an indication as to the role of culture in affecting differential survival rates. In 1980-1982 and 1985, the infant mortality rates of Muslim girls were somewhat higher than that of boys at the post-neonatal stage, possibly indicating selective neglect of girl children (see Table 6.6).

Table 6.6:   **Infant Mortality Rates per 1,000 Live Births, According to Population Group, Age, and Sex, Israel 1980-1982 and 1985**

| | Muslims | | Jews | |
	Males	Females	Males	Females
		1980-1982		
Total	24.9	23.4	13.7	11.0
0-1 week	10.7	8.3	8.0	6.0
0-1 month*	13.8	10.9	9.8	7.6
1-12 months	11.1	12.5	3.9	3.4
		1985		
Total	18.9	19.1	10.8	8.7
0-1 week	8.4	8.2	6.3	5.1
0-1 month*	11.3	10.4	7.8	6.3
1-12 months	7.6	8.7	3.0	2.4

* perinatal and neonatal

(SAI 1987;130)

In the data for 1985 and 1986, the higher rate of mortality from infectious diseases and from other unspecified causes (in 1986) among Arab girls than among Arab boys on the one hand, and the higher mortality rate from external causes of Arab boys on the other, should be noted along with the differences at all points in favor of Jewish infants (see Table 6.7).

Table 6.7:   **Infant Mortality Rates per 1,000 Live Births, According to Population Group, Sex, and Selected Cause of Death, Israel 1985 and 1986**

	Non-Jews		Jews	
	Males	*Females*	*Males*	*Females*
		1985		
Total*	18.9	17.8	10.8	8.7
infections	1.5	2.4	0.6	0.5
intestinal	0.3	0.5	0.1	0.0
other	0.7	1.0	0.3	0.3
pneumonia	0.5	0.9	0.2	0.2
congenital anomalies	5.9	4.8	2.7	2.1
perinatal causes	5.6	5.1	5.0	4.0
birth trauma	0.1	0.1	0.1	0.0
other	5.5	5.0	4.9	4.0
external causes	1.1	0.5	0.3	0.4
other and unspecified	5.0	5.0	2.3	1.7
		1986		
Total*	17.8	16.7	10.5	8.5
infections	2.0	2.5	0.5	0.3
intestinal	0.7	0.8	0.0	0.0
other	0.6	0.6	0.2	0.1
pneumonia	0.7	1.1	0.3	0.2
congenital anomalies	6.8	5.3	2.8	2.3
perinatal causes	5.6	4.1	5.0	4.2
birth trauma	—	—	—	0.1
other	5.6	4.1	5.0	4.1
external causes	1.0	0.6	0.5	0.5
other and unspecified	2.6	4.1	1.8	1.2

* See footnote to Table 6.4.

(SAI 1987:140, 1989:152)

'Notifiable' communicable diseases. The state's immunization programs and other health campaigns, which generally cover the Arab population, have succeeded in virtually eliminating the subtropical infective diseases (v. Yekutiel 1979, Grushka 1968). Nevertheless, the following diseases which the Israel Ministry of Health requires to be reported were, while quite rare, reported at a higher rate for Arab than for Jewish children in 1976-1980: measles, typhoid, polio, and whooping cough—all diseases against which children are vaccinated. Their incidence means either that the immunization program is not reaching all children (perhaps less well on second or booster immunizations) or that vaccines are not absorbed (CBS 1984 #722).

Data on hospitalizations of infants. A high rate of hospitalizations of Arabs infants (twice as high as expected, taking into account the higher proportion of infants in the Arab population)—in 1981-1985 12% of all Arab hospitalizations were in this age group, as compared to to 3.7% of Jews; a higher absolute number of hospitalizations of Arab children for anemia; and an almost equal absolute number of hospitalizations of Arab and Jewish infants for enteritis, are all consistent with cumulative incidence of disease rather than a single blow of great severity. It is likely that a pattern of repeated assaults of infection facilitated by and leading to malnutrition, to further infection and finally to death is the prevalent one (CBS 1988:#826).

Major Causes of Death
    In Israel mortality rates from infectious diseases have decreased in the population following improvements in public health, while there has been an increase in deaths from other causes, especially from chronic diseases (Davies 1979, Tulchinski et al. 1982, IMH 1985:63).
    Age-standardized mortality rates in 1987 were: Females: Jews 5.5, Druze 5.5, Christians 5.8, Muslims 6.6; Males: Druze 6.3 Jews 7.3 Christians 8.0, Muslims 8.0. Examination of age-specific mortality rates (Section 6.A., above) showed that while the difference in the death rates of Arabs and Jews was highest in infancy and childhood, Arabs had somewhat higher mortality rates than Jews at most later ages as well. Further comparison of the two populations in 1986 according to age-standardized causes of death shows that the rates of mortality from most major causes, while similar for the most part, were also somewhat higher for Arabs than for Jews.
    In Israel in 1985, four out of the five leading causes of death among Muslims and Jews were similar ones: ischemic heart disease, cancer, cerebrovascular disease, and external causes (official

statistics list only one cause per death). The possibility of differential diagnoses of Arabs and Jews exists (due, for example, to differences in existing medical files) but cannot be weighed on the basis of available data. The various causes were ranked somewhat differently in the different groups, but the major significant difference between the Jewish and Arab populations was that 'congenital defects and other perinatal causes,' high on the list among Muslim males and females (due to the young Muslim age composition and high infant mortality rates from these causes), were not among the leading causes of death among Jews (*SAI* 1987:134-35).

With regard to leading causes of death other than congenital defects and perinatal causes, comparison of age-standardized death rates by selected cause in 1986 shows overall similarity between Jews and Arabs (see Tables 6.8 and 6.9). However, among these causes Jewish men and women had mortality rates higher than Arabs only for cancer, and Jewish women—who are more likely than Arab women to be urban, employed and mobile—had a higher rate of death from external causes. The rates of mortality from ischemic heart disease were about equal for Jewish and Arab men. Arabs had higher death rates than Jews from all of the other causes listed.

Within the overall similarity between the causes of death of Jews and non-Jews, the highest dissimilarity is in deaths from infectious diseases; such deaths are mostly distributed between the very young and the elderly. Comparison of mortality from infectious diseases among Arabs and Jews points out a high rate of deaths of Arabs from some diseases that are less fatal for Jews. Thus, for the dangerous infectious diseases, physicians' notification of the illness to the Ministry of Health is obligatory. Although the rates of notification of some diseases among Arabs is relatively low compared to Jews, the rate of deaths from these diseases is higher. In the case of measles, the proportion of notifications of the disease among Arabs in 1981-1985 was 20% of the total number of notifications, but the proportion of deaths of Arabs out of the total number of deaths from this cause was 70%—a difference of 250%. In the cases of viral hepatitis, bacillary meningitis, and viral meningitis, the differences ranged from 80-50% more deaths than notifications of Arabs relative to Jews (computed from CBS 1988:#826).

The rate of deaths from external causes—relatively low among Arab women, is particularly high among Arab men. With regard to chronic diseases, from 1963-1975 there was a sharp rise in deaths from ischemic heart disease among Arabs of both sexes (Abramson and

Table 6.8: Age-Standardized Rates of Mortality (per 100,000) According to Population Group and Selected Cause of Death, Israel 1986*

	Total Population		Jews	
	Females	Males	Females	Males
Ischemic heart disease	90.0	158.2	88.7	158.5
Cancer	99.7	117.5	103.3	119.8
Cerebrovascular disease	49.1	49.9	46.7	49.0
External causes**	29.7	55.5	30.5	54.5
Pneumonia	12.5	15.6	12.2	15.4
Infectious Diseases	10.7	12.1	9.4	11.3

* CBS statistics for 1986 (unpublished). 'Total Population' combines rates for Jews, Muslims, Christians and Druze. Rates for each of the Arab groups and for the Arab group as a whole represent samples too small to be statistically significant.
** not including suicide and homicide; including deaths from unsuccessful operations.

Table 6.9: Excess Deaths (in %) in the Total Population Compared with the Jewish Population, According to Selected Cause of Death, Israel 1986 (Computed from Table 6.8)*

	Females	Males
Infectious Diseases	14	7
Cerebrovascular disease	5	2
Pneumonia	2	1
Ischemic heart disease	1	0
Cancer/malignancies	-3	-1
External causes	-3	2

* see footnote to Table 6.8.
'Excess deaths' — representing differences between the non-Jewish and the Jewish populations — is a calculation of:
(the rate for the total population, minus
the rate for the Jewish population),
divided by the rate for the Jewish population

Gofin 1979). From 1976-1982 mortality from ischemic heart disease among Arabs was a constant high. Ischemic heart disease has become the principal cause of death among Arabs as among Jews. While the rate through the early 1980s was higher among Jews (IMH 1982b), in 1986 mortality from ischemic heart disease of Arab men almost equalled that of Jews.

Israel as a whole has a mortality rate from ischemic heart disease higher than the European average, while mortality from all other causes is lower than the European averages (Rosen 1987:12, reporting the WHO's 'Quantitative Indicators for the European Region'). Given that the rate of mortality of men from this cause is higher than that of women, in Israel, as compared with Europe, the rate is particularly high among women, and among Arab women even more than among Jewish ones.

Cancer is the leading cause of death among Jewish and Arab women in Israel, and the second among men. In 1963-1975 there was a rise in the incidence of cancer (especially lung cancer) as a cause of mortality among Arab men; from 1976-1982 there was no further rise, but mortality from cancer remains high, especially among men, although at a lesser rate than among Jews (Abramson and Goffin 1979, IMH 1985).

During the period 1963-1975 deaths from cerebrovascular disease increased among Arabs of both sexes but especially among women (CBS 1983:#708). From 1976-1982 the rate of mortality of non-Jews from strokes was doubled, while there was a significant decrease among Jews (IMH 'Budget Proposal' 1985, from *SAI* 1976-1983). The current rate is especially high among Arab women.

Data on Hospitalizations

The relation between the causes of death and major health problems is salient enough to make consideration of the former relevant in indicating major medical trends and concerns. But there is no necessary overlap between the major causes of mortality and of morbidity in a population, and for individuals listed causes of death are not always the causes of most suffering in life. 'Causes of death' do not fully reflect the prevalence and consequences of not necessarily fatal diseases and conditions which affect the quality of life as well as the general state of health (McKinlay et al. 1989).

Currently available comprehensive data on hospitalization (from 1979, and not age-standardized) show rates of hospitalization for infective diseases, congenital malformations, and external causes higher among Arabs, while hospitalizations for the degenerative diseases were higher among Jews. These differentials to a great extent reflect the variant age composition among the two populations. While they do not in themselves indicate differential risks, they do indicate the extent of the problems of infections, congenital malformations and external causes for this population as whole.

While mortality from infective causes was decreasing in the mid 1970's, hospitalization rates of Arabs for endemic infectious diseases, including upper respiratory and enteric diseases, actually rose (CBS 1983:#708;xii). Since this was a period of intensive hospital expansion, the greater availability of hospital beds might have influenced treatment choice, although overall hospitalization rates did not rise. It is more likely that the high rate of hospitalization for infectious diseases was a function of inadequate primary care. The difference between Jews' and non-Jews' rates of hospitalization for enteritis and other diarrheal diseases—three and a half times as high among non-Jews—means that these illnesses constituted a much greater problem among Arabs. Similarly, bacillary dysentery rates in the total population increased by 27% from 1979 to 1980 (*SAI* 1981:111). While the 1980 data cover the whole population, the earlier reports include only data for Jews. The sharp rise may reflect a considerably higher rate among Arabs. Hospitalization rates for Jews and non-Jews for infective diseases in 1976 were highest among urban Arabs, high among Jews in settlements of low socioeconomic status, and particularly low among rural Arabs (Ellencweig and Slater 1986). Poor people—Arabs more than Jews—tended to be hospitalized at high rates (evidently because of a high incidence of infectious diseases among them) in urban locations where medical care was available, but not in Arab rural locations where treatment was less easily accessible and where people might delay or forgo it.

6.B.   Case Studies on Mortality and Disease in Infancy and Early Childhood

The following case studies appeared in Israeli and international medical and public health journals and other publications, and as theses done in medical schools in Israel. They vary greatly in their validity and reliability; some are based on samples of wards in particular hospitals while others employ strict sampling procedures. Many were done in the 1970s, and may represent conditions which have undergone some change. In spite of such shortcomings, they are

presented here in amplification of some of the issues discussed
previously through the use of national statistics.

Causes of Infants' and Children's Deaths and Diseases
Genetic and other congenital diseases. Congenital heart disease and
thalassemia have been shown to be related to consanguineous
marriages in Arab villages (Gev et al. 1986, Biener 1977, Rososhansky
1980, Omar 1978, Montag et al. 1980). Several villages have a high
prevalence of deaf-mutism and of mental retardation, possibly
attributable to nutritional and environmental factors as well.

Low birthweight. Comparison in 1983-1984 of Muslim, Christian and
Jewish infants according to mother's continent of birth, found that
while differences between groups in average weight at birth were
statistically significant, they were medically meaningless: High-risk
birthweights characterized 7% of the Arab infants, and 6.9% of the
Jews (Mor-Yosef et al. 1989).

Perinatal mortality. In the Upper Galilee, perinatal mortality declined
among both Jews and Arabs by the late 1970s but its rate among Arabs
was almost four times as high as the rate among Jews (Ballas et al.
1982). This was so in spite of intensive improvements in the neonatal
unit in the maternity department of the regional state hospital, and this
study attributes the difference to a lesser availability and use of the
state's preventive family health stations in Arab villages than in Jewish
settlements in the region.

Infective causes. Most systematically, a study of matched birth and
infant death files for 1977-1980 in the Center region showed large
disparity in post-neonatal rates—3.7/1,000 live births for Jews,
12.7/1,000 for Arabs. Deaths from infectious disease were 5.6 times
as high for Arab infants: This was the largest difference in cause of
death, and could not be explained by such risk-factors as maternal age
and parity or low birthweight (Bar-El 1985).
    Surveys of infant deaths in the Western Galilee in 1964-1986
showed that most were due to infectious diseases, and greatly
declined in recent years (Amit and Freundlich 1974, Freundlich et al.
1982, Biener et al. 1989). With regard to effect of environmental
conditions on infectious diseases, a link has been posited between
incidences of typhoid among children and specific serotypes said to
be endemic in open sewage in Umm al-Fahm (Levin 1980).

Infants' Deaths in Subgroups in the Population

A comparative case study of Jewish communities based on matched birth and death files showed that in the center district (of lowest infant mortality in the country), where there is good medical care and access to teaching hospitals, among Jewish towns the one town whose population is poor and preponderantly of Asian and African origin had an infant mortality rate much higher than the rest (15.7/1,000 live births, of which 5.6/1,000 were in the first month, and 10.1/1,000 post-neonatal; Modan and Bar-El 1981). Four other, more affluent, Jewish towns in the region had much lower rates ranging from 1.4--1.6/1,000 in the first month and from 1.6--3.8/1,000 in the period from one month to one year).

The low first-month mortality rates in the region as a whole must be accounted for by the particularly excellent access to prenatal care; even the first-month rate of 5.6/1,000 in the poor community was considerably lower than the national average among Jews. Nevertheless, the height of this rate relative to the other Jewish communities in the region is probably due to deficiencies in the poor community in mothers' health and nutrition.

The total rate of 15.7/1000 in this community was half-way between the average national infant mortality rates for Jews and for Arabs at the time of the study. The neonatal rate in the poor Jewish community was half the average rate among Arabs; that this ratio was more favorable to Jews than a comparison of the Arab rate with the national average among Jews evidently reflects the quality of the health services provided to Jews in this region.

The post-neonatal rate was not similarly affected by health care. The rate of 10.1/1,000 in the poor community was about four-fifths the average post-neonatal rate among Arabs. Thus while the greatest difference between Jews and Arabs nationally is in mortality at this phase, the rate among poor Jews in this study is so high, in comparison to other Jews, that they are closer to Arabs in this regard.

A case study of infants hospitalized in the Negev linked infections in infancy to poverty among both Jews and Arabs (Harlap et al. 1977). This study found that among Jews those of Asian and African origins and low socioeconomic status had more gastro-intestinal infections than the others. Hospital admission rates of Bedouin infants were especially high for gastro-enteritis, but also high for other infections and parasitic diseases, malnutrition, and external causes.

Poverty and Infants' Nutrition

Some chronic and acute undernutrition has been found among poor infants, Arabs and Jews, although at a higher prevalence among Arabs. Arab children from settled village and urban communities as well as Bedouin children have been found to be smaller and lighter than Jewish children (Nichaman and Reshef 1978, Palti et al. 1982).

In the cases of iron deficiency and of vitamin D deficiency, preventive supplements are in principle routinely available at the family health centers, so that high rates are secondarily attributable to a failure of the preventive programs.

A study in the Negev, where there are concentrations of Jews of low socioeconomic status (and of Asian and African origin) in state-established development towns as well as of semi-sedentarized and sedentarized Bedouin, found that one half of the Jewish and three-quarters of the Bedouin infants suffered from anemia, with acute cases accounting for 10% of both groups. This study attributed the high rate among Jews to lack of use of iron supplements, and the higher rate among Bedouin to other nutritional and health problems as well. The Bedouin's longer period of breast-feeding acted to protect against a higher prevalence of acute cases (Sofer et al. 1986). But breast-feeding only, during the first year, with low rates of nutrients from fruit, vegetables and meat, was found to cause undernutrition to the point of stunting among Bedouin babies (Dagan et al. 1983). The decline in breast-feeding, as traditional cultural practices are changed with sedentarization, further exacerbates nutritional problems (Dagan et al. 1984). In addition, hypothermia in low desert temperatures aggravates low resistance which contributes to repeated infections (Dagan and Gorodischer 1984).

Changes in breast-feeding practices, substituting routine cow's milk for mother's milk, affect not only the poor. A study of Arab and Jewish infants in a northern district in 1981-82 found high rates of iron-deficiency anemia among both groups (Lavon et al. 1985). While among Jews those in low-income families were most vulnerable, among Arabs infants from more prosperous villages were also affected, a finding which probably reflects a decline in breast-feeding together with inadequate preventive reach.

In several studies done in the 1970s there are reports of scurvy and rickets among Arabs and poor Jews. Scurvy reflects a faulty diet of child and/or (for breast-fed infants) mother, deficient in fruit and vegetables and resulting in a low level of vitamin C. Its occurrence in children may be linked to mental retardation, possibly as a consequence of low levels of vitamin C in the mother (Weizel 1975).

Rickets due to a vitamin D deficit and to lack of exposure to sunlight causes hypo-calcemia and stunted growth. Occurring even on a marginal level it facilitates infections in the gastro-intestinal tract and respiratory problems. Infants are especially vulnerable in winter when, with inadequate heating in houses, mothers tend to overwrap and overprotect them outdoors as well. There is not enough vitamin D in mothers' milk, and poor mothers in Arab villages tend to supplement babies' diets with vitamin-poor additions of potatoes, rice and bread. Since vitamin D is added to commercial milk, the inference is that such milk is not a significant part of the ill infants' nutrition.

Among both Jews and Arabs rickets was correlated with poverty. In 1970-1977, among children hospitalized in a state hospital in a northern region where many Arab patients are treated, a larger proportion of Arabs than Jews (and more males than females) had rickets, and at a higher degree. Most of these children suffered from malnutrition, and one quarter from anemia (Rinot 1978).

A survey in an Arab village in the Western Galilee revealed that three-fifths of infants aged 4-12 months had rickets, as well as a high rate of anemia. In this village most men worked as unskilled laborers, so that their families are assumed to be poor. The overwhelming majority of infants were found to be unexposed to the sun in the winter, and received no vitamin D supplements; this indicated lack of contact between the population and the center, and inadequate health education (upon subsequent instruction, most of the women in this case began to administer the supplements). Mostly affected were infants who were breast-fed only—generally boys (Zaharan 1980). Male infants also tended to be more overprotected from exposure to cold, and to sunlight In the case of rickets, a nurturing preference of boys may thus have effects in their disfavor.

It is possible that since the 1970s nutritional standards have improved; the continuing reductions in the rates of post-neonatal mortality especially would tend to indicate so, although the range and depth of poverty among Arabs may point otherwise. It has been shown elsewhere that infant mortality rates are subject to even short-range fluctuations in the standard of living (Wood 1982). Not enough is known about the nutrition of Arab infants, as of children and adults. A recent ethnographic study in an Arab community encapsulated as a neighborhood in a 'mixed city,' demonstrates that current problems in nutrition of infants are at least in part attributable to the fact that mothers' inadequate awareness of nutritional requirements is matched by the family health center personnel's untested and incorrect assumptions about these mothers' nurturing behavior (Rumney 1986).

Infant Mortality Rates of Males and Females
Excess male hospitalizations. A study in the Negev in 1978 found that twice as many Bedouin boys as girls were hospitalized for gastro-intestinal infections. In the context of high infant mortality (the highest in the country) in this region, this may indicate selective caring for male infants. Neglect of female infants may well be found among populations of the Jewish poor as well. A study in the 1970s found that while gastro-intestinal infections were high in the Jewish development towns in the Negev (as opposed to well-to-do urban areas), the rate of hospitalized boys to girls was 3:2 (Moshe 1983). Excess hospitalization rates of male infants, familiar through Asia and Africa, reflect both the greater biological vulnerability of males, and selective care. Since selective neglect of girl infants reflects the continued inferior status of women related to lags in education and employability, such neglect may be considered, along with poverty, a correlate of underdevelopment and class inferiority (Harris and Ross 1987).

Excess female infant mortality from infections. An earlier case study in the Western Galilee in 1970 found the infant mortality rate among Arabs to be higher for boys than girls (as expected considering the higher vulnerability of male infants) for all causes except for infections of the digestive tract; such infections, which generally occur in the post-neonatal stage as part of a pattern of repeated infections, undernutrition and lowered resistance, possibly imply that girls were less cared for (Amit and Freundlich 1974).

Utilization of Health Services
Several case studies in the 1970s noted a differential pattern (lower for Arabs than for Jews) of seeking and using prenatal as well as curative care for infants (Rogov 1980, Alpern 1976, Cohen 1983, Atad et al. 1986). Arab children were found to arrive at a hospital emergency room with more acute conditions than Jewish children; this was attributed to a lesser availability of primary health services in Arab communities and a greater distance of hospital from these communities, as well as to lesser education of Arab parents with regard to medical needs (Makhoul 1987; similarly Motro 1968).

6.C. Health Trends and Problems

The major tendencies indicated for the Arab population as a whole by the above discussion of national statistics and case studies are: first, the steep decline in infant mortality rates along with the remaining gap between Arab and Jewish infants; secondly, the drastic reduction in infectious diseases as causes of mortality at all ages as well as their overall decline—but with it the still higher incidence and greater severity, as compared with the Jewish population, of infective diseases among Arab infants, children and adults; and thirdly, the increasing general similarity in health status at later ages between Arabs and Jews, brought about by the rapid increase among Arabs of the chronic degenerative diseases. With regard to these tendencies, it is possible to point out, albeit not in a definitive manner, the relevance of various risk factors—behavioral, environmental and genetic—as well as to discuss the role of the health services.

The Decline in Infant Mortality Rates and the Gap between Arabs and Jews.

As has been previously said (see 2.E., and 5.B., above) the infant mortality rate in Palestine began to decline more than 100 years ago—before the development of the health services had significant impact—evidently as demographic controls on infant mortality were relaxed to enable peasant families—and, later, proletarized peasant families—to benefit from the relative advantages of larger households in an expanding colonial economy (cf. Harris and Ross 1987). The decline in infant mortality, along with a rather stable and high rate of fertility, resulted in an especially high rate of growth of the Arab population (Friedlander and Goldscheider 1979, Gilbar 1989).

The decline in birth rates in Israel as of the mid-1960s among Muslims, and 20 years earlier among Christians (see 5.B. above), is part of a 'demographic transition' to a low-fertility, low-mortality regime as the practice of birth control increased as the major means of regulating population. Contraception, as well as abortion until the fourth month, were sanctioned by Islamic law in premodern Islamic populations and are supported by Islamic medicine (Musallam 1983).

The transformation from a cultural pattern based on polygyny, high fertility, kinship endogamy, and a low age of marriage, to an increasingly nuclear family organization, lower fertility and rising age of marriage, characterize the Muslim family in the Middle East and elsewhere in recent years (Behnam 1985, Rosenfeld 1980). In Israel, the opening of some channels of socioeconomic mobility for Arabs as of the 1960s, the subsequent rise of a permanent Arab working class and the regeneration of a middle class, and the rise in the status of women have led to continuing reductions in the rate of fertility among Muslims and Druze; even sharper reductions have occurred among the more urban Christian population (see Table 6.10).

The new demographic regime, based on intensive efforts at preserving the life of infants as fewer children are wanted with more parental investment in the nurturing and care of each child, is probably the factor most responsible for the increasing rate of survival of infants (see Matras 1990). The continued decline in infant mortality from all causes, at a rate similar to that of Jews in the 30 years from the mid-1950s to the mid-1980s, is thus mainly due to the increasing participation of Arabs in the industrial economy and education in

Table 6.10:   Total Fertility Rates, by Population Group and Mother's Continent of Birth, Israel 1975 and 1985

	1975	1985
Arabs		
Muslims	7.75	4.63
Druze	6.85	4.47
Christians	3.35	2.12
Jews		
Born in Asia or Africa	3.77	3.21
Born in Israel	3.08	2.89
Born in Europe or America	2.82	2.79

(*SAI* 1987;120).

Israel, to a general increase in the standard of living, leading to improvements in mothers' health and in the care and nutrition of babies, and to increasing investment in the education of children (both male and female) as the primary channel for social mobility. The gap between Arabs and Jews is mainly due to lags and inequalities in the demographic transition, primarily in the poor, rural and underdeveloped sector. High reductions in rates of death from perinatal and infective causes are probably due in addition to improvements in sanitary conditions at birth and thereafter, and to the overall influence of the public health services in providing prenatal supervision and curative care.

With all that, it is necessary to explain the fact that the average infant mortality among Arabs has remained twice as high as that of Jews, and that, moreover, the average infant mortality rates of all Arab communities—even those which are in the top socioeconomic sector of Arab communities—are higher than the rates of even the bottom sector of Jewish communities (Dor et al. 1988).

The persistence of demographic control through allowing some infants to die (Scrimshaw 1983) might account for some of the higher rate of infant deaths. Although Islam explicitly prohibits infanticide, the practice is known to be ancient in the Middle East and documented in the Middle Ages (Giladi 1990). If such practices persist, they operate in conjunction with more primary differential risk factors which affect both the contracting of diseases (most importantly environmental and genetic risk factors), and their severity (poverty and insufficient availability or use of the health services).

Environmental risk factors. Substandard environmental conditions in Arab communities, due to the state's insufficient investment in infrastructure, affect Arab residents of all classes. Although water quality in Israel as a whole is far from good, it is worse in Arab communities. Open sewage increases the chances of exposure to infective agents.

Genetic risk factors. The persistence of high rates of mortality from congenital diseases is mainly attributed to genetic causes operating together with cultural patterns of kinship endogamy.

Age of marriage. Infants of very young mothers have lower chances of birth and survival. There has been a rise in the age of marriage among Arabs, but a difference of 2.5 years (in 1982) in the ages of Jewish (21.9) and non-Jewish brides (19.4; Eisenbach 1989).

Poverty. Poverty is directly related to mothers' health and to undernutrition, as well as to the need for selective care of infants. Anthropological studies elsewhere have shown the effect on infant mortality of health behavior situational to poverty, including selective neglect, forced upon the poor by limited opportunities (e.g. Wood 1982, Scheper-Hughes 1984, Harris and Ross 1987).

Poverty alone may account for much of the differences in rates of infant mortality between Arabs and Jews in Israel. The range and the depth of poverty are much higher among Arabs than among Jews, and the fact that the average infant mortality rates of even the most affluent Arab communities is higher than that of the poorest Jewish communities may be related to the fact that the average income in the most affluent Arab communities is lower than that of the poorest Jewish communities.

The role of the health services. Access to prenatal and primary care for infants affects the chances of birth and survival. As has been documented, such medical care, public and private, has been increasingly available at all levels, but at a lesser distribution and access in Arab communities, where services are often inferior in quantity and quality and in some places do not exist.

In addition, a lesser utilization of health services may be explained by reasons other than lack of access. Such reasons may include reliance on traditional medical culture, lack of insurance, as well as other pressing demands on time and resources, especially where local public facilities are not available or where people are not insured. All in all, lack of awareness and readiness to take advantage of available care, to the degree that it exists, must to some extent be considered a reflection of inadequate reach of the local public health services.

Infant mortality especially from infectious disease and most frequently in the post-neonatal phase, from causes which are often preventable and curable (Modan and Bar-El 1981) represents a variety of factors including the detrimental effects of class on nutrition and selective care, a failure of the environmental and personal preventive system, and an inadequate reach of curative care. Enteric infections resulting from poor environmental sanitation, to which infants and children in Arab villages are vulnerable, have—especially when complicated by dietary insufficiencies—further health consequences. For example, the absorption of vaccines may be prevented by diarrheas, so that even when immunizations are administered they may not be effective among infants and toddlers suffering from gastrointestinal infections.

Environmental Factors Affecting the Rate of Infectious Diseases and of Deaths from External Causes.

Because state investment in development of the infrastructure of Arab communities has been insufficient, the Arab population of Israel is subject, more than the Jewish population, to a set of medical problems characteristic of underdevelopment.

A decline in mortality from infectious diseases has, elsewhere, been found evidently to have been primarily due to improvements in public health—in environmental sanitation and personal hygiene—rather than to medical preventive or curative interventions. But especially where, as in Arab communities, water supply and sewage disposal are frequently substandard, and where a low standard of living may make for low personal immunity and resistance, inoculations as well as curative care take on special importance.

It is possible that the higher rate of death from external causes among Arab men may also be related to environmental factors, as well as to their working class status: Manual occupations, with daily commuting to the workplace on substandard roads in the periphery, and active participation in the construction of rural housing in communities without adequate planning and infrastructure, may all increase the risks of accidents leading to death.

The Rise in the Chronic Degenerative Diseases.

As more people survive infancy and early childhood to reach later ages, and in part as a function of the decline in infectious diseases as causes of death, there has been a rise in the rates of morbidity and mortality from the chronic diseases. In general, behavioral and environmental risk factors relevant to these increases are a fast rate of dietary change toward increased consumption of fats and sugars; a high rate of smoking; the stressful effects of bearing, caring and providing for households in a situation of class inferiority; and exposure to industrial pollution. All of these factors are tied to social class, and the mortality from the chronic degenerative diseases has been shown to be higher among working-class and poorer populations.

The risk factors for ischemic heart disease—diets high in sugars, cholesterol and other fats, smoking, and stress—have been found to be especially associated with low socioeconomic status (Susser 1983, Cooper et al 1981). Changes in lifestyle and diet affect these rates. Thus among the Bedouin (who traditionally ate meat and milk only in the spring), a low cholesterol and low fat diet, no reliance on processed foods, and a nomadic lifestyle evidently offered protection from heart disease through the 1960s. With sedentarization, heart disease began to be reported in the 1970s, and less rarely in the 1980s (Abu-Rabi'a 1976, 1987).

As to cerebrovascular disease, stroke as a cause of mortality is common especially in poor countries and among poor populations, but epidemiological knowledge as to how changes in socioeconomic conditions affect it is evidently inconclusive (Cooper et al. 1981, Susser 1983, McKinlay et al. 1989). Its greatest risk-factor is high blood pressure, for which nutrition based on the cheaper foods (fats and sugars) and psychosocial stress are the most widely accepted etiological hypotheses; genetic factors may also be operative (e.g. Shasha et al. 1986). With regard to cancer, the somewhat higher overall rate of deaths among Jews than among Arabs in Israel might possibly be related to the greater effects of industrially-created environmental pollution in Jewish urban residential communities than in most Arab communities, which tend to be rural and industrially underdeveloped.

With regard to the rate of mortality from all the chronic diseases, it must be said that these do not necessarily parallel the rates of morbidity in the population. Among Jews in Israel (as in the U.S.A.) mortality (but not necessarily morbidity) from ischemic heart disease and cerebrovascular disease had been declining (Epstein and Strulov 1986). Poorer populations—such as the Arabs in Israel—may benefit less from the contributions of the health services in delaying the deaths of those who are ill (Susser 1983, McKinlay et al. 1989). Access to preventive, curative and emergency care—less available in Arab communities—may reduce 'preventable deaths' (e.g. Woolhandler et al. 1985).

The rise in the prevalence of the chronic degenerative diseases is important not only in relation to mortality but perhaps even more because it has extended the years of life lived in poor health (McKinlay et al. 1989). Chronic diseases, no less than external injuries and congenital diseases, result in high rates of disability. In fact, the National Institute for Insurance reported a high rate of non-Jewish disabled in 1978 (National Institute for Insurance 1983). Congruently, comparison of a sample of rural Arabs over 65 years (in 1985) and of Jews over 65 (in 1982) found that twice as many Arabs as Jews reported themselves as confined to the house or to bed (Weihl 1986).

Here the health services also play a major role. Medical services affect adults more than infants, and morbidity more than mortality as a whole. Early discovery and control through medication of the chronic diseases, as well as the quality of medical care, its accessibility and comfort are crucial components of the sense of well-being at later ages. Older Arabs use the health services less than the Jews (Margolz et al. 1980), but it is not known whether this is due only to lesser access or also to cultural preferences for self help and traditional medicine. Much anthropological work remains to be done in Israel with regard to the comprehensive aspect of health, beyond what statistical indices of mortality and morbidity may tell. A study of aging women (Datan et al. 1981) indicates that traditional Muslim culture has facilitated Arab women's passage through menopause. Traditional patterns of family involvement in the care of the aged have been supportive, among Arabs in Israel as in other societies, but are undergoing change (Matras 1990; Rizek 1979, Al-Haj 1986).

An improving standard of living due to employment of the majority of Arab men in permanent labor, to the rise of an entrepreneurial sector, and to higher levels of education of both men and women, is reflected in higher levels of the economic prerequisites for health and in the growing awareness of this population of their own health needs. The increasing availability of state and state-subsidized public health services enables increased access to and use of public medical care. With respect to these factors, there is increasing equality between Arabs and Jews in Israel, as there is, less fortunately with regard to the degenerative diseases.

At the same time, a continued lag in the health status of Arab infants and children especially with regard to enteric infections, nutritional-deficiency caused diseases and conditions, and genetic diseases, reflect insufficient state investment in providing an adequate environmental infrastructure and sufficient local preventive and curative services the Arab communities, as well as the inferior conditions of health affecting a vulnerable sector of low socioeconomic status in particular. Most of the effects of poverty affect a poor sector in the Jewish population as well, but poverty is both wider and deeper among Arabs, and underdevelopment of Arab communities is more general. With regard to poverty, to environmental neglect and to the inferior access to local services in Arab communities, the state's universalistic asserted goals continue to be challenged.

CONCLUSION

In the Basic Laws of the Israel Government there is no law requiring provision by the state of health services or participation of citizens in such provision through compulsory health insurance. The state is not, for example, obliged by law to provide a family health station or center in every community, but may do so out of motivations arising from universalistic commitments and the exigencies of democratic politics.

In principle, the Israel Health Ministry is a supra-political state agency dedicated to promoting the health of all Israel's citizens, while voluntary agencies are factional and thus responsible only to their insurees. The state is formally responsible for equal rights and for equal communal development, while the Histadrut is responsible only for the conditions of employment and well-being of its members. In both cases this obligation arises not simply out of goodwill toward either citizens or members but because of the taxes or fees they pay, and in both cases, too, only some of these rights—individual but not communal—are legally (IMH) or contractually (HSF) defined.

Both the government and the voluntary agencies act according to political and economic interests and agendas. These interests sometimes are common for Jews and Arabs, but more often have a special reflection upon the Arab population in Israel. In practice, while the voluntary agencies have functioned as political arms of political parties and institutions, so has the IMH; the state has taken direct responsibility for individual citizens as insurees under its partial national social insurance, as members of local communities, and as residents of regional units of administration, while the HSF—extending services to communities in its own behalf and as the state's surrogate—focuses on them as Histadrut members. The HSF has been the primary provider of curative health services to Arab individuals and communities, but the Histadrut itself, which has had the power to promote equal opportunity through industrial development of these communities, has instead allowed less than equal opportunity for organized expression to its Arab members and has provided them with local health care which is too frequently inferior.

Contrary to general opinion which considers the Israeli health services system to be deficient in planning, the system has produced many plans; it is the systematic implementation of such plans which has been problematic, in part because of general budgetary constraints but in greater part due to conflicts between vested interests (Margolis 1977). The medical arena in Israel is characterized by public crises (e.g. Modan 1985).

The major structural flaws in the health services in Israel are their fragmentation between levels of care, which hinders continuity; the partiality of consistent preventive approaches; over-centralization within each service-providing agency, leaving little influence to community needs and decisions; the lack of compulsory health insurance which now allows for a sector of citizens—particularly Arabs—to be unprotected at need; and the very complexity of the entire system which leads to inefficiency and inconvenience. The main structural flaw in the environmental services is the division of responsibilities between different government ministries and between the government and local authorities, and the dependence of these services on wider national priorities and policies and on non-governmental agencies which have their own agendas, often unfavorable to Arabs.

Although overemphasis on costly curative care at the expense of environmental and even personal prevention is part of the developmental trajectory of Western bio-medicine as a whole, the pattern of the structural flaws in the Israeli health system has been further charted by the particular path of the politics of health institutions in Israel. With regard to the Arabs, national policies and politics which determine all other institutional approaches have been discriminatory in their principal guideline—the very legitimacy attributed to delays in development of Arab communities by the responsible bureaucracies on the basis of Jewish primacy. If clinics cannot be opened without municipal councils, roads and telephones, and these are late to come; if good health is impossible with low standards of water, sanitation and housing and these are not improved; if local development is impossible without adequate government participation and this is not forthcoming, national priorities are responsible.

The state has succeeded in guaranteeing access to hospitals (and to associated diagnostic, consultative and guidance services) on universalistic criteria; in practice, hospitals in some areas of Arab population concentrations are less developed and substandard in facilities and on the whole are understaffed. Social welfare benefits (income-maintenance supplements and social insurance benefits), which positively affect the standard of living and thus health, are also part of the civil rights of Arab citizens. Not quite equal since they are computed on a lesser basis since the Arabs do not do Army service, these are nevertheless ameliorative and universalistically applied. But gross inequalities in allocation of resources for community development (environmental sanitation and public housing especially) and inequalities in local health services—both those within the state's realm of activities and those which are not but which it nevertheless could influence—deprive the Arab population fundamentally. Precisely because health services have not been anchored in law, the state and the Histadrut have been able to present achievements vis-à-vis Arabs as a function of goodwill. It may well be that the state and the Histadrut have achieved more equality for Arabs in the area of health services than in any other area in which they have been active among them. If so, it is in itself a notable fact that even with regard to the right to well-being, perhaps the most universal of human rights, accomplishments are critically shadowed by significant lags.

Arabs (excepting the Druze) have not only been excluded from employment in the military and defense sectors, but have also not been equally employed in the public health services as in the public sector in general. The absolute improvement in their economic situation, which has been expressed in increased rates of medical insurance and in demands for sick fund services and for equality within the HSF, is expressed as well in an increase in communal services including an increased use of private medical practitioners in Arab villages. As private medical services in Israel began to flourish in the 1970s and 1980s as a result of the rise of the middle class, they have done so in Arab communities also. Beyond the 'mixed' urban centers, an increasing number of Arab medical personnel now practices in Arab urban and village communities. A growing political awareness and civic involvement in the Arab population have led to a recent proliferation of Arab voluntary associations focussed on environmental and health service improvements.

The social history of interaction between Jewish and Arab society in Israel as it was mediated by medical institutions has barely been mapped. Its beginnings are surely characterized by Arab ambivalence—need and respect, mixed with suspicion and fear—toward Jewish health providers, as well as by a Jewish ambivalence toward Arab patients and, increasingly lately, toward Arab physicians. The social impact especially on Arab women—because they had fewer other opportunities than Arab men to interact with Jews, not only of local services but even more so of out-of-village clinics and hospitals—must have been considerable. The study of the role of the HSF during its phase of expansion among the Jewish immigrant population has shown that it was an important agent for socialization (Shuval 1970). Arab patients' alienation from non-Arabic-speaking physicians and nurses is only a limited and negative aspect of this interaction; another, positive, side are the cross-cultural human and social contacts arrived at through medical encounters, at first mostly by introducing Arab patients and Jewish professionals, but then with the development of Arab manpower more and more by serving to dispel discriminatory stereotypes among the Jewish public. On the one hand, the separation of services on the local level has had a negative dynamic. For example, aid to Bedouins arriving for care at clinics in Jewish settlements in the Negev was freely given until Jews in these settlements became more self-conscious of their own improved condition vis-à vis the Bedouin's poverty. Their self-consciousness was appeased by requiring Bedouin to use only separate clinics (Kressel 1981).   On the other hand, consultative clinics and hospitals have been arenas for sympathetic interaction—on the universal ground of illness— between populations which might otherwise not have come in contact (women and children even less so than men) in their roles as patients and as concerned families and friends. The intensive growth of Arab medical manpower in Israel is a crucial aspect of this interaction.

Both access to health care and the health status of the Arab population are functions of their minority status and class position in Israel. In terms of the health of a population, health services are secondary to the primary conditions of health defined by standards of living and of nutrition and by environmental conditions, as well as by the awareness of the importance of these factors (e.g. Townsend and Davidson 1982). For the state, investment in health services, while important, is relatively cheap in comparison to the investment required for improving the socioeconomic status of a poor population, for reducing the economic production of disease-causing agents, or for eradicating poverty altogether and obliterating class distinctions. The historical direction taken in Israel has rather been away from socialism toward increasing class differentiation (Carmi and Rosenfeld 1989). Nevertheless—with all the skepticism which the priorities and efficacy of Western medical care elicit when historically observed—these services are a part of the criteria which are perceived to constitute the quality of life. While alternative, traditional health care may be available and used, the fact is that the Arabs in Israel—and especially those who have come of age during the period of the existence of the state—want and demand equal participation within the medical culture which is prevalent. As Arab leadership makes public stands adequate to representing the needs of the Arab population in Israel, this population's increasing political and financial weight can be expected to be applied toward achieving equality within the health services system.

REFERENCES CITED

Abramson J. and R. Gofin 1979, 'Mortality and Its Causes among Moslems, Druze and Christians in Israel,' *Israel Journal of Medical Sciences* 15:965-972.

Abu-Rabi'a A. 1979, *Traditional Medicine as Compared with Modern Medicine among the Bedouin* (Hebrew), M.Sc. Thesis, Department of Social Medicine, Hadassah Medical School, Jerusalem.

Abu-Rabi'a Y. 1976, *Saturation of Fatty Acids in Sub-Epidermal Fat and the Frequency of Ischemic Heart Disease among the Bedouin of the Negev* (Hebrew), M.D. Thesis, Hadassah Medical School, Jerusalem.

—— 1987, 'Health Status and Health Needs of the Bedouin of the Negev' in H. Kana'aneh, S. Al-Hadj and S. Rabi (eds.), *Proceedings of the First Health Conference in the Arab Community* (Arabic), Nazareth.

Adams (Stockler) R. 1987, 'Nurses as a Social Force in the Yishuv,' unpublished ms.

Aharoni Y. 1979, 'The Histadrut Sick Fund in the Arab Sector in Israel (Hebrew), *Meida la-Rofe* 19:23-29.

—— 1981, 'The Arab Sector in the Yizra'el Valley' (Hebrew), *Meida la-Rofe* 21:61.

Al-Haj M. 1986, *Social Change and Family Patterns in Arab Communities in Israel,* Westview, Boulder.

Al ha-Mishmar 9 September 1976, 'Top Secret: A Proposal for the Treatment of the Arabs of Israel' (Hebrew).

Alpern Y. 1977, *Toxemia of Pregnancy: A Demographic Comparison in the Mixed Population of the Western Galilee* (Hebrew), M.D. Thesis, Tel Aviv University.

Amit S. and E. Freundlich 1974, 'Infant Mortality in the Western Galilee,' (Hebrew) *Harefua* 1974:179-181.

Arian A. 1981, 'Health Care in Israel: Political and Administrative Aspects,' *International Political Science Review* 2/1:43-56.

Arnon-Ohana Y. 1978, *The Internal Political Struggle in Palestinian Arab Society* (Hebrew), Ph.D. Thesis, Tel Aviv University.

Assaf M. 1970, *Relations Between Arabs and Jews in the Land of Israel 1860-1948* (Hebrew), Mif'alei Tarbut ve-Hinukh, Tel Aviv.

Atad J., R. Auslander, L. Epstein, A. Cohen, Y. Sorokin, and H. Abramovici 1986, 'Premature Labor Contractions and Preterm Labor: A Comparative Study of Jewish and Arab Populations in Israel,' *Israel Journal of Medical Sciences* 22:470-472.

Avitzur Sh. 1972, *Everyday Life in the Land of Israel in the Nineteenth Century* (Hebrew), Am Ha-Sefer, Tel Aviv.

Awad A. and H. Kana'aneh 1987, 'Health Manpower Supply in the Arab Sector' (Arabic), in H. Kana'aneh et al.

Bachi R. 1945, 'The Decline of Child Mortality in Palestine,' *Acta Medica Orientalia*, January 1945/1.

Baer G. 1963, *The Arabs of the Middle East*, (Hebrew), Ha-Kibbutz Ha-Meuhad, Tel Aviv.

—— 1969, *Studies in the Social History of Modern Egypt*, Aldine, Chicago.

Ballas S., S. Zohar A. Gottfried and M. Borshtein 1982, 'A Model of a Regional System of Obstetrics, and Perinatal Report on 4000 Infants' (Hebrew), *Harefua* 51 (May 1982):365-369.

Bar-El V. 1985, 'Israel: The National Program for reduction of Infant Mortality,' *Proceedings, International Collaborative Effort on Perinatal and Infant Mortality* vol. 1.

Bar-El Y. 1985, *The History of Modern Medicine in the North of the Land of Israel During the Ottoman Period*, (Hebrew), M.D. Thesis, The Technion School of Medicine, Haifa.

Barer M., A. Gafni and J. Lomas 1989, 'Accommodating Rapid Growth in Physician Supply: Lessons from Israel, Warnings from Canada,' *International Journal of Health Services* 19/1:95-115.

Baruch, N. 1973, *The Institutional Organization of Health Services in Israel*, (Hebrew), Center for Policy Research, Jerusalem.

Bar-Yitzhak Y. 1981, *Social Services in the Arab Sector* (Hebrew), Ha-Hevra le-Sherut Sotziologi, Ramat Gan.

Behnam D. 1985 'The Muslim Family and the Modern World: Papers from an International Conference: The Tunis Conference,' *Current Anthropology* 26 #5 (Dec. 1985).

Ben-Dor G. 1979, *The Druzes in Israel: A Political Study*, Magnes, Jerusalem.

Bernstein D. 1987, *The Struggle for Equality: Urban Women Workers in Pre-state Israeli Society*, Praeger, New York.

Berriman Sh. 1962, 'The General Association of Workers in the Land of Israel,' (Hebrew), *Ha-Enciclopedia ha-'Ivrit*, vol. 15:28-63.

Bilu Y. 1980, 'The Morrocan Demon in Israel: The Case of Evil Spirit Disease,' *Ethos* 8:24-39.

Biener R. 1977, *Thalassemia Major Among the Arab Population of the Western Galilee* (Hebrew), M.D. Thesis, The Technion School of Medicine, Haifa.

Biener R., E. Freundlich and Z. Greif 1986, 'Infant Mortality in the Western Galilee 1964-86,' *Israel Journal of Medical Sciences* 25:87-91.

Cagan H. n.d., *My Beginning in Jerusalem* (Hebrew), WIZO, Tel Yizhak.

Canaan T. 1914, *Aberglaube und Volksmedizin im Lande der Bibel*, L. Friederichsen, Hamburg.

———— 1949, 'Conflict in the Land of Peace,' *Journal of the Palestine Arab Medical Association*.

Carmi Sh. and Rosenfeld, H. 1974, 'The Origins of the Process of Proletarization and Urbanization of Arab Peasants in Palestine' in *City and Peasant: A Study in Sociocultural Dynamics, Annals of the New York Academy of Sciences*, 220, New York.

———— 1989, 'The Emergence of Militaristic Nationalism in Israel,' *International Journal of Politics, Culture and Society* 3/1, (Fall 1989).

CBS, see Israel Government Central Bureau of Statistics.

Chimansky P., R. Jubran and R. Tamaisi 1984, *Job Potential for University Graduates in Arab Communities in Israel (a Survey)* (Hebrew), The Technion, Haifa.

Cohen, A. 1983, *The Treatment of Premature Labor and Its Influence on Early Birth: Comparative Survey among the Jewish Population and in the Arab Sector* (Hebrew), M.D. Thesis, Tel Aviv University Medical School, Tel Aviv.

Cooper R. M. Steinhauer, W. Miller, R. David and A. Schazkin 1981, 'Racism, Society and Disease: An Exploration of the Social and Biological Mechanisms of Differential Mortality,' *International Journal of the Health Services* 11/3.

Dagan R., S. Sofer, W. Klish, G. Hundt, H. Saltz and S. Moses 1983, 'Growth and Nutritional Status of Bedouin Infants in the Negev Desert, Israel: Evidence for Marked Stunting in the Presence of Only Mild Malnutrition,' *American Journal of Clinical Nutrition* 38 (Nov. 1983):747-456.

———— 1984, 'Infant Feeding Practices among Bedouin in Transition from Seminomadic to Settlement Conditions in the Negev Area of Israel,' *Israel Journal of Medical Sciences* 20:1029.

Dagan R. and R. Gorodischer 1984, 'Infections in Hypothermic Infants Younger than 3 Months Old,' *American Journal of Diseases of Children* (May 1984).

Datan N., A. Antonovsky, and B. Maoz 1981, *A Time to Reap: The Middle Age of Women in Five Israeli Subcultures*, Johns Hopkins Press, Baltimore.

Davidov D. et al. 1981, *Planning of Health Services in the Western Galilee Region* (Hebrew), University of Haifa, Department of Medical Administration, External Studies, Haifa.

Davies A.M. 1979, 'Demography, Morbidity and Mortality in Israel: Changes Over 30 Years,' *Israel Journal of Medical Sciences* 15:959-964.

Dor I., S. Ben-Tuvia, and E. Deychev 1988, *Classification of Local Authorities According to the Socio-economic Characteristics of the Population*, Ministry of the Interior and the Central Bureau of Statistics, Jerusalem.

Doron A. 1975, *The Struggle for National Insurance 1948-1953* (Hebrew), Baerwald School of Social Work, Hebrew University of Jerusalem, Jerusalem.

—— 1979, 'Medical Services in Israel, a View from a Different perspective' (Hebrew), *Bitahon Sotziali* 17(March 1979):51-62.

Eisenbach Z. 1978, *Trends in Fertility of the Moslem Population* (Hebrew), Ph.D. Thesis, The Hebrew University of Jerusalem, Jerusalem.

—— 1989, 'Changes in Fertility of the Muslim Woman in Recent Years' (Hebrew), *Hamizrakh Hahadash*, 32/1:80-96.

Eisenstadt S. N. 1967, *Israeli Society*, Weidenfeld and Nicolson, London.

Eliav M. 1978, *The Land of Israel and its Settlement in the 19th Century 1777-1917* (Hebrew), Keter, Jerusalem.

Ellencweig A. 1982, 'Patterns of Utilization of the Health Services as Compared to Other Countries—Doctor-Patient Contacts' (Hebrew), *Bitahon Sotziali* 23 (June 1982):90-100.

Ellencweig A. and P. Slater 1986, 'Factors Affecting Hospitalization for Selected Diseases in Israel,' *Israel Journal of Medical Sciences* 22:417-425.

Epstein, L. and A. Strulov 1986, 'Possible Influence of Changes in Risk Factors on Cardiovascular Morbidity and Mortality in Israel: Need for an Information System,' *Israel Journal of Medical Sciences* 22:301-306.

ESCO Foundation for Palestine 1947, *A Study of Jewish Arab and British Policies*, Yale University Press, New Haven.

Evang K. 1960, *Report on a General Evaluation of the Health Services in Israel*, WHO Regional Office for the Eastern Mediterranean.

Fakhouri C. 1980, *Dental Caries among an Arab and Jewish Urban Population: Comparative Survey of School children in Akko* (Hebrew), D.D.S.   Thesis, Hadassah School of Dentistry, Jerusalem.

Farah F. 1987, 'Environmental Health in the Arab Sector: Water and Sewage Disposal' (Arabic), in H. Kana'aneh et al.

Fieldhouse D. 1981, *Colonialism 1870-1945, an Introduction*, Weidenfeld and Nicolson, London.

Finkel M. 1983, 'Sanitation Systems and Structures' (Hebrew), *Mivnim Akhshav* 13:34-35.

Freundlich E., S. Amit and A. Regev 1982, 'Infant Mortality in the Western Galilee in the Years 1965-1980' (Hebrew), *Harefua* (April 1982).

Freundlich E. and R. Hino 1984, 'Consanguineous Marriage among Rural Arabs in Israel,' *Israel Journal of Medical Sciences* 20:1035-1038.

Friedlander D. and C. Goldscheider 1979, *The Population of Israel*, Columbia, New York.

GDH, see Government of Palestine Department of Health.

GDS, see Government of Palestine Department of Statistics.

Geraissy N. and H. Kana'aneh 1987, 'Curative Health Services in the Arab Sector' (Arabic), in H. Kana'aneh, et al.

Geraissy S. 1987, 'The Role of local Councils in the Health Sphere' (Arabic), in H. Kana'aneh et .al.

Gertz A. (ed.) 1947, *Statistical Handbook of Jewish Palestine*, The Jewish Agency, Department of Statistics.

Gev D., N. Roguin and E. Freundlich 1986, 'Consanguinity and Congenital Heart Disease in the Rural Arab Population in Northern Israel,' *Human Heredity* 36:213-217.

Ghattas B. and J. Nahas 1987, 'Environmental Health in the Arab Sector: Solid Waste' (Arabic), in H. Kana'aneh et al.

Giladi A. 1990, 'Some Observations on Infanticide in Medieval Muslim Society,' *International Journal of Middle East Studies* 22:185-200.

Gilbar G. 1989, 'Trends in the Demographic Development of the Palestinians 1870-1987,' *Skirot* (Hebrew), 108(Sept. 1989), Shiloah Institute, Tel Aviv University.

Glick L. and A. Reshef 1973, 'Vitamin A Status and Related Nutritional Parameters of Children in East Jerusalem,' *American Journal of Clinical Nutrition* 26(Nov. 1973):1229-1233.

Government of Palestine
—— 1936-1937, *Memoranda*, prepared by the Government of Palestine for use of the Palestine Royal Commission, vol. 1, Jerusalem.
—— 1946, *A Survey of Palestine*, prepared for the Anglo-American Committee of Inquiry, The Government Printer, Palestine.
Committee on Development and Welfare Services 1940, *Report*, Jerusalem.
Committee on Village Administration and Responsibility, 1941, *Report*, Jerusalem.
Department of Health (GDH) 1923-27, 1929-35, 1937-40, 1942, 1946, *Annual Report*, mimeographed until 1929, printed from 1930, Jerusalem.
—— 1944, *A Nutritional Economic Survey of Wartime Palestine 1942-43*, W.J. Vickers.
Department of Statistics (GDS) 1931, *Census* vol. 2, chapter 2.
—— 1946, *Statistical Abstract of Palestine* 1944-45, Jerusalem.
—— 1947, *Vital Statistics Tables* 1922-1945, Jerusalem.
Economic Advisory Council, Committee on Nutrition in the Colonial Empire 1939, *Summary of Information Regarding Nutrition in the Colonial Empire: First Report, Part II*, London.
GDH, see Government of Palestine Department of Health.
Gran P. 1979, 'Medical Pluralism in Arab and Egyptian History: An Overview of Class Structures and Philosophies of the Main Phases,' *Social Science and Medicine* 138-339-348.
Granquist H. 1931, *Marriage Conditions in a Palestinian Village*, Helsingfors and Leipzig.
Grant E. 1921, *The People of Palestine*, Lippincott, Philadelphia.
Greenberg O. 1982, *Development of Health Services Under Conditions of Social Change--Mutual Relations Between Town Residents and the Health Services in Qiriat Shemona* (Hebrew), Ph.D. Dissertation, Department of Anthropology, University of Tel Aviv.
Grushka Th. (ed.) 1959, *Health Services in Israel, A Ten Year Survey 1948-1958*, Israel Ministry of Health, Jerusalem.
—— (ed.) 1968, *Health Services in Israel* , Israel Ministry of Health, Jerusalem.
Ha-Ahot be-Israel (Hebrew), 1988, 133(Jan. 1980):40-45, 135(Sept. 1988):29.
Hadassah Medical Organization 1939, *Hadassah Medical Organization, Twenty Years of Medical Service to Palestine 1918-38*, Jerusalem.

Halevi H.S. 1961, 'Hadassah' (Hebrew), *Ha-Enciclopedia ha-'Ivrit*, vol. 14:615-617.

────── 1962, 'Health Services in Schools in the School Year 1960-61,' *Statistical Bulletin of Israel* 13(Oct. 1982):10 (supplement).

────── 1979, 'The Pluralistic Organization of Health Services in Israel' (Hebrew), *Bitahon Sotziali* 17(March 1959):5:50.

────── 1980, *The Bumpy Road to national Health Insurance: The Case of Israel* The Brookdale Institute, Jerusalem.

Harlap S. R. Prywes, N Grover and A.M. Davies 1977, 'Maternal, Perinatal and Infant Death in Bedouin and Jews in Southern Israel,' *Israel Journal of Medical Sciences* 13.

Harris M. and E. Ross 1987, *Death, Sex and Fertility: Population Regulation in Pre-industrial and Developing Societies*, Columbia Press, New York.

Hett J. 1981, *Statistical Analysis of the Demographic Characteristics of Sick Fund Insurees 1976* (Hebrew), Central Bureau of Statistics Special Publication #659, Jerusalem.

Histadrut (the General Association of the Workers in Israel)

────── 1985, *Report to the XV Conference of the Histadrut, for the Years 1981-1985* (Hebrew), G. Bartel (ed.), Histadrut Acting Committee, Tel Aviv.

────── Guiding Committee for Local Conferences, XV Histadrut Conference 1985 (Hebrew), *Book of Local Conferences*, Tel Aviv.

Histadrut Sick Fund 1957, *The HSF in the State* (Hebrew), Histadrut Sick Fund Center, Tel Aviv.

────── 1984, 1986, *Institutions and Services* (Hebrew), Department for Research and Medical Economics, Histadrut Sick Fund Center, Tel Aviv.

────── 1984, *XI Conference* (Hebrew), Tel Aviv.

────── 1985, *A Twenty Year Study 1965-1985* (Hebrew), Introduction by N. Shavit, Department for Research and Medical Economics, Tel Aviv.

Horowitz D. and Lissak, M. 1977, *From Yishuv to State* (Hebrew), Am Oved, Tel Aviv.

HSF, see Histadrut Sick Fund.

IGA, see Israel Government Archives.

IGY, see *Israel Government Yearbook*.

IMH, see Israel Ministry of Health.

ISCAR, see *Israel State Comptroller's Annual Report*.

Israel Government
    Archives (IGA)

——— Israel Ministry of Health 1948-1958 G4264, G4245, G4223,
——— Israel Foreign Ministry HZ 2402/23b 1953.
Central Bureau of Statistics (CBS)
——— 1976-1989, *Statistical Abstract of Israel (SAI)*, #27-40, Ha-Makor, Jerusalem.
——— 1980, *Survey of Use of Health Services* 1977 (Hebrew) Special Publication #639, Jerusalem.
——— 1981, (#659) see Hett.
——— 1981, *Family Expenditure Survey 1979/80* (Hebrew), (Pt. 1) #691.
——— 1983, (#708) *Diagnostic Statistics of Hospitalized Patients (and Hospitalization)* (Hebrew), Jerusalem.
——— 1983, *Use of Health Services (1981)* (Hebrew), Special Publications #717, Jerusalem.
——— 1984, *Statistical Tables of Infectious Disease 1976-1980* (Hebrew), Special Publications #722, Jerusalem.
——— 1985a, *A List of Localities, Geographic References and Population, 1983* (Hebrew), Census of Population and Housing 1983 #6, Jerusalem.
——— 1985, *Causes of Death 1981-82* (Hebrew), Special Publications #763, Jerusalem.
——— 1986a, *List of Localities and Their Population and Codes 31 December 1985*, Technical Publication #53:1-13, 31-34.
——— 1986b, *Labor Force Survey*.
——— 1988, *Statistical Tables on Selected Infectious Diseases 1981-1985*, Special Series #826, Jerusalem.
Committee for Planning General Health Insurance, 1959, *Plan for General Insurance for Israel* (Hebrew), Ahva, Jerusalem.
Knesset 1973, 1981, *Hatza'ot Hok ha-knesset, Reshumot* (Hebrew), Jerusalem.
Ministry of Health (IMH)
——— 1968, *The Health System in Israel 1948-1968* (Hebrew), Jerusalem.
——— 1979, *Profile of Health Services in Israel, Survey of Preventive and Ambulatory Services According to Localities 1/1/1978* (Hebrew), The Department for Planning, Budgeting and Medical Economics.
——— 1982a, *Incidence of Cancer in Israel: Facts and Numbers 1972-76* (Hebrew), Jerusalem
——— 1982b, 1985, 'Budget Proposal' (Hebrew), Jerusalem.
——— 1985, *Statistical Bulletin* (Hebrew), Jerusalem.
Department of Dental Health 1985, *Personnel Resources and Provision of Services 12/85* (Hebrew), Jerusalem.

National Insurance Institute 1983, *Recipients of Unemployment Benefits 1976-1983* (Hebrew), Survey #41.

—— 1982, *Annual Survey, 1987*, L. Achdut and G. Yaniv eds., Bureau of Research and Planning, Jerusalem.

Prime Minister's Office 1976 'Health Status of the Arab Population' (Hebrew), mimeo, Jerusalem.

Israel State Comptroller's Annual Report (ISCAR), 1950-1984 (1-35).

Yearbook (IGY) 1957-1987.

Johnson, T. 1973, 'Imperialism and the Professions: Notes on the Development of Professional Occupations in Britain's Colonies and the New States,' in H. Paul (ed.), *Professionalization and Social Change*, University of Keele, England.

Journal of Palestine Studies 1976, 'Special Report' 1(Autumn 1976):190-200.

Kana'aneh H., S. Rabi and S. Badarneh 1976, 'The Eradication of a Large Scabies Outbreak Using Community-Wide Health Education,' *American Journal of Public Health* 66/6(June 1976):564-567.

Kana'aneh H., S. Al-Hadj and S. Rabi, (eds.) 1987, *Proceedings of the First Health Conference in the Arab Community (1986)* (Arabic), Nazareth.

Kanev (Kanievski) I. 1942, *Social Insurance in the Land of Israel* (Hebrew), Bri'ut ha-Oved, Tel Aviv,

—— 1965, *Mutual Aid and Social Medicine in Israel* (Hebrew), HSF and the Social research Institute of the General Association of Labor in Israel.

Kass A. 1989, 'Western Medicine in Nineteenth Century Jerusalem,' *The Journal of the History of Medicine and Allied Sciences* 44:447-461.

Kawar M. 1987, 'Preventive Health Services in the Arab Sector' (Arabic), in H. Kana'aneh et al.

Kayman, Ch. 1984, *After the Catastrophe: The Arabs in The State of Israel 1948-1950* (Hebrew), Mahbarot le-Mehkar ule-Bikoret #10, December 1984, Haifa.

Kopp, J. 1985, 'The Social Services in Israel' in J. Kopp (ed.), *Allocation of Resources to the Social Services 1984* (Hebrew), The Center for Study of Social Policy in Israel, Jerusalem.

Kraus, V. 1990, *Promises in the Promised Land: Mobility and Inequality in Israel*, Greenwood Press, Connecticut.

Kressel G. 1981, 'The Ecological and Cultural Adaptation of Sedentarized Bedouin in Israel' (Hebrew) in A. Layish (ed.), *Ha-Aravim be-Israel: Retzifut u-Tmurah*, Magnes, Jerusalem.

Kurland S. 1947, *Cooperative Palestine: the Story of the Histadrut*, National Committee for Labor Palestine, Sharon Books, New York.

Landau J. 1969, *The Arabs in Israel*, Oxford University Press, Oxford.

Lavon B., T. Tulchinski, M. Preger, S. Rabi and S. Kaufman 1985, 'Iron Deficiency Anemia among Jewish and Arab Infants at 6 and 12 Months of Age in Hadera Israel,' *Israel Journal of Medical Sciences* 1:197-112.

Levin Y. 1980, 'Viral Hepatitis in Israel' (Hebrew), Israel Ministry of Health, Department of Epidemiology, Jerusalem.

Linenberg R. 1971, 'The Penetration of National Political Parties to the Druze Village Daliat al-Karmel' (Hebrew), *Medina ve-Mimshal* 125-144.

Livingstone W.P. 1925, *A Galilee Doctor*, Hodder and Stoughton, London.

Lustick I. 1980, *Arabs in the Jewish State: Israel's Control of a National Minority*, University of Texas Press, Austin.

McKinlay J., S. McKinlay and R. Beaglehole 1989, 'A Review of the Evidence Concerning the Impact of Medical Measures on Recent mortality and Morbidity in the United States,' *International Journal of Health Services* 19/2:181-208.

Maccabi Sick Fund 1986, *Guide to Services, Haifa and the North* (Hebrew).

Machnes Y. 1980, 'Consumption of Private Medical Services by Israeli Households with Full Coverage of Health Insurance,' *Public Health* 4.

Makhoul E. 1987, 'Hospital Utilization by Arab Children' (Arabic) in H. Kana'aneh et al.

Mani, A. 1965, 'Health Services to the Arab Population' (Hebrew), *Briut ha-Tzibur #3*, Israel Ministry of Health, Jerusalem.

Mansur G. 1937, *The Arab Worker under the Palestine Mandate*, Jerusalem.

Margalith, D. 1970, *The Jewish View of Medicine* (Hebrew), Shokeid, Jerusalem, 266-375.

Margolis, E. 1977, 'National Health Planning and the 'Medical Model': The Case of Israel,' *Social Science and Medicine* 11:181-186.

Margolz I., S. Nashif and H. Friedan 1983, 'Elderly Moslem Arabs in Rural Areas (Approaches and Needs)' (Hebrew), *Bitahon Sotziali* 24(Feb. 1983):131-141.

Matras J. 1990, *Dependency, Obligations and Entitlements: A New Sociology of Aging, the Life Course, and the Elderly*, Prentice Hall, Englewood Cliffs, New Jersey.

Modan B. and Bar-el V. 1981, 'Epidemiology in Health Policy,' *Israel Journal of Medical Sciences* 17:80-85.

Modan B. 1985, *Medicine under Siege: The Doctor's Strike and the Crisis in Israeli Medicine* (Hebrew), Adam Publications, Tel Aviv.

Montag Y., S. Winter, Ch. Dar and M. Barak 1980, 'Frequency of Congenital Anomalies among Jews, Arabs, and Druze' (Hebrew), *Harefua* (Dec. 1980).

Mor-Yosef Sh., A Samuelov and D, Weinstein 1989, 'Distributions of Birth-weights among the Various Sub-populations of Israel, 1929-1984' (Hebrew), *Harefua* 116/4:208-210.

Moshe, N. 1983, *Survey of Certain Demographic, Medical and Socioeconomic Characteristics of Children Hospitalized in the Soroka Medical Center in 1978* (Hebrew), M.D. Thesis, University of Tel Aviv Medical School, Tel Aviv.

Motro, M. 1968, *Hospitalized Morbidity among Bedouin Children in the Negev: Survey and Distribution of Hospitalizations and Mortality in Comparison to a Jewish Population* (Hebrew), M.D. Thesis, University of Tel Aviv Medical School, Tel Aviv.

Musallam, B. 1983, *Sex and Society in Islam*, Cambridge University Press, Cambridge.

Navarro V. 1973, *Health and Medical Care in the U.S.: A Critical Analysis*, Baywood, New York.

—— 1976, 'Social Class, Political Power, and the State and Their Implications in Medicine,' *Social Science and Medicine* 10: 451-457.

—— 1978, *Class Struggle, the State, and Medicine: An Historical and Contemporary Analysis of the Medical Sector in Great Britain*, Martin Robertson, London.

—— 1989, 'Why some Countries have Health Insurance, Others have National Health Services, and the United States has Neither,' *International Journal of Health Services*, 19 #3:383-404.

Nichaman M. and A. Reshef 1978, 'Attained Growth Status of Selected groups of Israeli Children,' *American Journal of Clinical Nutrition* 31:895-903.

Nudelman Juli 1986, *Bloodshed in Israeli Medicine: Personal Evidence* (Hebrew), ha-Negev, Be'er Sheva.

Ofer G. 1967, *The Service Industries in a Developing Economy: Israel as a Case Study*, Praeger in cooperation with the Bank of Israel, New York.

—— 1985, 'National Expenditures on the Social Services' (Hebrew), in Kopp J. (ed.), *Haktza'at Mash'avim la-Sherutim ha-Hevratiim 1984*, Ha-Mercaz Leheker ha-Mediniut ha-Hevratit be-Israel, Jerusalem.

Omar D. 1978, *Thalassemia Beta: A Survey among Arab Families in Emeq Yizra'el* (Hebrew), M.D. Thesis, Tel Aviv University Medical School, Tel Aviv.

Oppenheimer, J. 1979, 'The Druze in Israel as Arabs and as Non-Arabs,' Mahbarot le-Mehkar ule-Bikoret #3, December 1979, Haifa, reprinted in A. Haidar, H. Rosenfeld and R. Cahana (eds.) 1983, *Arab Society* (Hebrew), Jerusalem.

Palley H., Y. Yishai and P. Ever ha-Dani 1983, 'Pluralist Social Constraints on the Development of a Health Care System: The Case of Israel,' *Inquiry* 20/1.

Palti H., B. Strozzi and M. Avitzour 1982, 'Growth Patterns of Children in in a Moslem Semirural Community Near Jerusalem,' *Journal of Epidemiology and Community Health* 36:187-191.

Rabi S. 1987, 'Awareness and Education for Health in the Arab Sector' (Arabic), in H. Kana'aneh et al.

Reiss N. 1989, 'Processes Affecting the Distribution of Public Health Services to the Arabs in Israel,' *Asian and African Studies* 23/2-3.

Rinot M. 1978, *Rickets among Young Children in Shomron County: A Clinical and Epidemiological Survey* (Hebrew), M.D. Thesis, The Technion School of Medicine, Haifa.

Rizek S. 1979, 'Old Age in Nazareth: Conditions of Life and Needs for Services' (Hebrew), *Gerontologia* 13-16 (1979-1980):20-25.

Rogov I. 1980, *Infant Mortality in the Western Galilee in the Years 1975-76* (Hebrew), M.D. Thesis, The Technion School of Medicine, Haifa.

Rosen, B. 1987, *The Health of the Israeli People: An International Comparison Based on the WHO's 'Quantitative Indicators for the European Region,'* The Brookdale Institute, Jerusalem.

Rosen G. 1974, *From Medical Police to Social Medicine: Essays in the History of Health Care*, Science History Publications, New York.

Rosenau M., and Ch. Wilinski, 1928, *Reports of the Experts Submitted to the Joint Palestine Commission*, Daniels, Boston.

Rosenfeld H. 1964, 'From Peasantry to Wage-Labor and Residual Peasantry: The Economic and occupational Transformation of Arab Villages' in R. Manners (ed.), *Process and Pattern in Culture*, Aldine, Chicago.

—— 1976, 'Social Factors in the Explanation of the Increased Rate of Patrilineal Endogamy in the Arab Village in Israel' in J. Peristiany (ed.), *Mediterranean Family Structures*, Cambridge University Press, Cambridge.

—— 1978, 'The Class Situation of the Arab National Minority in Israel,' *Comparative Studies in Society and History* 20/3.

—— 1980, 'Men and Women in Arab Peasant to Proletariat Transformation' in S. Diamond (ed.), *Theory and Practice*, Mouton, the Hague.

Rosenfeld H. and M. Al-Haj 1989, 'The Emergence of an Indigenous Political Framework in Israel: The National Committee of Chairmen of Arab Local Authorities,' *Asian and African Studies* 23/2-3:205-244.

Rosenfeld H. and S. Carmi 1976, 'The Privatization of Public Means, the State-Made Middle Class, and the Realization of Family Value in Israel' in J. Peristiany (ed.), *Kinship and Modernization in Mediterranean Society*, The Center for Mediterranean Studies, American Universities Field Staff, Rome.

Rososhanski S. 1980, *Thalassemia among a Hamula from Kafr Qara* (Hebrew), M.D. Thesis, Tel Aviv University Medical School, Tel Aviv.

Rumney S. 1986, *Nutritional Habits and Treatment of Infants: Continuity and Change in an Arab Neighborhood in Haifa* (Hebrew), M.A. Thesis, Department of Sociology and Anthropology, University of Haifa.

Saeb Y. and H. Kornfeld-Keller 1962, 'The Health Center in Baqa el-Gharbiyye' (Hebrew), *Bri'ut ha-Tzibur*, Israel Ministry of Health Jerusalem.

SAI, see Israel Government Central Bureau of Statistics, *Statistical Abstracts of Israel*.

Samuel H. 1925, *Report of the High Commissioner on the Administration of Palestine 1920-25*, Colonial Offices (#15), London.

Scheper-Hughes N. 1984, 'Infant Mortality and Infant Care: Cultural and Economic Constraints on Nurturing in Northeast Brazil,' *Social Science and Medicine* 19:535-546.

Schmelz U. 1974, 'Mortality in Infancy and Early Childhood among the Non-Jewish Population in Palestine and Israel' (Hebrew) in *Births and Deaths of Infants in Israel 1948-72*, Central Bureau of Statistics Special Publications Series #453:55-59, Jerusalem.

Scrimshaw S. 1983, 'Infanticide as Deliberate Fertility Control,' in R. Bulatao and R. Lee (eds.), *Determinants of Fertility in Developing Countries: Fertility Regulation and Institutional Influences*, vol. 2:245-266, Academic Press, New York.

Semyonov M. and N. Epstein-Levin 1987, *Hewers of Wood and Drawers of Water: Noncitizen Arabs in the Israeli Labor Market*, Institute of Labor Relations, Cornell University Press, Ithaca.

Shafir G. 1989, *Land, Labor, and the Formation of the Israeli Palestinian Conflict 1982-1914*, Cambridge University Press. Cambridge.

Shapira Yosef 1961, *Land and Labor* (Hebrew), Am Oved, Tel Aviv.

Shapira Yonatan 1980, 'The End of a Dominant Party System' in A. Arian (ed.), *The Elections in Israel, 1977*, Jerusalem Academic Press, Jerusalem.

Shasha Sh., L. Epstein, A. Saab and A. Tamir 1989, 'Blood Pressure Measurements in Druze Children: An Extension of the Nahariya Study,' *Israel Journal of Medical Sciences* 25:463-464.

Shim'oni Y. 1947, *The Arabs of Israel* (Hebrew), Am Oved, Tel Aviv.

Shuval Y. 1970, in collaboration with A. Antonovski and A.M. Davies, *Social Functions of Medical Practice*, Jossey Bass, San Francisco.

—— 1979, 'Primary Care and Social Control,' *Medical Care* 17/6:631-638.

Smith H. 1964, *Manpower Survey: Physicians*, Israel Ministry of Labor.

Smooha S. 1978, *Israel: Pluralism and Conflict*, University of California Press, Berkeley.

Sofer S., R. Dagan, G. Hundt, H. Salz-Rennert, H. Kaplan, and S. Moses 1986, 'Frequency of Anemia among Jewish and Bedouin Infants in the Negev' (Hebrew), *Harefua* 61/9:217-219.

Stark H. 1970, 'Childhood Urolithiasis in Northern Israel,' *Israel Journal of Medical Science* 6:341-345.

Survey, see Government of Palestine 1946.

Susser M., K. Hopper and J. Richman 1983, 'Society, Culture and Health,' D. Mechanic (ed.), *Handbook of Health, Health Care, and the Health Professions* 23-49, The Free Press, New York.

Swirski Sh. 1981, *Orientals and Ashkenazim in Israel: Ethnic Division of Labour* (Hebrew), Mahbarot le-Mehkar ule-Bikoret, Haifa.

Tadmor Y. 1981, *The Palestine Labor League 1940-1947* (Hebrew), M.A. Thesis, University of Tel Aviv.

Taqqu R. 1987, *Arab Labor in Mandatory Palestine 1920-1948*, Ph.D. Dissertation, Columbia University, New York.

Townsend, P. and N. Davidson 1982, *Inequalities in Health: The Black Report*, Penguin, New York.

Tulchinski T., B. Lunenfeld, S. Haber and M. Handelsman 1982, 'Israel Health Review,' *Israel Journal of Medical Sciences* 18.

——— 1985, 'Israel's Health System: Structure and Content Issues,' *Journal of Public Health Policy* 6/2.

Tzadka P. 1978, 'Infant Mortality 1975-1977' (Hebrew), CBS *Musaf la-Yarhon ha-Statisti le-Israel* #9, Jerusalem.

——— 1985, 'Perinatal and Infant Mortality: Recent Trends in Israel,' *Proceedings, International Collaborative Effort on Perinatal and Infant Mortality* 1. DHHS Publications (PHS) 1952, U.S. Government Printing Office.

Tzahor Z. 1981, *The Road to Leadership of the Yishuv, the Histadrut at its Beginning* (Hebrew), Yad Yitzhak Ben-Zvi, Jerusalem.

Ullmann M. 1978, *Islamic Medicine*, Edinburgh University Press, Edinburgh.

Waitzkin H. 1983, 'A Marxist View of Health and Health Care' in D. Mechanic (ed.), *Handbook of Health, Health Care, and the Health Professions* 657-682, The Free Press, New York.

Washitz Y. 1947, *The Arabs in the Land of Israel* (Hebrew), Sifriat Poalim, Merhavia.

Weihl H. 1986, *Living Conditions and Needs of the Rural Arab Elderly in Israel*, The Brookdale Institute, Jerusalem.

Weil P. 1986, 'Agricultural Intensification and Fertility in Gambia (West Africa)' in W. P. Handwerker (ed.), *Culture and Reproduction: An Anthropological Critique of Demographic Transition Theory* 294-320, Westview, Boulder.

Weizell A. 1975, *Scurvy and Mental Retardation* (Hebrew), M.D. Thesis, The Technion School of Medicine, Haifa.

Wellesley, W.R. Lord Peel, Chairman 1937, Palestine Royal Commission, *Report*, HM Stationery Office, London.

White B. 1976, *Production and Reproduction in a Javanese Village*, Ph.D. Dissertation, Columbia University, New York.

Wood C. 1982, 'The Political Economy of Infant Mortality in Sao Paulo, Brazil,' *International Journal of the Health Services* 12/2:215-229.

Woolhandler S., D. Himmelstein, R. Silber, M. Bader, M. Harnly, and A. Jones, 1985, 'Medical Care and Mortality, Racial Differences in Preventable Deaths,' *International Journal of the health Services* 15/1:1-22

Worsley P. 1982, 'Non-Western Medical Systems,' *Annual Review of Anthropology* 11:313-48.

Yekutiel P. 1979, 'Infective Diseases in Israel: Changing Patterns over 30 Years,' *Israel Journal of Medical Sciences* 15:976-982.

Yishai R. 1986, *Physicians Strike* (Hebrew), Zmorah Bitan, Tel Aviv.

Yishai Y. 1982, 'Politics and Medicine: The Case of Israeli National Health Insurance,' *Social Science and Medicine* 16:285-291.

Yofe H. 1971, *A Generation of Pioneers*, Alpha Press, Jerusalem.

Zaharan, Y. 1980, *Nutritional-Deficiency Rickets among Children of the Arab Village 'Ibillin in the Western Galilee* (Hebrew), M. Sc. Thesis, Department of Nutrition, Hadassah Medical School, Jerusalem.

Zalmanovitch Y. 1983, *Histadrut, Kupat Holim, Government: The Conflictual and Consensual Exchange Approaches as a Political Explanation*, M.A. Thesis, Department of Political Science, University of Haifa.

Zureik E. 1980, 'Reflections on Twentieth-Century Palestinian Class Structure' in K. Nakhleh and E. Zureik, (eds.), *The Sociology of the Palestinians*, St. Martin's Press, New York.

NAME INDEX

A

Abramovici H. 188
Abramson J. 158, 160, 166, 168, 187
Abu Rabi'a A. 147, 187
Abu-Rabi'a Y. 126, 148, 179, 187
Abu Sinan 120, 132
Achdut L. 195
Adams (Stockler) R. 187
Adulam 67
Afula 25, 30
Aharoni Y. 111, 187
Akko 1, 20, 21, 81, 84, 88, 112, 113,
   114, 121, 122, 129, 147, 148, 150,
   151, 191
Al-Hadj S. 193
Al-Haj M. 152, 154, 180, 187, 199
Alpern Y. 174, 187
Amin (Dr.) 10
Amit S. 170, 174, 187 191
Antonovski A. 190, 200
Ar'ara 118, 121, 132, 150
Arian A. 55, 59, 60, 62, 63, 65, 95, 187
Arnon-Ohana Y. 22, 188
Arrabe 116, 120, 129, 132
Assaf M. 5, 6, 12, 17, 19, 32, 37, 38,
   40, 41, 42, 43, 44, 45, 49, 188
Atad J. 174, 188
Auerbach (Dr.) 12
Auslander R. 188
Avitzour M. 198
Avitzur Sh. 1, 2, 4, 5, 188
Awad A. 146, 148, 188

B

Bachi R. 51, 188
Badarneh S. 195
Bader M. 202
Baer G. 3, 188
Ballas S. 170, 188
Baqa al-Gharbiyye 67, 80, 82, 120
   129, 132, 151, 199
Barak M. 197
Bar-El V. 170, 171, 178, 188, 197
Bar-El Y. 3, 4, 7, 8, 9, 10, 14, 15, 188
Barer M. 99, 188
Bartel G. 193
Baruch N. 55, 62, 70, 188
Bar-Yitzhak Y. 142, 188
Beaglehole R. 196
Beer Sheva 20, 21, 66, 81, 148
Behnam D. 175, 188
Beirut 10, 36-37
Beishan (Bet Shean) 21
Ben-Dor G. 119, 188
Ben-Gurion D. 58, 61, 64
Ben-Tuvia S. 190
Bene Beraq 20
Bernstein D. 27, 189
Berriman Sh. 24, 25, 189
Bet Jann 120, 132
Bet Shean 67
Bethlehem 5, 121
Bir El-Maxur 120
Bilu Y. 147, 189
Biener R. 170, 189
Borshtein M. 188

SUBJECT INDEX